THE ROOTS AND SOUL OF THE CHINESE PEOPLE

BY XU JUN

Published by
ACA Publishing Ltd.
University House
11-13 Lower Grosvenor Place,
London SW1W 0EX, UK
Tel: +44 (0)20 7834 7676
Fax: +44 (0)20 7973 0076
E-mail: info@alaincharlesasia.com
Web: www.alaincharlesasia.com
Beijing Office
Tel: +86(0)10 8472 1250
Fax: +86(0)10 5885 0639

Author: Xu Jun
Editor: Martin Savery
Translator: Jiang Lin
Cover art: Daniel Li

Published by ACA Publishing Ltd in association
with the People's Publishing House

© 2014, by People's Publishing House, Beijing, China
ALL RIGHTS RESERVED. NO PART OF THIS
PUBLICATION MAY BE REPRODUCED IN MATERIAL FORM,
BY ANY MEANS, WHETHER GRAPHIC,
ELECTRONIC, MECHANICAL OR OTHER, INCLUDING
PHOTOCOPYING OR INFORMATION STORAGE, IN WHOLE OR IN PART, AND
MAY NOT BE USED TO PREPARE
OTHER PUBLICATIONS WITHOUT WRITTEN
PERMISSION FROM THE PUBLISHER.

The greatest care has been taken to ensure accuracy but the
publisher can accept no responsibility for errors or omissions, or
for any liability occasioned by relying on its content.

ISBN 978-1-910760-31-4

A catalogue record for *The Roots and Soul of the Chinese People* is available from
the National Bibliographic Service of the British Library.

Contents

Preface   Strengthen Cultural Self-Confidence to Extend a Spiritual Lifeline XIII

Volume I

Chapter 1   **The Historical Origin of Fine Traditional Chinese Culture** 3

     1. The meaning of the words 'traditional' and 'culture' 3

         (1) Tradition: Passed on from generation to generation and deeply embedded in a long history 3

         (2) Culture: Human culture constitutes social ethics 4

         (3) Traditional culture: the culture of the Chinese nation and the international community 5

     2. Where are the four major ancient civilisations now? 6

         (1) Mesopotamian culture, the cradle of civilisation 6

         (2) Egyptian civilisation, a wonder of the world 7

         (3) Indian civilisation, the home of Buddhism 8

         (4) Chinese civilisation, continuous vitality 9

     3. The continuity of Chinese culture in ancient and modern times 10

         (1) The Chinese are descended from the same roots and share a common origin 11

         (2) The descendants of the Yan Emperor and the Yellow Emperor come from the same family 13

         (3) The values that the descendants of the Yan Emperor and the Yellow Emperor identify with 14

     4. The cultural community of multi-ethnic integration 15

         (1) 56 ethnic minorities bloom like 56 flowers 15

         (2) 56 ethnic minorities, one communal family 17

         (3) 56 ethnic minorities jointly create Chinese culture 18

Chapter 2 **The Development Thread of Fine Traditional Chinese Culture** 21

1. The pre-Qin period: The emergence of culture and all schools of thought contending for attention................. 21
   (1) The primitive stage: the germination of culture............ 21
   (2) The Xia-Shang-Zhou period: vigorous cultural growth . 23
   (3) The Spring and Autumn and Warring States period: All schools of thought contended for attention 26

2. The Qin and Han dynasties: the thriving of original Chinese culture 29
   (1) Unification of the country and culture 29
   (2) Respect for the Yellow Emperor and Lao Tzu with Confucianism the sole orthodoxy 30
   (3) Diverse development of literature during the Han dynasty 32

3. The period of the Wei, Jin, and Southern and Northern Dynasties: More contention over cultural links between past and present 34
   (1) The rise of metaphysics and focus on reasoning............. 34
   (2) Multiple collisions assimilating 'as rivers flow to the sea' .. 35
   (3) Literature and history unrestrained, painting and calligraphy rampant 37

4. The Tang and Song dynasties: the pinnacle of cultural development 40
   (1) Taoism and Buddhism equally revered, pursuit of Confucian inheritance theories 40
   (2) Emergence of neo-Confucianism and renaissance of Confucianism 41
   (3) Tang poetry and Song Ci (poems) shining like the glittering milky way 43
   (4) History compilation system established, historians emerge 46

5. Multicultural clashes and fusion during the Liao, Xia, Jin and Yuan dynasties 46

	(1)	Territorial expansion by military force and state rule in accordance with Confucianism 47
	(2)	Religious freedom and cultural innovation 48
	(3)	Rapidly gaining momentum and turning outward to the world 49
6.	The Ming and Qing dynasties: Seeking revival amid cultural decline 50
	(1)	Rise of 'literary inquisition', Confucianism still revered .. 50
	(2)	Magnificent spectacle of cultural integration 51
	(3)	Rise of schools of thought and cultural revival 52
7.	Transformation of modern and contemporary culture .. 54
	(1)	Internal and external pressure and the Cultural Revolution .. 54
	(2)	The eastward transmission of Western science and enlightenment 55
	(3)	The New Culture movement, a new start 57

Chapter 3 Basic Tendency of Fine Traditional Chinese Culture ... 59

1.	China's cultural development strategy against the backdrop of globalisation 59
	(1) Economic globalisation and cultural diversification 59
	(2) Cultural development and strategic advance 60
	(3) Opportunities and challenges for a strong cultural country . 62
2.	Stick to the roots and march towards modernisation 65
	(1) Socialism revives culture 65
	(2) The Chinese characteristics manifested in culture 67
	(3) Cultural modernisation needs further endeavours 69
3.	Cultural revival and fulfilling the Chinese dream 70
	(1) Revitalisation of the Chinese nation through cultural revival 70
	(2) Cultural revival, a dream of 100 years 72
	(3) The 'three selfs' of culture and the fulfillment of the Chinese dream 73

Chapter 4   The Unique Creation of Fine Traditional Chinese Culture 76

    1. A unique historic fate has nourished unique humanistic feelings 76

        (1) The endless thread of culture 76

        (2) An agrarian civilisation with a unique moral character .. 77

        (3) Historical destiny bred unique humanistic feelings 79

    2. The unique fundamental realities of China cultivated its unique cultural genes 82

        (1) The collective consciousness generates 'genes' 82

        (2) Cultural genes carry tradition 83

        (3) Cultural genes mold the Chinese heart 84

    3. Unique cultural paradigm fostered by unique path of development 87

        (1) The cultural paradigm of a unique style 87

        (2) Cultural paradigms differ in history and in modern times . 88

        (3) Modern China and a new paradigm 90

Chapter 5   The Value Proposition of Fine Traditional Chinese Culture 92

    1. Political ambition intrinsic in fine traditional Chinese culture 92

        (1) Unselfishly return to propriety and the path of benevolent government 93

        (2) Taking overall responsibility and maintaining one's own integrity 94

        (3) The universal community and pursuit of great harmony .. 95

    2. Fine traditional Chinese culture fosters feelings of dedication to serving one's country 96

        (1) If it is good for the country, no need for fame and fortune .. 97

        (2) Serve the country with supreme loyalty and even at the cost of hundreds of lives 98

        (3) Grieve first, rejoice later and be concerned for the world .. 99

3. The awe-inspiring righteousness reflected in fine traditional Chinese culture 100

    (1) Serve unyieldingly and stick steadfastly to the mission .. 100

    (2) Upright and straightforward, not afraid to confront danger 101

    (3) Poor but with lofty ideals and immune to temptation. 102

4. Dedication demonstrated in fine traditional Chinese culture 103

    (1) Sacrifice and selflessness 103

    (2) Fear no hardships to benefit people around the world ... 104

    (3) Be true to your convictions and vehemently save the country from danger 105

5. The path of self-cultivation shown by fine traditional Chinese culture 106

    (1) The decrees of heaven are not unchanging and god helps men of virtue 106

    (2) Inner cultivation and exterior action, self-discipline to calm others 108

    (3) Internal self-examination, external action and the unity of knowledge and action 109

Chapter 6 Distinctive Characteristics of Fine Traditional Chinese Culture 112

1. National character: People are my brothers and all things are my kind, rooted in rites and morality 112

    (1) The culture of family names and blood being thicker than water 112

    (2) Civil administration and cultural influence on Chinese people 114

    (3) Cultural backbone dates back to ancient times 115

2. Tenacity: Constant self-improvement with high aspirations and diligence 117

    (1) Know what is impossible but dare to struggle against heaven and earth 117

  (2) Strive ambitiously and diligently to make the country prosperous 118

  (3) Make determined efforts despite suffering setbacks 119

 3. Inclusiveness: Self-discipline, social commitment and kind-heartedness 121

  (1) Inclusiveness of a hundred schools of thought 121

  (2) Adopt best practices from all quarters and coexist harmoniously with thousands of other countries 121

  (3) Communication, combination and advancing in unison . 122

 4. Matter-of-fact spirit: studying the nature of things for humanistic pragmatism 124

  (1) Scrupulously abide by one's duty and come down to earth.. 124

  (2) The matter-of-fact spirit, practical actions, and emphasis on practical results 125

  (3) Humanistic pragmatism and unification of ontology and function 126

 5. Continuity: Pursue reform to add or subtract for an orderly inheritance 127

  (1) Trace back to its source and bear ancestry in mind 127

  (2) Protection, utilisation, inheritance and development .. 128

  (3) Pursue reform to remove or supplement, and make innovative expansion 129

Volume 2

Chapter 1 **Benevolence - Doctrine of Conducting Self-Perfection of the Chinese People 133**

 1. Benevolence and boundless love 133

  (1) Benevolent people always care for and love others 134

  (2) Benevolence depends on oneself rather than others 136

  (3) Consider and do good to others 137

 2. The spirit of great love handed down from generation to generation 138

	(1)	Return parental love with filial piety 138
	(2)	Love and sympathise with people to foster world peace.... 140
	(3)	Thousands of years of continuous patriotism............... 142
3.	Consolidate the moral foundation of the modern Chinese people with benevolence 143	
	(1)	Practice benevolence entirely of one's own accord with caution and self-discipline 143
	(2)	Consider others and help others 144
	(3)	Be concerned about people all over the world and be determined to serve the country worthily.................... 146

Chapter 2 Focus on 'People-Oriented' Thought - The Foundation of the Chinese People's National Security 149

1. Trace back to the source of 'people-oriented' 149
   (1) The rudiments of 'people-oriented' thought in the period of Three Emperors and Five Sovereigns 150
   (2) Lessons from the fall of the Xia dynasty: loss of the foundation of the country 151
   (3) The chorus of many schools of thought and surge of 'people-oriented' thought 152
   (4) The failure of 'people-oriented' thought: publicity and fall 155

2. 'People-oriented' thought: A political doctrine amplifying benevolence 158
   (1) Attaching great importance to the people: The people are more important than the monarch 158
   (2) Love the people: Take the common aspirations of the people as those of the monarch 159
   (3) Benefit the people: Bestow virtue on the people 160
   (4) Favour people: Do not go against people's will............ 162

3. Integrating 'people-oriented' thought and democracy in China in the new century 163
   (1) A clear-cut stand of serving the people 163
   (2) Serve the people as public servants 164

	(3)	Manage affairs for the people and let them be their own masters 165
	(4)	Whether rulers love the people or not can be measured by the level of popular support 167

Chapter 3   Honesty - The Foundation of the Chinese People .. 168

	1.	Honesty is the bond that unites people and holds them together 168
		(1) Consistence of sincerity and faithfulness 168
		(2) Cultivation of oneself and others rests in honesty 170
		(3) Loyalty, courage and utmost honesty 172
	2.	Honesty: The timeless practice of the Chinese people 174
		(1) Conduct oneself in society based on honesty and honouring commitments 174
		(2) Honest management of family affairs and the paramount value of family harmony 175
		(3) Start business with honesty and take it as the source of abundant wealth 176
		(4) Honest governance and happy people living in a peaceful country 177
	3.	Modern trends of thought on honesty 179
		(1) Lack of honesty is the concern of the times 179
		(2) Return of honesty a call of the times 180
		(3) Build an honest society with joint efforts 182

Chapter 4   Uphold Righteousness - The Selfless Kindness of the Chinese People 185

	1.	The long history of the theory of 'righteousness' 185
		(1) Explanation of the meanings of 'righteousness' and 'justice' in Analytical Dictionary of Characters 185
		(2) 'Of the four dimensions', one's 'righteous spirit' reaches up to the clouds 187
		(3) Difficulty of handling people who talk frivolously 189

2. Righteousness, the common value historically pursued by Chinese nationals 192
   (1) Ancient legends eulogised righteousness 192
   (2) Twenty-five histories manifesting justice 193
   (3) Song of the Guerrilla resounds through the ages 196
3. Revitalise modern society with the spirit of fearlessness and positive energy 198
   (1) Socialist core values refresh traditional just values 198
   (2) The light of justice shines on the Chinese Dream 200
   (3) Develop awe-inspiring righteousness and energise modern society 201

Chapter 5 Concord - The Beautiful Harmony of the Chinese People 203

1. A historical interpretation of harmonious interaction and sincere cooperation 203
   (1) Concord of Yin and Yang, endless growth and multiplication 204
   (2) Etiquette and harmony secures peace for family and country 207
   (3) Harmony of body and mind and concord of knowledge and action 208
2. Benign interaction between the Chinese people and the universe 209
   (1) Man and nature stand aloof from worldly success 209
   (2) Artistic harmony like nature itself 210
   (3) Social harmony and each in their proper position 212
   (4) Physical and mental harmony aim at supreme goodness .. 213
3. Modern practice of the idea that 'harmony and peacefulness are prized' 214
   (1) Harmony and common prosperity of man and nature 214
   (2) The harmonious interaction of humans and society 215
   (3) A strong country without hegemony for harmony and win-win 217

Chapter 6 Quest for Great Unity - The Ideal Situation for the Chinese People 220

1. The dream of the sages for great unity 220
    (1) The whole world is one community and selection should be done on merit.. 221
    (2) Treat others like relatives and love indiscriminately 223
    (3) Universal harmony with good neighbourly relations ... 225
2. Tracing the history of the Chinese people's pursuit of great unity 226
    (1) Uphold virtue and harmony, and the pursuit of equality .. 226
    (2) Great unity, reform and 'continual etiquette' 227
    (3) The whole world as one community settled by the Three People's Principles. 229
3. Contemporary interpretation of great unity 230
    (1) 'Two centenaries' and the Chinese Dream 230
    (2) People's splendid lives and fulfilling the dream 232
    (3) Common destiny and big power responsibility 233

Conclusion Good Management of the World and Flourishing Culture 237

1. Three waves of craze for traditional Chinese culture ... 237
2. Inspired by the 'craze for traditional Chinese culture' ... 240
3. Seek the outstanding 'cultural yeast' 241

Postscript 243

Preface

Strengthen Cultural Self-Confidence to Extend a Spiritual Lifeline

The Vitality[1] *of the Chinese People – a Citizen's Textbook on Socialist Core Values*, published by the People's Publishing House in October 2014, aroused considerable interest in society. This prompted some readers to wonder about the origin of socialist core values and their relationship with the vitality of the Chinese people and with traditional Chinese culture. It also motivated the author to trace back to the source.

In the 13th collective learning of the political bureau of the central committee of the Communist Party of China (CPC), General Secretary Xi Jinping pointed out: "Fostering and carrying forward socialist core values must take root in the fine traditions of Chinese culture. Solid core values must be sourced from their intrinsic roots. Discarding one's traditions and roots is tantamount to severing one's own spiritual lifeline. The profound, fine traditional Chinese culture serves as the foundation for us to gain a firm foothold among the torrents of global culture." He stressed: "Efforts should be made to clarify the history, development thread and basic orientation of fine traditional Chinese culture and to clarify the unique creativity, value, ideas and distinctive features of fine traditional Chinese culture in a bid to boost our self-confidence in our own culture and values." At a forum on philosophy and social science work in May 2016, Xi Jinping emphasised once again: "Our steadfast confidence in the road, theories and institutions of socialism with Chinese characteristics is in essence the

---

[1] Vitality – the Chinese characters used here 精气神 (*jing qi shen*) actually embody a much deeper meaning than just 'vitality' or 'life force'. In the Taoist tradition, which forms the foundation of the traditional Oriental healing and health-promoting arts, there are said to be Three Treasures (三宝 *sanbao*), also known as Three Jewels or Triratna, that in effect constitute life, namely, *jing*, *qi* and *shen*, which are generally translated as essence, vitality and spirit. They form the cornerstones of Traditional Chinese Medicine and practices such as *Neidan*, *Qigong* and *Taiqi*. The ultimate goal of all of the Oriental healing and health-promoting arts is to cultivate, balance and expand the Three Treasures. Source: *Theory of Jing, Qi and Shen* – http://tcm.chinesecio.com/en/article/2009-08/24/content_11728.htm

firm confidence in our culture. Cultural confidence functions as the most fundamental, deepest and most enduring power." "The Chinese nation boasts profound cultural traditions and an ideological system laden with special characteristics which reflect the knowledge, wisdom and rational thinking of the Chinese people accumulated over thousands of years and foster China's unique advantages."

Ruminating on the series of important speeches addressed by General Secretary Xi Jinping, we have increasingly become aware of the fact that it is a vital, significant and far-reaching mission for the modern Chinese people to stand steadfast to our 'foundation' and to inherit and carry forward fine traditional Chinese culture. For this reason, the author has further probed into the source of the 'roots' and the 'soul' of the Chinese people on the basis of *The Vitality of the Chinese People — a Citizen's Textbook on Socialist Core Values*, and strove day and night for years, finally completing it after making numerous modifications. A companion volume, *The Roots and Soul of the Chinese People — The Common Sense of Fine Traditional Chinese Culture* is an attempt to respond to the 'two clarifications' raised by Xi Jinping to clarify the inherent relationship between modern Chinese culture and fine traditional Chinese culture. The research achievements can be finally concluded in the following two sentences: The vitality of the Chinese people has been accumulated over a long period of Chinese civilisation spanning 5,000 years; socialist core values are rooted in the fertile, fine traditional Chinese culture.

1. Fine traditional Chinese culture possesses infinite charm

Fine traditional Chinese culture is the Chinese culture in a stable form generated, formed and inherited during the long evolution of the Chinese nation. It generally refers to the ancient Chinese culture constantly settled, accumulated and formed in the long history of the Chinese nation before the Opium Wars which broke out in 1840. Some people also define it as lasting until the end of the modern era of Chinese history, designating it as the fusion of ancient and modern Chinese culture.

Deeply rooted in China's vast hinterland, fine traditional Chinese culture was passed on from generation to generation in the minds of the Chinese people and exerted worldwide influence. Even now, people still take delight in talking about the opening ceremony of the 29th Olympic Games held

Preface

in Beijing on 8 August 2008 whose ingenious design, magnificent scenes, majestic momentum and gorgeous colours incisively and vividly displayed the details and glamour of fine traditional Chinese culture, presented an exquisite cultural feast to millions upon millions of audience worldwide, showcased the connotations of Chinese cultural harmony and shocked both China and even the entire world.

For more than 5,000 years, fine traditional Chinese culture has exerted tremendous influence on the inner world and the code of conduct of the Chinese people, favourably impacting all aspects of people's production and lives. For instance, the sages and men of virtue in previous generations advocated that 'people are the foundation of the state', and called for making the people wealthy, in the belief that wealth prompts etiquette and that 'well fed means well bred' and led to a modified code of conduct for the state and its people guided by moral principles. For another example, the state concept of 'grand unification', the people-based ideology that 'the people are more important than the ruler', the system design of clan and country isomorphism (similar structure) and the value of life in innovative application with reality all had significant effects on China's political process; the updating, progress and deduction of culture itself inaugurated a system of discourse with Chinese characteristics, style and manners, enriched the spiritual life of the Chinese people and boosted the cultural soft power of modern China…

Fine traditional Chinese culture has made indelible contributions to the progress and development of human society and exercised wide influence in the international community. The 'four great inventions' of China (the compass, papermaking, gunpowder, and printing) did not simply propel the political, economic and cultural development of ancient China but were spread to the West by various means and impacted world civilisation. The world-renowned 'Silk Road' brought China's products and production technologies, including silk and tea, to other parts of the world in the period of Emperor Wu. Zheng He of the Ming dynasty visited Asian and African countries seven times, conducted economic, trading and cultural exchanges, and sowed the seed of peace all along the way. China always goes out to the outside world with sincere smiles and presents an elegant, friendly nation to the whole world.

China fever first hit Europe in the 17th and 18th centuries and many intellectuals demonstrated a strong interest in Chinese culture. German

mathematician and philosopher Gottfried Leibniz, the inventor of differential and integral calculus, paid close attention to and deeply respected Chinese culture. He highly praised Confucian ethical education and the social order and national unity it fostered, saying: "China should dispatch missionaries to teach us the tenets of natural philosophy and their practical application, just like we dispatched missionaries to teach them the philosophy enlightened by God." His explanation of the diagram of *The Book of Changes* and his evaluation of Chinese characters tremendously impacted the research on *The Book of Changes* and Chinese characters, and generated far-reaching influence on Sino-Western cultural exchanges.

Mr Ji Xianlin once promoted the idea that 'the 21st century is the era of Eastern culture'. British scholar Arnold Joseph Toynbee said the 21st century would be the era of the Chinese, and that he would live in China in the afterlife, if possible. In January 1988, 75 Nobel Prize winners wrote in a joint declaration in Paris, France: if human beings are to live on in the 21st century, they should learn from the wisdom of Confucius developed 2,500 years ago. Now the 'Chinese Bridge' project implemented by the Chinese government has yielded brilliant fruits and the Confucius Institutes all over the world provide a vital platform for foreigners to learn Chinese, to gain knowledge about China and have stimulated Sino-foreign cultural exchanges.

The fine traditional Chinese culture is displaying its ever-growing appeal in the modern world!

2. Fine traditional Chinese culture comprises the roots and soul of the Chinese people

Fine traditional Chinese culture comprises the roots and soul of the Chinese people and serves as an indispensable mental prop handed down by the Chinese from generation to generation. The reproduction of the Chinese nation, the progress of Chinese civilisation and the spiritual lifeline of the Chinese people all originate from traditional Chinese culture in the long run. The formation and development of traditional Chinese culture originated in the germination of cultural awareness, derived from cultural factors, cultural differences, cultural conflicts and cultural identification, evolved into a cultural type, while the inheritance of cultural relics and cultural deposits over thousands of years became the roots of China and the soul of the Chinese nation.

Preface

Cultural awareness blossomed in the Yan and Huang era[1] which is deemed to be the starting point of Chinese culture. The dragon culture is one of the origins of Chinese culture. In the *Book of Changes*, the earliest mention of dragons, a record was kept of 'dragons flying' and 'dragons roaming the valleys'. China is a 'dragon country' and the Chinese people are reputed to be the 'descendants of dragons (metaphor for the Chinese nation)'. When Cheung Ming-man[2] sang *My Chinese Heart* in a long gown of dragon design, the fascination for the magnificent Yangtze and Yellow rivers and the eulogy for the oriental dragon touched the soul of millions upon millions of descendants of the dragon worldwide.

All schools of thought contended for attention in the pre-Qin period in China. The exchanges, contention, collision and study of different ideologies gave rise to various schools of learning exerting a significant influence on future generations, such as Confucianism, Taoism, Mohism, Legalism, the school of logicians, the Yin-Yang school, the school of diplomacy, the eclectics and the agriculturalist school. Among them, Confucianism became the backbone of the basic value system of traditional Chinese culture and provided the fundamental precepts for governing ancient China. Since the time of Confucius, Confucianism has experienced ups and downs. In their long history of development and propagation, Buddhism and Taoism took on national Chinese characteristics and developed into Chinese Buddhism and native Taoism. The harmonious cultural values formed during the long blending of Confucianism, Buddhism and Taoism stretch back thousands of years, resulting in concepts such as, the 'theory that man is an integral part of nature' in terms of the relationship between man and nature; the 'application of etiquette and cherishing of peace' and that 'time isn't as important as terrain; but terrain isn't as important as unity with the people' in dealing with the relationship between man and society; 'the benevolent love others', that one should respect the aged and take good care of children and 'do unto others as you would have them do unto you' in handling human relations; 'all nations live side by side in perfect harmony' and 'harmony in diversity and peaceful coexistence' in terms of the relations between states; 'a peaceful family will prosper' and filial obedience to parents in terms of family ties; 'harmony brings

---

[1] The Yan and Huang era (炎黄时代 *yanhuang shidai*) – this refers to the legendary ancient times when the Yan Emperor and the Yellow Emperor - the ancestors of the Chinese nation - established civilisation. This period is reckoned to be the starting point of Chinese culture.

[2] Cheung Ming-man (张明敏) – a Cantonese singer from Hong Kong well known in China for singing patriotic Chinese songs in Mandarin.

wealth' and neither the young nor the old should be cheated in business contacts. It is a common cultural phenomenon in China which is rarely seen in other countries: that Confucius, Lord Lao Tzu and the Goddess of Mercy can coexist harmoniously and believers of different religions can be on good and sincere terms. It is often said that the Chinese people are fairly happy and that they follow Confucianism when they have their moment, Taoism when they are dejected and Buddhism when they are lost in despair. The Chinese people can find spiritual consolation in any case from traditional Chinese culture. It is the influence of a happy outlook in traditional Chinese culture on the Chinese people which also demonstrates the importance of Confucianism, Taoism and Buddhism in the minds of the Chinese.

Fine traditional Chinese cultural relics are the inheritance of Chinese culture and the world's cultural heritage attracting the attention of Chinese and foreigners is its prominent manifestation. The world cultural heritage is the crystal, representation and witness of human civilisation. Data shows that as of July 2015, there were a total of 48 world heritage sites in China, a world-renowned ancient civilisation, which had been nominated by UNESCO to the World Heritage List since China joined the Convention on the Protection of World Cultural and Natural Heritage in 1985, second only to Italy (with 51) worldwide. Among them, 30 are world cultural heritage sites, 10 world natural heritage sites, 4 world cultural and natural heritage sites and 4 world cultural landscape heritage sites. In 2004, the 11th session of the 10th NPC standing committee approved the Chinese government to join UNESCO's Convention on the Protection of Intangible Cultural Heritage. As of late 2013, a total of 38 intangible cultural heritage sites in China had been nominated in the Intangible World Heritage Sites List, ranking top in the world. The valuable world heritage sites, intangible world cultural heritage sites, and above-ground and underground immovable cultural relics embody indelible historical value and the eternal value of life, showcasing the profound deposits of fine traditional Chinese culture and its tenacious vitality.

The tenacious vitality of fine traditional Chinese culture can be proved by historical records. According to the calculation of British historian Arnold Joseph Toynbee, in the human history of up to 6,000 years, 21 (or 26 calculated by someone else) forms of civilisation have appeared, 14 have vanished, 6 were lifeless and only the Chinese culture has continued to thrive. Karl Marx once compared the social structure based on the feudal natural economy to 'a bag of potatoes' which were separated from each other in the same bag. Then what is the powerful impetus that firmly holds the Chinese nation together? Chinese and foreign scholars have racked their brains to decipher the mystery of the 'grand unification'. As an expert has described, the map of China looks like a rooster singing with a resounding voice and China will 'sing loudly at the cock-crow' as led by Confucian culture.

Traditional culture is the bloodline of the Chinese nation and will not change as people's clothes or the times change. Even if any change does occur, it is just the appearance, representation and the carrier whose core spirit will not be eclipsed in the wind. Especially, the mnemonic symbol of culture will not vanish with the passage of time. Chinese culture is a towering ancient tree with its roots extending to the past, the present and the future; Chinese culture is the spirit and the soul providing inexhaustible energy for the existence and development of the Chinese nation.

3. Let fine traditional Chinese culture dazzle the youth of the times

'Later generations should learn from historical experience.' Traditional culture is the source while modern culture is the flow. As to traditional Chinese culture, Mao Zedong once said: "We should summarise and inherit the valuable legacy left over from Confucius to Sun Yat-sen." On 1 March 2013, General Secretary Xi Jinping gave an important speech in the central party school and stressed: "History reveals success and failure, gains and losses, ups and downs; poetry can elevate people's emotions, make them high-spirited and delicately beautiful; ethics dictate to us a sense of honour and distinguishes between honour or disgrace and between true and false." Nevertheless, traditional Chinese culture is not perfect, featuring both essence and dross. We should get rid of the dross and keep the essence, and endow traditional culture with new vigour and vitality by means of new thoughts, ideas and modes of expression. In the journey of building socialism with Chinese characteristics in the 21st century, we should constantly strengthen our self-confidence in culture and values, launch cultural innovation and reinvigorate the essence of fine traditional Chinese culture in the new era.

'New wine in an old bottle', meaning new concepts in an old framework, comprises a key part of China's cultural innovation. 'New wine in an old bottle' is a metaphor for the practice of creative efforts to present new contents in an old form or to interpret old contents in a new way (also regarded as 'plausible innovation'). New concepts in an old framework reflect the new contents of the spirit of modern society and extend the genes of traditional culture. It is manifested to some extent in aspects of the cultural category, dimension and style. For instance, Guan Zi[1] was the earliest to publicise the concept of the 'rule of law': 'The ruler of a country should not base his authority on multiple elements. Only by rule of law can he govern the country effectively.' The ancients were deeply aware of the efficacy of the rule of law. However, the subjects of the rule were the people and the law was simply applied as a tool for the 'rule of man'. Today, we propose to launch overall running of the country according to law by critically evaluating and developing the contents of the 'rule of law'. There is a difference of only a single word in Chinese between 'running the country according to law' and 'rule of law' but there is an essential difference in connotation. The subjects of 'running the country according to law' are the people but the objects of the 'rule of law' may be the authorities abusing state power. It is a fundamental change from 'rule by man' to 'rule of law'. Another example is the proposition of socialist core values, which is the practice of socialism with Chinese characteristics, which absorbs the essence of fine traditional Chinese culture, learns from the achievements of human civilisation, realises the transformation of traditional core values in the new century and raises China's traditional cultural ethics to a higher level.

It is another vital part of China's cultural innovation to put new wine in a new bottle and endow new wine with new contents. In terms of cultural innovation, it is most evident in primary theoretical innovation (also called 'genuine innovation'), unearthing theoretical innovation and methodological theoretical innovation. It strives to realise innovative transformation and development of traditional Chinese virtues amid the excavation and elucidation of fine traditional Chinese culture. For instance, to uncover the potential of the national spirit, the Chinese nation has developed a great national spirit featuring unity and solidarity, love of peace, industry, courage and self-improvement with patriotism as the core. The national spirit is intertwined with the spirit of the times and carried

---

1 The *Guanzi* (管子) – At over 135,000 characters long, the *Guanzi* is one of the longest early Chinese philosophical texts attributed to Guan Zhong, a 7th century BCE philosopher who was prime minister to Duke Huan of Qi. Most *Guanzi* chapters deal with the art of governance comprising a blend of Legalistic, Confucian and Taoist philosophy.

Preface

forward in the new historical circumstances. The Jinggangshan spirit, the spirit of the Long March, the Yan'an spirit, the anti-fascist spirit and the Xibaipo[1] spirit were formed in the period of democratic revolution; the Daqing spirit, the Lei Feng spirit and the 'two bombs and one satellite'[2] spirit were developed in the period of socialist construction; the spirit of combating floods, the spirit of combating 'SARS'[3], the Qinghai-Tibet railway spirit, the astronauts spirit and the earthquake relief spirit were fostered in the new period of reform and opening up.

Efforts should be made to inherit fine traditional Chinese culture, keep the roots and strengthen self-confidence in Chinese culture and values. Cultural self-confidence is having the confidence and conviction in one's cultural vitality and cultural self-understanding. It entails firm adherence to the ideals and faith in the cultural vitality of the Chinese nation based on cultural self-awareness and on persisting in the path of self-confidence, theory and institutions. With cultural self-confidence, we can rationally examine the historical traditions and culture, the national and folk culture, and modern Chinese culture, and tolerate and learn from the accomplishments of the world's historical culture and modern civilisation in a drive to establish the basis to correctly master the road, direction and soul of culture, invigorate cultural innovation, transmission, enterprise and industry, to spur on collaboration in the cultivation of cultural human resources and to realise cultural self-improvement.

Self-confidence in one's values is the concentrated reflection of cultural self-confidence. The strengthening of self-confidence in culture and values is now the concentrated reflection of the self-confidence in socialist core values. Values refer to the sum of people's viewpoints, opinions and attitude in coping with problems relating to universal values and are a deeper manifestation of culture. Socialist core values are the unique culture of society and the spiritual support of civilisation. *The Decision on the Major Issues for the CPC Central Committee to Build a Socialist Harmonious*

---

[1] The Xibaipo (西柏坡) spirit – The village of Xibaipo, some 80km northwest of Shijiazhuang, Hebei province, was the final base from which the CPC launched its victorious campaigns to defeat the KMT in 1947-1948 before winning the revolutionary war, unifying the country and founding the PRC.

[2] The strategy of self-reliance in cutting-edge science and technology for national defense which led China to detonate its first atomic bomb in October 1964 and to launch its first satellite '*Dongfanghong* I' ('The East Is Red') in April 1970 using a 'Long March' carrier rocket.

[3] The SARS (severe acute respiratory syndrome) or 'bird flu' epidemic hit southern China and Hong Kong in late 2002 through mid-2003 causing deaths and illness on a large scale before it was overcome.

Society made at the sixth plenary session of the 16th Central Committee of the CPC proposed the concept of a socialist core value system and the 18th NPC of the CPC brought forward the idea of socialist core values. Cultivating and practicing socialist core values has become the major pathway to boosting self-confidence in culture and values.

The strengthening of self-confidence in culture and values must run counter to the historical nihilism and national nihilism which belittle and defame Chinese culture and deny the great contributions delivered by the Chinese nation to human civilisation. Throughout the ages, no nation has ever defamed itself or denigrated all of its traditional culture. Conversely, the world's nations highly value their own history and take pride in their historical heritage. To combat historical nihilism and national nihilism, endeavours should be primarily made to correctly treat traditional culture, to be fully aware of the gigantic historical role of traditional culture, to discard the practice of scorning tradition and forgetting one's origins, to adhere to the policy of making the past serve the present and to inherit the quintessence of fine traditional Chinese culture. Second, it is necessary to rationally recognise foreign culture, to insist on cultural opening with a broad global vision and an inclusive and all-embracing attitude, to avoid acting arrogantly and narrow-mindedly, to adapt foreign things to Chinese needs and to absorb the essence of foreign culture for cultural innovation and renewal. Third, we should uncover the potential of the world's value of Chinese culture which not only belongs to China but also to the whole world and the whole of mankind. We should tap the vitality and glamour of Chinese culture amid cultural exchanges in a move to influence the world and mankind.

Volume I

Efforts should be made to clarify history, the development thread and the basic orientation of fine traditional Chinese culture and to clarify the unique creativity, values, ideas and distinctive features of fine traditional Chinese culture in a bid to boost self-confidence in our own culture and values.

— Xi Jinping

Chapter 1

The Historical Origin of Fine Traditional Chinese Culture

China's history of 5,000 years or more bears witness to the fact that the Chinese nation stands majestically in the world simply benefitting from the spiritual nourishment of its fine traditional Chinese culture. Every Chinese person can find the roots and soul of the Chinese nation from a long history of traditional culture.

1. The meaning of the words 'traditional' and 'culture'

'Traditional culture' has been a buzzword in recent years, where 'culture' is the tenet and 'traditional' modifies, defines and stresses 'culture'.

(1) Tradition: Passed on from generation to generation and deeply embedded in a long history

In *Ci Hai*, the comprehensive Chinese dictionary, 'tradition' is interpreted to be the thinking, culture, ethics, customs, art, institutions and behavioural patterns handed down from generation to generation during a long history that exert an intangible influence and control on people's social behaviour.

The main characteristic of tradition is its historic nature. All sorts of 'traditions' are handed down from one's ancestors and boast profound historical deposits. Not only does the value of inheritance play a certain role in the present but it also provides some help for future generations and determines the thought processes and actions of one's descendants. For instance, eating and dress codes, or local celebrations in some places often generate longstanding influence. Sometimes, people are subconsciously under the influence of traditions. Furthermore, some traditions have become instinctive for people and deeds naturally follow without the need to be taught. For example, the ethnic minorities are good at singing and dancing and cannot help dancing with joy on festive occasions, which is an example of instinctive actions stemming from traditions.

As times develop and change, traditions also have positive and negative effects. For example, the glorious tradition of patriotism and the national spirit of constantly seeking self-improvement are all positive traditions; for instance, the practice of ancestor worship on the grave-sweeping day (the Qingming festival) each year is a good tradition conveying later generations' reverence for their ancestors and should be carried forward. Nevertheless, some negative elements of traditions should be properly addressed and discarded. For instance, the feudal ethical code that 'it is improper for men and women to touch each other's hands when passing objects' and the filial piety that prohibits the son from criticising his father's wrongdoings are now incompatible with social progress. For this reason, traditions should be meticulously selected, transformed and updated while fine traditions should be passed on for generations.

Since 'traditional' and 'culture' are usually used together, some people mistake 'traditions' for 'traditional culture'. From the perspective of the concept of 'great culture', all social creations can be deemed as culture. But with 'traditional' before 'culture', the extension of 'culture' is actually narrowed to the scope of culture 'handed down for generations and identified by people'. In this sense, the so-called traditions are the culture handed down through history and identified relatively uniformly in society.

(2) Culture: Human culture constitutes social ethics

In ancient Chinese, 'wenhua' (meaning 'culture') referred to 'civil administration' and 'enlightenment'. 'Wen' and 'Hua' were used together in *The Book of Changes* • *Hexagram Bi* • *Lines and Hexagrams*: Firmness and gentleness comprise heavenly culture while civilisation refers to human culture. Heavenly culture shows the changes in nature while human culture constitutes social ethics. Culture is the achievement of civilisation produced by human beings. For instance, writing systems were invented by men and have served as a better tool for the exchange of ideas. Concurrently, writing systems are the carriers of culture, which can record history without the limitations of time and help later generations access the production experiences and cultural and technical knowledge gained by their predecessors; they also break through the limitations of space so that civilisations in different regions can communicate and integrate with each other. These all demonstrate how, with the promotion of culture, human beings have undergone constant advancement from obscurity during which they have not only rebuilt the world but also transformed themselves.

'Culture' is the object of research of many disciplines such as philosophy, sociology, anthropology and politics, and which are unable to decide which one of its myriad definitions is right. The word 'culture' is derived from the Latin word 'cultura' originally meaning land and crop cultivation and refers to material production activities such as farming and horticulture. With the progress of human society, this original meaning was extended to refer to spiritual production activities. Later, the meaning of culture was further expanded and came to refer to all the knowledge and even all the contents of social life in general.

In modern society, culture has become one of the most commonly used words in people's lives and academic activities, and has been defined from different perspectives. The culture in our present discussion does not refer to culture in a broad sense or that in our daily expression but the thoughts, ideas, spirit and value system with knowledge as the carrier in the material activities of rebuilding the world. As Ji Xianlin, a renowned Chinese linguist and literary translator, once pointed out, the deeper sense of Chinese culture was the characteristic of Chinese culture most evidently manifested in its ethical quality, the three cardinal bonds and the six lesser bonds (the six lesser bonds being: the first is the kinsmen of the father's generation on the father's side including the brothers and sisters of the father; the second is the brothers; the third is the clansmen; the fourth is the mother's brothers, namely, the kinsmen of the mother's generation on the mother's side; the fifth is the teachers and the sixth is the friends) and the mentality of solving the interpersonal ties advocated by Chinese culture; it is the most conspicuous feature of Chinese culture that differentiates it from that of other countries.

(3) Traditional culture: the culture of the Chinese nation and the international community

Traditional culture is the national culture developed as the civilisation evolves reflecting the characteristics, style and features of a nation. It is the overall manifestation of various aspects of ideology and culture in the national history. Compared with modern culture and foreign culture, it contains the cultural entities and consciousness of the materials, systems and spirit existing throughout history, for instance, national dress, life style and customs, classical poetry and essays, and concepts of loyalty and filial piety, namely, the qualities generally known as cultural legacy. Each nation or country with a long history has its unique traditional national culture; the longer the history of the nation or country, the deeper the ingrained cultural tradition and the greater the cultural influence on future generations.

There is a saying in the cultural domain: The more national it is, the more international it is. That is to say that the more distinct a culture is, the stronger is its international appeal. Definitely, whether or not the traditional culture of a nation is international depends on whether it conflicts with that of other countries or with social modernisation. Conversely, however unique a national culture is, it is difficult to gain international recognition and its internationalisation can end up merely being a self-hypothesis.

2. Where are the four major ancient civilisations now?

The entry of the human race into the era of civilisation was chiefly marked by the emergence of cities, metal products and writing systems. Ancient Babylon, ancient Egypt, ancient China and ancient India were the earliest birthplaces of human civilisation and hence acquired the reputation as the 'four major ancient civilisations', and the source of knowledge about philosophy, science, literature and art of the human race today.

(1) Mesopotamian culture, the cradle of civilisation

The area between the ancient Tigris and Euphrates rivers was one of the cradles of human civilisation and Western civilisation. The ancient Greeks called it 'Mesopotamia' meaning 'the place between two rivers' (the Tigris and Euphrates). With the present city of Baghdad as the boundary, Mesopotamia was divided into southern and northern parts. The ancient Assyrian city was the centre of the northern part, which was called Silesia or briefly Assyria; Babylon stood in the centre of the southern part, which was called Babylonia. Babylonia was further divided into two areas, namely, Sumer in the south close to the mouth of the Persian Gulf and Akkad, to the north of Sumer. The citizens of both places were respectively called Sumerians and Akkadians. The earliest Mesopotamian civilisation was created by the Sumerians. In the reign of King Hammurabi, the ancient kingdom of Babylon flourished and unified the Tigris and the Euphrates. For this, people were accustomed to calling the civilisation of the Tigris and Euphrates the Babylonian civilisation.

The world's earliest cities, schools, writing systems and libraries emerged between the Tigris and Euphrates. Especially, the first reformer in human history created the earliest and most intact ancient law book in human history, namely, the *Code of Hammurabi* there. Furthermore, the earliest proverbs, myths and epic poems were born there and the decimal and sexagesimal systems of mathematics were invented there. Especially, in the 6th century BC, Nebuchadnezzar of the Babylonian Empire built the Hanging Gardens of Babylon for the homesick Princess Armyitis. Noted as one of the eight wonders of the world, how the 'hanging' garden in the air was built remains a mystery to this day. The ups and downs of history, splendidly colourful literature, mysterious religion, sacred laws, lavish buildings, colourful art and daily life, and prominently successful science and technology all amazed and surprised people.

Mesopotamian civilisation hit its heyday in the 8th century BC and the Assyrian kingdom expanded into a huge military empire conquering Babylon, Syria, Phoenicia, Palestine, Asia Minor and Egypt successively and occupied almost all the countries bordering the Mediterranean coast except Greece and Italy. The year 612BC witnessed the attack on Assyria by the Chaldeans residing in Babylon and the Medes living in the east. Sin-shar-ishkun, the last king of Assyria, and his palace were burnt to ashes. The ancient Babylonian civilisation was not brought to light again until the 18th century thanks to incessant archaeological excavation and research by scholars.

(2) Egyptian civilisation, a wonder of the world

The pyramids, one of the eight wonders of the world, are the symbol of the civilisation of ancient Egypt. Egyptian civilisation has a history of more than 5,000 years which is known as the era of Egyptian civilisation in Western historical circles. However, generally speaking, Egyptian civilisation traditionally refers to the period from 3100BC to 332BC, namely, the period generally known as the civilisation of the Pharaoh era. 'Pharaoh' originally meant 'large house', referring to the palaces in the ancient kingdom and began to be used as a form of address for the king in the new kingdom simply because it was taboo for ordinary Egyptians to call the king by name. Now 'Pharaoh' customarily serves as the title for the king of Egypt.

The Egyptians in the era of the Pharaohs created one of the most brilliant civilisations in human history comprising: the ingenious hieroglyphics (pictographic writing system), resplendent literature, characteristic religious features, world-renowned pyramids, architectural marvels represented by masonry-built temples, eternal artistry exhibited by carvings and paintings, unique medicine showcased by mummification and amazing astronomy and mathematics.

In the year 332BC, King Alexander of Macedonia conquered Egypt and brought an end to the rule of the Persians. From then on, none of the kings reigning in Egypt was of Egyptian blood lineage and this marked the end of the era of the Egyptian Pharaohs boasting a history of up to 3,000 years. In 642, the Crescent banner rose along the Nile, symbolising that Egypt, the origin of human civilization, had entered the sphere of Islamic civilisation. For this reason, the full title of Egypt today is 'the Arab Republic of Egypt'.

(3) Indian civilisation, the hometown of Buddhism

India was formerly said to boast a history of 5,000 years of civilisation. Nevertheless, deduced from the latest underwater archaeological discovery, the history of India's civilisation may date back to between 8,000 and 9,000 years ago, surpassing that of Egypt. As early as 2300BC, city-states and the glorious Harappa civilisation had emerged along the Indus River Valley. The Gupta Empire sprang up in the 4th century and the ancient Indian civilisation went through a process of development of more than 2,600 years. Ancient India was the homeland of cotton and Buddhism, featuring the unique caste system and the slavery system, developed handicraft industry and commerce, profound literature and art, Buddhist architecture with its characteristic shapes, remarkable mathematical achievements, superior astronomy and unique medicine.

What most distinguished ancient Indian civilisation from other civilisations was its city design. The city planning of ancient India featured a grand scale and clear-cut boundaries between downtown areas and the citadel. The citadel had not merely protective high walls but also granaries and public facilities prepared for war; the downtown areas were arranged in order and drainage systems were established under almost every street; most of the houses were equipped with facilities indispensable for life such as wells, bathrooms and waste discharge pipes. It should also be mentioned that all the architecture in the downtown areas was built with bricks hardened in brick kilns, which was more advanced than the civilisations of ancient Egypt (applying stones) and Mesopotamia (using naturally dried bricks).

India was invaded and harassed by foreign forces during its history. The

British conquered the French in the 1760s and occupied India exclusively for 190 years. Despite countless intrusions by other nations and the impact of various external cultures, Indian culture has always prevailed with an uninterrupted principal line, namely, Hinduism encompassing Vedism, Brahmanism and Hinduism. The incessant enrichment of the Indian culture itself and the constant integration of foreign cultures fostered the diversity of Indian culture.

(4) Chinese civilisation, continuous vitality

Among the four great ancient civilisations worldwide, China is the only country whose process of development and traditions have not been interrupted.

As early as 10,000 years ago, the people of Yuchanyan (Jade Frog Cave) of Daoxian county, Hunan province began to domesticate rice (in recent years, some scholars reckon that the ancient Luoyue people residing in Long'an, Guangxi more than 10,000 years ago were the earliest to domesticate rice, see *'People's Daily Online* • Intellectual Property Rights' on 19 November 2012), which was the initial period of Chinese civilisation. Approximately 8,000 years ago, our ancestors were able to fabricate jade articles and carve symbols, which was the origin of Chinese characters. At least 7,000 years ago, our ancestors began to use lacquerware and smelt metals. China made a complete entry into the age of civilisation when the Xia dynasty (around the 21st century BC-16th century BC, the first dynasty of China) was founded and had an uninterrupted record of history in writing from the Shang dynasty (about 1600BC-1046BC).

Throughout its history, China has achieved a myriad of scientific, technological and cultural accomplishments represented by the four great inventions of ancient China (the compass, gunpowder, papermaking and printing) and delivered pivotal contributions to human civilisation. Historians hold the view that the times of Yao and Shun, mythical Chinese rulers and emperors, and the three dynasties[1] comprised the period of the birth and growth of Chinese culture and legend attributes the appearance of Chinese culture to a remoter stage of time, namely, the times of Emperor Yan and Emperor Huang 5,000 years ago when brilliant civilisation was created, such as the invention of the southward pointing cart (using a cart-

---

[1] Refers to the times of Yao and Shun who were the mythical heads of two united tribes and three dynasties, namely, the Xia, Shang and Zhou dynasties, which lasted for more than 2,000 years.

mounted gear and clutch mechanism to indicate south rather than the magnetic field of a compass) and the creation of medical science based on tasting hundreds of different types of herbs. Although the history of Emperor Yan and Emperor Huang cannot be traced, Chinese people have always firmly deemed themselves to be the descendants of Emperor Yan and Emperor Huang and believe that the descendants of the Chinese nation have always been rooted in native China and constantly carried forward the indigenous culture.

What merits special mention is the culture of the Zhou dynasty (1046BC-256BC) when Chinese culture was almost developed to its fullest. Moreover, the culture of that period laid a solid foundation for the later feudal Chinese culture of more than 2,000 years. The first tide of mind emancipation arose in the pre-Qin period (21st century BC-221BC) in Chinese history, which tapped the vitality of academic thinking and formed the basic pattern of traditional Chinese culture. The unification of the thinking and culture of the Chinese nation appeared in the Qin (221BC-207BC) and Han (202BC-220AD) dynasties which enjoyed sound economic development and advanced science and technology. The Tang (618AD-907AD) and Song (960AD-1279AD) dynasties were the pinnacle of Chinese feudal society and the mature period of traditional Chinese culture. The period from the Yuan (1271AD-1368AD) and Ming (1368AD-1644AD) dynasties until the mid-Qing (1636AD-1912AD) dynasty saw the decline of Chinese feudal society and constituted the period of the conclusion of traditional Chinese culture. Due to the invasion by Western powers, the eastward transmission of western sciences and the violent collision between the Chinese and Western cultures after the Opium Wars[2], traditional Chinese culture entered a transitional period. After enduring trials and tribulations, Chinese culture has not ever discarded the roots and the soul of its native culture.

3. The continuity of Chinese culture in ancient and modern times

How did the Chinese nation get its name? Two major explanations prevail about the word 'China'. First, China was initially defined to be the central area of the Yellow River. Two mountain ranges meet at

---

[2] After two invasions of China by Western countries, the Opium Wars ended in failure, the cession of territories and payment of indemnities by the Qing government which signed a series of unequal treaties with Western invaders and fell into a semi-colonial and semi-feudal society.

the border between Shanxi and Shaanxi. One is Zhongtiao Mountain frequented by Yao, Shun, Yu and Tang among the Three Emperors and Five Sovereigns in ancient China. The other is Huashan Mountain in the territory of Shaanxi, one of the origins of Chinese national culture. Connected together, the two mountains were called China (*zhonghua* is one of the words for China in Chinese – the '*zhong*' derived from Zhongtiao Mountain and the '*hua*' derived from 'Huashan Mountain). Second, the word 'China' was first seen in the ancient literature of the Wei and Jin dynasties. *The Book of Jin* • *The Biography of Chen Jun* records that Chen submitted a written statement to Wang Dao, saying: "China declines and the whole country collapses because of the wrong talent policy…" Here 'China' was relative to 'frontier', just like a county of a country. Emperor Hongwu was the first to apply 'China' in the political arena in ancient times. In the official call to arms he released to the Central Plains after he ordered Xu Da and others to launch the northern expedition in October of the first year of Wu, a state in the Zhou dynasty (1367), Zhu Yuanzhang (Emperor Hongwu) put forward the slogan 'expel the Northern barbarian tribes from ancient China and recover China'. In the late Qing dynasty, Sun Yat-sen borrowed it and proposed the slogan 'drive out the foreign invaders and recover China', led the campaigns to overturn the Qing dynasty and founded the 'Republic of China'.

(1) The Chinese are descended from the same roots and share a common origin

Emperor Shen Nung and Emperor Huang from the Xiong family represent the ancestors of the Chinese nation and the forefathers of Chinese culture. Chinese descendants refer to later generations of the Chinese nation who are also called 'the posterity of Emperor Huang and Emperor Yan'. Legend has it that from the ancient emperors until the emperors of the Xia, Shang and Zhou dynasties, all their descendants were regarded as linear descendants of Emperor Huang and that even the aboriginal tribes and ethnic minorities in ancient China were all included in the system. The later emperors all claimed to be the descendants of Emperor Huang. People of almost all family names can trace their remote ancestors back to Emperor Yan, Emperor Huang or their courtiers. And the ethnic minorities who were assimilated into Chinese culture (for instance, the Xiongnu, Xianbei and Qidan) also claimed to be the descendants of Emperor Huang and Emperor Yan. In the face of the invasion and encroachment of Western powers in the late Qing dynasty, some far-sighted people including ethnic minorities called for the barriers between ethnic groups to be broken to restore cohesion in China among the 'descendants of Emperor Yan and Emperor Huang'. Amid the invasion by formidable foreign enemies and the crisis of the threat of national extinction, the notion of the 'descendants of Emperor Yan and Emperor Huang' became the symbol for the Chinese whose basic culture was based on ancestor worship to build national cohesion. During the War of Resistance against Japanese Aggression (1937-1945), the label 'descendants of Emperor Yan and Emperor Huang' became synonymous with the Chinese nation in the flames of war against the Japanese enemy and served as a clarion call to stimulate Chinese at home and abroad to jointly rise up against the Japanese invaders. The CPC central committee said in a telegram to the Kuomintang (KMT) that: "We are all the descendants of Emperor Huang and the Chinese nation. With the national calamities before our eyes, we have no alternative but to reject all preconceived ideas, enter into close cooperation and march hand in hand on a great journey to emancipate the Chinese nation." Chiang Kai-shek pointed out in *To All the Soldiers in the Anti-Japanese War* that: "We are all descendants of Emperor Huang hurling ourselves into revolution." Both the KMT and the CPC held memorial ceremonies for the Mausoleum of Emperor Huang. Mao Zedong autographed the funeral oration and Chiang Kai-shek autographed the three characters '黄帝陵' (*huangdiling* – the Mausoleum of Emperor Huang). They all called themselves the 'descendants' of Emperor Yan and Emperor Huang. With pens as their weapon, scholars wrote articles eulogising the meritorious achievements of Emperor Yan and Emperor Huang and to mobilise the morale of soldiers and civilians to fight in the anti-Japanese war. Chen Ziyi said in an article that: "Those who were not the descendants of Emperor Huang were encompassed as the descendants of Emperor Huang no matter what their surnames were"; "the later generations of the Chinese nation were all descendants of Emperor Huang." Mr Qian Mu, a master of Chinese learning, held the view in his book Emperor Huang that it is sensible for us all to call ourselves the 'descendants of Emperor Yan and Emperor Huang', expressing his agreement with the appellations of 'the descendants of Emperor Yan and Emperor Huang' and 'the descendants of Emperor Huang'.

Even to this day, the appellation of 'the descendants of Emperor Yan and

Emperor Huang' is more of a cultural symbol than a symbol of bloodline. Overseas Chinese call themselves 'the descendants of Emperor Yan and Emperor Huang', which actually identifies with Chinese culture. As long as that psychological recognition continues, the appellation will continue to be used.

(2) The descendants of the Yan Emperor and the Yellow Emperor come from the same family

The title of descendants of the Yan Emperor and the Yellow Emperor stresses the unification of the blood relationship and culture, which reflects the extension of history and culture from ancient times until now. During the 5,000 years of China's development, the union of tribes of Yan and Huang evolved from the Huaxia (an ancient name for China) nation to the Chinese nation. They intermarried, integrated and learnt from cultural exchanges with one another with the blood of Yan and Huang flowing in their veins. This was also the basis for us to call ourselves the descendants of Yan and Huang.

Xie Junxiang, a renowned cultural expert on family names, has conducted special research on the family names of people on the Central Plains. His research results indicate that among the 4,820 family names whose source can be traced, 1,834 originated in Henan, accounting for 38%; among the top 120 major surnames sequenced according to the population and taking up 90.14% of the Han population, 52 could be dated back to Henan and 45 partially to Henan. The population of surnames originated in Henan covered more than 80% of the Han population. Whether in primitive society when matriarchy prevailed and the 'surname' was originated or in patriarchal society where the 'family name' was originated, Henan served as the focal area for human activities. In terms of the blood relationship, the present 120 major surnames respectively belonged to three clan families, namely, the family of Emperor Huang, the Emperor Yan and the Dongyi clan, with Henan as the centre of the long-term activities of the three families. During the Xia and Shang dynasties when surnames developed fast, Henan was the location of the nation's capital. The Xia and Shang dynasties also witnessed the emergence and thriving of slavery and the burgeoning development of Chinese surnames, with present Henan as the centre of the activities of the two dynasties.

(3) The values that the descendants of the Yan Emperor and the Yellow Emperor identify with

The moral qualities jointly honoured and pursued by the descendants of the Yan Emperor and the Yellow Emperor refer to benevolence, righteousness, etiquette, knowledge (wisdom), faith, filial piety, loyalty, honesty, lenience and harmony that encompass extensive cultural connotations. Benevolence refers to the basic principle of handling interpersonal relationships advocating 'love of others' and caring for everyone; righteousness, essentially meaning 'kindness' or 'beauty', refers to the fact that the behaviour of every individual should benefit others and society; etiquette is the code of conduct for people to jointly abide by in their social life since it is the foundation for individuals to get on in the world and for the state to be established and maintain peace; knowledge, pronounced 'zhi' in ancient China, has three implications, namely, to know oneself, to know others and to know about the world; faith refers to sincerity without cheating; filial piety, usually referring to 'filial obedience', essentially means treating parents, kinsfolk and elders well, and most fundamentally waiting on and supporting one's parents; loyalty in essence represents selfless dedication, commitment, sincerity and all-out effort; honesty implies sincerity without cheating; lenience hints at generosity, broadmindedness, having a relaxed attitude, and being comforting, tolerant and magnanimous; harmony means being accommodating and willing to act in concert.

The descendants of the Yan Emperor and the Yellow Emperor have a cultural spirit they jointly abide by and pursue: the spirit of seeking truth from facts and proceeding from reality; the humanist spirit of the unity of heaven and mankind and living in harmony with nature; the struggling spirit of being bold in practice and innovation, being vigorous, and promising and seeking self-improvement; the ethnic spirit of valuing benevolence and righteousness, focusing on openness based on sincerity, upholding harmony and 'the mean', and stressing courtesy; the patriotic and collective spirit of being concerned about the country and the people, being indifferent to fame and fortune, putting the interests of the whole above everything else and making selfless contributions.

From a superficial perspective, the descendants of the Yan Emperor and the Yellow Emperor have some tokens and cultural totemic symbols that they mutually recognise and abide by. For instance, the ancestors created the dragon totem and activities including the dragon lantern dance are often held in celebration of traditional Chinese festivals. The dragon can soar up into the heavens and down into the depths of the earth, speed across the sky, control the forces of nature and brew up storms on rivers and seas. Therefore, the dragon totem symbolises the lofty personality and ambitions of the Chinese nation.

For another example, the Chinese nation has always pursued safety, luck and happiness and has endowed many articles with strong symbolic meanings which imply complex emotions that are difficult to part with. For instance, the auspicious red Chinese knot, the red lanterns hung during festivals, the red character 'fortune' pasted on the door and the plum blossom, orchid, bamboo and chrysanthemum as themes frequently selected in traditional Chinese paintings all reflect connotations of the ideals and pursuits of the Chinese people.

Just as the lyrics in the song 'My Chinese Heart' describe: "My ancestors long ago imbued me with all the Chinese attributes." Wherever they go, as long as they are the descendants of the Chinese nation, they will be tightly linked together by symbols strongly imbued with Chinese culture.

4. The cultural community of multi-ethnic integration

China is a big, unified, multi-ethnic family and the integrated development of the culture of all ethnic minorities is indispensable for the development of the root system of Chinese culture. The shared prosperity of the 56 ethnic minorities has fostered the present thriving culture of the Chinese nation.

(1) 56 ethnic minorities bloom like 56 flowers

The big family of the Chinese nation comprises 56 fraternal ethnic nationalities with unique characteristics. The culture of all the ethnic minorities boasts commonality and distinctive features which add radiant splendour and amazing beauty to the culture of the whole Chinese nation.

The totem of the Han nationality features the design of a dragon and a phoenix respectively representing *yin* and *yang*, namely, female and male. The flying dragon and dancing phoenix symbolise the ethnic minorities in the central plains and southern China. The builder of most regimes in history, the Han nationality created a brilliant culture based on absorbing the culture of other ethnic minorities.

The Li nationality residing on Hainan island created oral literature, lively forms of song and dance, extensive themes and abundant contents handed down from generation to generation. The brocade craftsmanship of the Li ethnic minority has a unique style and the four major crafts such as spinning, weaving, dyeing and embroidery enable a wide range of designs including exotic flowers and rare herbs, fowls, beasts and figures. Enjoying considerable fame since the Spring and Autumn period, it is reputed as a 'living fossil' in the history of textile technology and production in China and has been nominated into 'UNESCO's intangible cultural heritage in urgent need of protection'.

The Tibetan people living on the Qinghai-Tibet plateau created the splendid national culture represented by the Potala Palace, the most massive and intact ancient palace architecture existing in China.

The Yi nationality are good at song and dance performances featuring numerous sorts of clothes with a riot of colours concretely manifesting the traditional culture and the aesthetic consciousness of the Yi people. The year 2006 saw the nomination of the 'Haicai tune of the Yi nationality' and the 'cigarette case dance of the Yi nationality' into the first group of China's State-level Intangible Cultural Heritage List.

The ethnic enclaves of the Naxi nationality have abundant cultural heritage. For the ancient documents of Dongba, the Naxi nationality was nominated to the Memory of the World Register in 2003, and the paintings and manual papermaking skills of the Naxi nationality were nominated to be included as part of China's Intangible Cultural Heritage in 2006.

The Dragon Boat Tune is one of the world's 25 major folk songs. Tujia brocade, also called Xilan Kapu brocade, meaning 'bedding of decorative design' in Tujia language, is reputed to be one of China's five major types of brocade thanks to its unique craftsmanship and fantastic composition.

The Qiang nationality, the oldest nationality in southeastern China, is renowned as 'a nationality amid the clouds' because of the position of Qiang village stockades halfway up the sides of hills, and was mentioned in the oracle bone scripts. The most famous musical instrument of the Qiang people is the characteristic *qiangdi* (Qiang flute) boasting a history of more than 2,000 years and a wide range of contents. Wang Zhihuan, a poet of the Tang dynasty, created the verses in his poem:

Chapter 1

'Why should the Qiang flute play that sad broken willow tune beyond the Jade Gate where the spring wind never blows?'.

The Drung ethnic minority (literally *dulongzu* 独龙族 or 'independent dragon people') with a population of about 7,000 living in Yunnan province still maintains the tradition of not installing any door locks on most houses but latching them with two sticks or casually closing doors without any fear of being burgled. They regard stealing as shameful, despicable behaviour and as something that should be punished by clansmen. For this reason, the Drung nationality features good social morality and a prevailing honesty.

The Uygur nationality has its unique culture and art, most represented by the Mukam art. The large, comprehensive art form integrating song and dance entertainment was nominated into the first group of the China Intangible Cultural Heritage List in 2006.

The Mongol ethnic minority, with its long history, has left behind abundant spiritual wealth represented by *The Secret History of the Mongols*, the oldest historical records of the Mongol ethnic minority and *Jangar*, one of the three great epic tales of China's ethnic minorities…

As the Chinese saying goes: "A mother gave birth to nine children of different personalities." The above examples show that any ethnic minority from the big family of the Chinese nation has its own uniqueness. It is precisely the distinctive characteristics of all ethnic minority cultures that adds to the diversity and richness of Chinese culture.

(2) 56 ethnic minorities, one communal family

The 56 ethnic minorities share the same family name 'China'.

The word 'China' arose in the Spring and Autumn period, originally a territorial concept referring to the areas directly under the jurisdiction of the emperor of the Zhou dynasty and the vassal states in the middle and lower reaches of the Yellow River such as the State of Jin, the State of Zheng, the State of Song, the State of Lu and the State of Wei, and extending to the Guanzhong area along the Wei river basin in the Qin and Han dynasties. For quite a long time, the concept of 'China' was vague and did not become clear as a country concept until the invasion by Western colonial powers in the late Qing dynasty. Nevertheless, it was still called 'the Great Qing Dynasty' at that time. After the Republic of China was established in January 1912, 'China' became the abbreviated title of the country. After the People's Republic of China was founded in October 1949, 'China' was still used for short.

Although 'China' is a territorial concept, it is the title of a social community. In the big family formed by 56 ethnic minorities living together, each ethnic minority has its own lifestyle and ethnic culture. As Feng Youlan, a renowned Chinese philosopher and philosophical historian, said: "The culture of a nation is the crystallization of its spiritual activities." People in different countries and territories have their own lifestyles and their own culture or traditions. Nonetheless, people of different ethnic minorities living together harmoniously in a big family need to share a common mentality and sense of identity. In this respect, although the ethnic cultures are different, they are unified in the culture of the big family of China. That sort of unification implies abundant individuality, which is also a Chinese cultural trait, namely, unity without uniformity.

(3) 56 ethnic minorities jointly create Chinese culture

The culture created jointly by the 56 ethnic minorities within the borders of China is called 'Chinese culture'. The Han nationality, which evolved from the Huaxia nationality, is the main constituent of the Chinese nation while the culture of the Han nationality is the main constituent of Chinese culture. Many ethnic minorities were integrated into the Han nationality during its historical development and their own national cultural characteristics were assimilated into Han culture. Therefore, the glorious Chinese culture is the ethnic culture jointly created by the Chinese ethnic minorities with the Han nationality being the main constituent which can be called accordingly 'Huaxia culture' or 'Chinese culture'.

In the long evolution of cultural history, people of all ethnic minorities lived together in minority areas in northern and southern China. The cultural forms of the Han nationality and the ethnic minorities influenced each other in terms of lifestyle, political systems, customs, conventions and religious beliefs due to historical migration patterns. Meanwhile, people of all ethnic minorities in China went through multiple intersection and integration through migration, aggregation, trading and even war, for instance, the integration of the farming culture in the Central Plains into the nomadic culture in northern China and the shifting farming culture in the mountainous regions of southern China. The ethnic minorities in northern and southern China made multifaceted contributions to Chinese culture. Many patterns of basic necessities of life, singing, dancing and entertainment were introduced from ethnic minority areas, for instance, such vegetables and fruits as cucumbers (originally called 'pepino'), walnuts (originally called 'Juglans regia') and pomegranates were brought to the Central Plains via the ethnic minorities in the northwest. In addition, mutton shashlik, Chinese-style baked rolls, grape wine and brewing techniques for distilling Chinese spirits also originated from ethnic minority areas in the western region of China. Even the earliest seat for daily living was the 'campstool' introduced by the nomads.

In terms of music and dancing, ethnic minorities are all good at singing and dancing. The musical instruments unearthed in the minority areas in northwestern and southwestern China in recent years have a long history and a wide variety, as exemplified by such superb material objects as the Neolithic stone chime unearthed in Dongdu, Qinghai province and the bronze drum from the Warring States period discovered in Chuxiong, Yunnan province. What's more, the Qiang flute, the frame drum of the Uygurs, the *sheng* (a reed pipe wind instrument) of the Zhuang and Miao ethnic minorities, the *konghou* (an ancient plucked stringed instrument), the 4-stringed Chinese lute, the brass cymbals, the *suona* horn (a wooden wind instrument), the *huqin* (a general term for certain two-stringed bowed instruments) and horse-hair string instruments are all indispensable musical instruments for traditional Chinese orchestras.

Dancing is part of the unique culture of an ethnic minority and almost every ethnic minority has its own traditional dances for religious worship and folk dances as well as classical and entertainment dances handed down for generations. For instance, the *Buluoto* fable of the Zhuang nationality has been nominated to the China Intangible Cultural Heritage List. *Buluoto* is a mythological figure in the oral literature of the ancestors of the Zhuang people, meaning 'omniscient senior citizen'. The Zhuang people are adept at singing and dancing and hold singing contests at fixed or irregular intervals; for instance, originating in the Spring and Autumn and the Warring States period and with a history of more than 2,500 years, the Kam Grand Choir is a multi-voice, naturally symphonic folk chorus without conductor or accompanying music played by folk song troupes in the Chinese area inhabited by the Dong people. The moment the Kam Grand Choirs of Liping county's Dong people struck a pose on the stage at the Autumn Festival in Paris, France in 1986, they astounded the audience with their singing skill which was considered to be 'glittering music like a clear spring with melodies skimming over the edge of ancient dreams'...

How humdrum and boring it would be without the song and dance performances by ethnic minorities on China's culture and art stage!

As for literature, 53 of the 55 ethnic minorities have their unique languages and only the Hui people and the Manchus speak mandarin. Additionally, many ethnic minorities have their own writing systems and have created numerous literary works in their own languages. Tibet has a long cultural tradition and the Tibetan language was invented in the 7th century BC. With its own alphabet, it is called the Sino-Tibetan language together with the Chinese language, and *The Epic of King Gesar* written in Tibetan is the world's longest heroic epic. *Jangar*, a long epic tale of the Mongol nationality, fills the blanks in the heroic epics of the Han nationality. The long verses of the *Kutadgu Bilig* and the widely known *The Tales of the Effendi* are both treasures of the Uygur nationality.

Throughout history, all China's ethnic minorities have made due contributions to the development of Chinese culture. In terms of the essence of the ethnic minorities, it is the nation, namely, the Chinese nation. Both as the descendants of the Yan Emperor and the Yellow Emperor and the dragon, the Han nationality and other ethnic minorities of the Chinese nation have complemented each other for generations, are renowned far and wide, and always uphold the lofty moral integrity of ancestor worship and remembering their roots. The spirits of the Chinese ancestors represented by the Yan Emperor and the Yellow Emperor creating the world and arduously starting businesses constitute the source of the power that motivates the people of all ethnic minorities to strive for unity, progress, active exploitation and self-improvement.

Chapter 2

The Development Thread of Fine Traditional Chinese Culture

Culture is the crystallisation of human beings' social activities. For a nation with a long history of continuous development, the long accumulation and inheritance of culture forms its tradition. Culture forming tradition is just like a river running for thousands of years where modern people nourished by a culture can still feel the vicissitudes and mellowness of history and absorb richer spiritual nutrition from it.

1. The pre-Qin period: The emergence of culture and all schools of thought contending for attention

A dividing line can be drawn between Chinese culture before and after the unification by the Qin dynasty universally known as the pre-Qin culture. It can be further divided into three stages of development: the primitive stage, the Xia-Shang-Zhou period, and the Spring and Autumn and Warring States period (770BC-221BC).

(1) The primitive stage: the germination of culture

The record of the earliest paintings of the Chinese ancestors in *Mister Lü's Spring and Autumn Annals* indicates that painting appeared quite early in China. In the prosperous matriarchal society, plants, animals and decorative geometric designs were well proportioned and beautiful, realistic and abstract. Ivory combs, ivory carved cylinders and terracotta zoomorphic ware unearthed in Dawenkou show the exquisite carving art and the quality of pottery products in those years.

The traditions of 'keeping records by tying knots' and 'wood engraving' in ancient times have been verified by archaeological discovery. The earthenware unearthed in Banpo, Xi'an province, comprised 32 types of carved symbols. Similar symbols were discovered on cultural relics such as the earthenware excavated at historic sites. The neat and orderly graphic symbol strokes on the earthenware of the Dawenkou culture and the Liangzhu culture were thought to be the earliest graphic characters in China. Later, pictographic paintings evolved to become pictographic characters, gradually became divorced from graphics and developed into Chinese characters. A complete system of Chinese characters was formed in the Shang dynasty.

Historical records, unearthed musical instruments and primitive paintings can help us to know about the music and dancing in primitive society. *The Origin of the World* mentions that: 'the drum was invented by a person of the Yi ethnic minority in ancient times'. It is a pity that no such drum has been kept. The voluminous Song-era unofficial history of China *Road History* (*Lushi* 路史 or *The Path of History*) recorded: 'Paoxi burnt the earth and made the *Xun* (an ancient egg-shaped instrument); Fu Hsi cut the *tung* tree to make a musical instrument; Ling Lun made the *Pan*, a musical instrument, with stone.' Ancient musical instruments such as the *Xun* and *Pan* were often unearthed. Excavated cultural relics and ancient frescos contain many drawings of dancing. On the ancient coloured pottery unearthed in the Ma Family's Kiln, 15 dancing figures were painted.

The ancestors in primitive society devoutly worshiped nature, totems and their forefathers. The ancient Chinese chiefly worshiped such natural elements as the sun, the moon, mountains, stones, fire, water, earth, heaven and the stars, and such natural phenomena as wind, rain, thunder and electricity. The worship of totems originated in the pursuit of ancestral roots and prevailed in the matriarchal period. People believed that the clans stemmed from some animals, plants or inanimate matter and took them as clan emblems. Totems were also considered to be the ancestors and patron saints of the clans. Ancestor worship was rooted in the idea that ancestors' souls were imperishable. Female ancestor worship prevailed in matriarchal society. Nü Wa in Chinese mythology was the icon in the age of feminism. After patriarchy was set up, the legendary Pan Gu, Fu Hsi, the Yan Emperor and the Yellow Emperor were worshiped as icons in the paternally-dominated era. Primitive witchcraft was a religious faith and a primitive culture. In the early stage of religion, there were no specialised sorcerers or priests and the rites were usually directed by tribal elders. Afterwards, the masters (a title of respect for a Buddhist or Taoist priest), sorcerers, priests or Shamans were given special responsibility for contacts with the mysterious and the supernatural, and became the predecessors of intellectuals.

(2) The Xia-Shang-Zhou period: vigorous cultural growth

The project of the division of the history of the Shang and Zhou dynasties presided over by Li Xueqin, director of the Ancient Civilisation Research Centre of the Chinese Academy of Social Sciences (CASS) and the release of the Xia-Shang-Zhou Chronological Table showed that in 2070BC, Yu the Great founded the Xia dynasty, the first dynasty in Chinese history. It marked the end of the primitive society ruled by the 'Three Sovereigns and Five Emperors[1]' in China.

The Xia dynasty spanned 470 years, 14 generations and 17 emperors. The Shang dynasty was founded in 1600BC spanning a period of 554 years, 17 generations and witnessed the reign of 31 emperors. The Shang dynasty came to an end in 1046BC and was replaced by the Zhou dynasty. The Western Zhou dynasty lasted 275 years, 11 generations and the reigns of 12 emperors.

The patriarchal system was the dominant cultural feature of the Xia, Shang and Zhou dynasties. Germinating in the Xia dynasty, the complete patriarchal system was established in the Western Zhou dynasty. It was marked by the lineal primogeniture system, the feudal system of landholding and a rigorous sacrificial system. Under the patriarchal system, 'rites' were compulsory and binding on each clansman. As a matter of fact, the patriarchal system became an unwritten common law, and although it began to collapse in the late Western Zhou dynasty, it had a long-term influence on Chinese society. The feudal patriarchal clan system of the Western Zhou dynasty left scholars in the Spring and Autumn and Warring States period with the notion that 'society was ruled by a collective master'. That idea laid the foundation for the establishment and unification of the kingdoms of Qin and Han. The

---

[1] The Three Sovereigns and the Five Emperors: The Three Sovereigns were said to be god-kings or demigods who used their magical powers to improve the lives of their people. Because of their lofty virtue they lived to a great age and ruled over a period of great peace. They included the Heavenly King who ruled for 18,000 years, the Earthly King who rule for 11,000 years and the Human King who ruled for 45,600 years. The Five Emperors were legendary, morally perfect sage-kings. They included the Yellow Emperor, Zhuanxu, Ku, Yao and Shun.

patriarchal system influenced not only politics but also the ruling class. It was later universally inherited as the basic concept of the patriarchal clan in civil society.

Ancient history records that: 'The politics of the Xia dynasty were corrupt and hence the *Law of the Xia Dynasty Ruled by Yu the Great* was prepared'. It was the first law book in Chinese history. Ancient historical legend noted that: 'Gao Yao made the law', 'Gao Yao established criminal punishment' and 'Gao Yao set up prisons'. Consequently, Gao Yao was worshiped by later generations as the forefather of the prison system, namely, the God of Prisons. Legend has it that when Gao Yao found it difficult to handle lawsuits, he would decide by means of the *Xie Zhi*, a unicorn or mythical creature like a bull or a sheep. The judges wore '*Xie Zhi* caps' in the Han and Tang dynasties and *Xie Zhi*-design clothes in the Ming and Qing dynasties. Now the head of a unicorn is still engraved on the judicial mallet in court symbolising impartial law enforcement. The *Xie Zhi* has become a remarkable emblem of the legal and political culture of China for thousands of years.

In the ages of Yao, Shun and Yu, primitive democratic conventions were applied to discussions of official business. According to legend, Yao set up a drum for protestation, Shun set up a board for protestation and Yu arranged for five musical instruments (drum, bell, big bell, chime stone and rattle drum) so that people could toll to state their ideas or grievances in court trials. These ancient customs gradually died out. Only the practice of 'beating the drum' outside the yamen, a government office in feudal China for filing a suit, continued for quite a long time.

The sacrificial vessels of the Shang and Zhou dynasties were predominantly represented by bronze ware and jade ware. It is said that bronze ware making techniques reached their peak in the Xia dynasty. Yu the Great once had nine tripod cauldrons forged and they were adopted as a national treasure. The tripod cauldron served as a token of nobility. The ancient books record that it was the prevailing system for the emperor to be represented by nine tripod cauldrons, the feudal princes by seven, senior officials by five, and junior officials by three or one. In addition, the tripod cauldron was also the symbol of state power. The bronze *simuwu fangding*, the largest and heaviest four-legged cauldron of its kind, was cast in the latter period of the Shang dynasty, namely, from the 14th to the 11th century BC. It signified that

China's bronze-working technology was advanced and mature as early as the Shang dynasty. The handicraft industry saw an increase in variety and more detailed categorisation in the Zhou dynasty and featured a multitude of craftsmanship.

The Yin and Yang and Five Elements theories that matured in the Shang and Zhou dynasties marked the earliest induction of natural phenomena into Chinese culture. The Five Elements[1] and Eight Trigrams[2] theory became one of the thought patterns of the Chinese. Tortoise shells or bones were used as divination tools in the Shang dynasty and the people of the Zhou dynasty used the Eight Trigrams comprising the Yin and Yang symbols and the supplemented hexagram as tools to predict good or bad luck. The work recording the Eight Trigrams was named *The Book of Changes* which is thought to be the 'origin of Chinese culture', the 'source of Oriental wisdom' and the 'algebra of the universe'. *The Book of Changes* boasts a longer history than The Bible and has been enshrined as the top of the classics for more than 2,000 years since Confucius made modifications and deletions to the 'six classics' (the six Confucian classics including *The Book of Poetry, The Book of History, The Book of Rites, The Book of Music, The Book of Changes* and *The Spring and Autumn Annals*).

The tortoise shells used for divination were also applied for letters, keeping a record of events and writing articles. The oracle bone inscriptions of the Shang dynasty are the earliest characters discovered so far, boasting a history of more than 3,300 years. The characters recorded on the tortoise shells laid a foundation for the phonograms, namely, the basis of the main Chinese characters.

In the late Shang dynasty, the Zhou people gradually rose under the benevolent rule of Emperor Wen of Zhou. After the Duke of Zhou named Dan acted as regent, he made rituals and music and formulated a series of political guidelines, a code of ethics and ancient laws and regulations. These rites, musical systems and ideology, after being supplemented and improved by later generations, formed a distinctive ritual and musical culture and civilization, and exercised a huge, far-reaching influence on the Chinese culture of all dynasties. They also

---

[1] The Five Elements refer to metal, wood, water, fire and earth.
[2] The Eight Trigrams refer to the three combinations of three whole or broken lines formerly used in divination.

guaranteed the powerful cohesion of the Chinese nation in the face of natural and man-made disasters, domestic strife and foreign aggression for thousands of years.

(3) The Spring and Autumn and Warring States period: All schools of thought contended for attention

With the decline of the Zhou dynasty, the old ideologies, rites and musical systems collapsed one after another. The ideas advocated and theories and views on social reform became dynamic and led to a situation where 'all schools of thought contended for attention'. It was the first age of ideological and cultural prosperity in Chinese history.

In that period, the educational structure of learning among feudal officials was broken. The idea of 'making no social distinctions in teaching' took shape. It was the cultural environment that fueled the development and invigoration of the intellectuals, namely, the 'scholar' class.

The 'scholar' class was a special class among the four main occupations, namely, the scholar, farmer, artisan and merchant. The 'scholars' appeared in China very early, in the Shang and Zhou dynasties. It referred to all levels of aristocrats including the feudal princes in general and to the lowest level of aristocrats in particular. Most of the time, it referred to the middle and lower ranking officials of the government departments. After the patriarchal clan system was shaken up, the scholar class experienced many changes and became a general reference to intellectuals. Going through the education in six classical arts such as standards of morality and etiquette, music and dance rituals, shooting techniques, carriage harnessing, calligraphy (now literature) and algorithms, most of the intellectuals developed cultural literacy. In the Spring and Autumn and the Warring States period, the scholar class expanded. The scholars were dynamic in that period. Unlike their past counterparts, they were less bound by the relationships of the patriarchal clan system and freer to take action: 'The prime minister of the State of Qi today may suddenly move to serve in the same position in the State of Wu later on.'

The campaign 'All schools of thought contend for attention' was the contention of a hundred schools of thought, such as the Confucian school, the Taoist school, the Mohist school, the School of Logicians, the Legalists, the military strategists in ancient China and the political strategists. According to the *History of the Han Dynasty - The History of Art and Literature*, a total of 189 schools contributing 4,324 articles participated in the contention. Afterwards, about 10 of them developed to become schools. These schools wrote and proposed ideas, discussed political affairs, influenced and criticised each other. They jointly presented a splendid, flourishing cultural development, just like flowers of every kind in bloom.

Some representative schools are highlighted as follows:

The Mohist school was founded by Mo Di. He studied Confucianism in his early years. After that, he abandoned it and established the Mohist school most fiercely against Confucianism. The leading thoughts of Mo Zi (Mo Di) were 'universal love' and 'non-offence', aiming to save the world in accordance with the principles of 'universal love and mutual benefit'. Mo Zi's thinking had enormous influence and was regarded as monstrous by the Confucians.

Confucianism was established by Confucius, which highly valued blood relations, human relations according to feudal ethics, worldly achievements, practical reason and moral cultivation with distinction. It took the responsibility to inherit and carry forward the rites, music and traditions of the Western Zhou dynasty. 'Benevolence' was the uppermost ideal state and the centre of Confucian ethical thinking. Mencius was the direct successor of Confucianism and was addressed respectfully by later generations as a 'secondary saint'. The thinking of Mencius primarily advocated 'applying benevolent government' in a kindly way and 'modeling oneself after the deceased king'. And Mencius also proposed the 'doctrine of good human nature'. In stark contrast, Xun Kuang, another successor of Confucianism, integrated Confucianism and Legalism as well as the ideology of military power, learning from the kings of recent antiquity and unification of the Legalist school, and strongly advocated the doctrine of evil human nature.

Lao Tzu and Chuang Tzu were the representative figures of Taoism. In the *Tao Te Ching* (the sacred text of Buddhism), Lao Tzu put forward a virtual nihilistic concept surpassing everything called the 'way' (the Tao or the path) or 'bigness'. The 'way' was the core philosophical idea of Lao Tzu. Lao Tzu's advocacy of social politics and life was 'inactivity' (meaning letting things take their own course). He held the view that only 'letting things take their own course' could 'make everything possible' (Chapter 25 of the *Tao Te Ching*). Chuang Tzu inherited Lao Tzu's thoughts and *Chuang Tzu* further shaped the 'way' advocated by Lao Tzu. The Taoist ideology of 'standing aloof from worldly affairs' and the thought of 'going into society' jointly fostered the attitude towards life with Chinese characteristics. Rulers could register political and military achievements by means of Confucian doctrines and rehabilitate themselves with Taoism. The 'compatibility of Confucianism and Taoism' constituted the basic framework and feature of Chinese culture.

Legalism originated from the ideologies of Guan Zhong and Zi Chan. The representatives in the early stage included Li Li, Wu Qi and Shang Yang in the early Warring States period. Their ideology was predicated on 'political reform' and they advocated replacing the ancient rites with the present laws. The representative in the later stage was Han Feizi in the last years of the Warring States period. He inherited the magic arts of Lao Tzu and the laws and the magic arts of the early Legalists. He also proposed basing everything on law. In addition, he stood for the extreme idea of monarchical power. The Qin dynasty, the first unified empire of China, was founded based on the political blueprint of centralised autocratic government provided in such representative works of the Legalist school as *The Book of Shang Yang* and *Han Feizi*.

In addition to the Confucian school, the Mohist school, the Legalist school and the Taoist school, other schools of the pre-Qin dynasty also scored accomplishments. For instance, the Yin and Yang school developed the primitive Five Element Theory, advocating that the five elements mutually reinforced and neutralised each other and linked everything in the world to Yin and Yang and the Five Elements to determine good or bad luck, weal and woe. Zou Yan, a representative of the School of Logicians, explained dynastic changes with the theory of the mutual generation of five elements and established the theory of five cyclical virtues. It was a fusion of both theology and mystical historicism. Zou Yan initiated the theory of 'nine states' and his global thinking integrating all the elements had a great impact on later generations.

Although all the philosophical schools of thought were different, they shared the same or similar theme, namely, the relationship between 'natural law' and 'humanity', that is, 'the relation between heaven and mankind'. They comprehensively and dialectically expounded the source and law of the natural universe (heaven and earth) and the reason for the improvement of mankind and the harmonious coexistence between mankind and nature. It was markedly different from the Western philosophical thought represented by ancient Greece based on experiential knowledge and cherishing science, knowledge and wisdom.

2. The Qin and Han dynasties: the thriving of original Chinese culture

Emperor Ying Zheng of the Qin dynasty unified China in 221BC. Afterwards, the First Emperor of Qin followed Li Si's suggestions, promoted the system of prefectures and counties all over the country, and founded the first centralised country featuring feudal autocracy in Chinese history. Although the Qin dynasty perished in the reign of the second emperor, the regime of centralism it established had a long-term influence on later generations. It was carried on by succeeding dynasties and lasted for more than 2,000 years in China. As to culture, the descendants believed that the orders of the First Emperor of Qin to burn the books and bury the literati in pits led to cultural retrogression. Actually, many of his cultural achievements went down in history.

(1) Unification of the country and culture

After unifying the country, the Qin dynasty resolutely carried out a series of new moves to fuel cultural development, which also unified the cultural community. These major moves included: first, the unification of the writing system, namely, 'moving toward one system of Chinese characters'. After long-term evolution, Chinese characters gradually evolved differently in the last years of the Zhou dynasty. The First Emperor of Qin ordered Li Si to preside over the project of 'unifying the writing system'. Li Si changed the complex and troublesome big-seal script into evenly round and orderly 'small-seal script' (namely, Qinzhuan, an ancient style of calligraphy adopted in the Qin dynasty) as the official standard font used in laws and decrees. Concurrently, Prison Officer Cheng Miao, according to the simplified Chinese characters prevailing among the common people, invented the clerical script. It was simpler than the seal script and was popularised nationwide as the writing system for daily use. 'Unifying the writing system' made a substantial contribution to cultural transmission and development. Second, was to unify the currency. The Qin dynasty stipulated that the currency be divided into gold coins with round outer edges and square holes in the middle. Gold was the dominant currency with *yi* as the unit (1 *yi* = 1,000g); the coin with a round edge and a square hole in the middle was the auxiliary currency with half a *liang* (25g) as the unit. Third was to unify the measurement system. It was necessary to promote a unified measuring system, to carve scales on the measuring instruments and to regularly check the accuracy and unification of the scale. Fourth was to unify the laws. Based on the original criminal laws, the Qin dynasty enacted a unified legal system, 'made clearly defined and scientific laws' and implemented the laws nationwide. Some articles of the *Law of the Qin Dynasty* in the bamboo slips of the Qin dynasty were unearthed in Yunmeng county, Hubei province. They indicated that the laws of the Qin dynasty were complicated, detailed and complete.

Moves by the Qin dynasty to unify the culture were aimed at reinforcing absolute centralization of the monarchy. But they objectively accelerated people's identity in social life and even cultural psychology and laid a firm foundation for China's cultural community. To resist invasion by northern nomads, the First Emperor of Qin linked the sections of the Great Wall in the State of Qin, the State of Zhao and the State of Yan during the Warring States period. The connected Great Wall extended for thousands of miles. From then on, the 'Great Wall' symbolised China and stood as the backbone of the unyielding Chinese nation. Whenever the country was in danger, the Chinese would think of 'the Great Wall built with flesh and blood'. Now, the Great Wall has been nominated as one of the Eight Wonders of the World and one of the Ten World Cultural Heritage sites.

(2) Respect for the Yellow Emperor and Lao Tzu with Confucianism the sole orthodoxy

Absorbing the profound lessons from the collapse of the Qin dynasty, Liu Bang, the moment he entered the pass, declared he would simplify the laws, loosen the legal network and 'abolish all the laws of the Qin dynasty' (*Record of the Grand Historian - Biographic Sketches of Emperor Liu Bang of the Han Dynasty*). After the regime was established, Liu Bang adopted the 'Doctrine of the Yellow Emperor and Lao Tzu' advocating the supplementation of rule by torture with benevolent rule and laissez-faire governance. The successor of Liu Bang carried forward Taoism and further advanced the golden era of the 'rule of the western Han emperor Han Jingdi'.

The so-called 'Doctrine of the Yellow Emperor and Lao Tzu' was a derivative of Taoism, namely, one of the two schools of Taoism. 'Huang' referred to the doctrines of the Yellow Emperor and 'Lao' referred to the theory of Lao Tzu, putting aside the difference that the doctrine of the Yellow Emperor not only preached but also stated ideas or facts. The doctrine of the Yellow Emperor and Lao Tzu stressed 'governing by non-interference' and advocated reducing government interference by the rulers in people's natural living status so that they could live and work in peace and contentment. It was both advantageous and disadvantageous for the governance of the country. 'Making peace with rulers of ethnic minorities in the border areas by marriage' could not eradicate the trouble brought about by the Xiongnu, an ancient nationality in China and the subinfeudation system gave rise to local separatist forces and especially the rapid expansion of the forces of feudal kings. A succession of rebellions took place, threatening the Han regime.

In October of the first year in the Jian-Yuan era (140BC), Liu Che, Emperor Wu of Han, not long before succeeding to the throne, demanded the upright imperial censors air their views on 'governance' in the capital city. Dong Zhongshu's three schemes (namely the 'three schemes about heaven and people') stressed the advocacy of 'upholding only Confucianism' which enjoyed the favour of Emperor Wu. Afterwards, through a series of measures including establishing the Bright Hall (the place for the emperor to meet feudal princes or hold memorial ceremonies), enabling ceremonies and music to prosper, elevating Confucianism to the highest position, respecting Confucianism and education as well as softening the institutions, the unified position of Confucianism was secured. Moreover, education, examinations and official selection were combined and the study of Confucianism gradually came to be equated with the study of Chinese civilisation. Hence Confucianism achieved pre-eminent status. For the first time Confucianism also became recognized as a basis for state governance.

In the sixth year of Emperor Zhao of the Western Han (81BC), Assistant Minister Huo Guang convened the Salt & Iron Meeting to debate termination of the salt and iron franchise, wine monopoly and unified commodity transportation and equalisation. It was in effect a general evaluation and summation of the policies in the period of Emperor Wu. After the meeting, the state policies were changed, bringing to an end years of warfare. The country entered another rehabilitation phase. After that, Huan Kuan 'deduced' and classified these policies and compiled *The Salt and Iron Theory*. Thanks to it, Confucianism became more comprehensive and systematic, and became the ruling economic phililosophy in feudal Chinese society.

(3) Diverse development of literature during the Han dynasty

Literature with a cultural symbolic meaning underwent new development in the Han era. A new genre of poetry, namely, 'Fu', came into being, became popular, flourished in the 400 years of the Han dynasty and was called ' Han poetry' in literary history. The Fu genre was of the Sao style in the early period. Later, the prosaic style became popular. Featuring ornate diction, extravagant techniques and abundant vocabulary, it mostly depicted the bustling spectacle of the Great World and influenced the style and technique of later literary works. The earliest prosody composers included Jia Yi and Mei Cheng. The former was noted for his *A Chinese Raven* and *Mourning for Qu Yuan* and the latter for the resplendent rhetoric, grand structure and momentum of his *Remonstration with Seven Stories*. Some scholars held the view that the formal poetry in the Han dynasty was inaugurated from Mei Cheng's *Remonstration with Seven Stories*. When the prosaic Da Fu of Han reached the pinnacle of its development, some prosody composers became well known, such as Sima Xiangru, Yang Xiong and Dongfang Shuo, especially Sima Xiangru who was most famous and whose works *Master Zixu* and *Imperial Forest* were masterpieces of those times.

The Yuefu folk ballads were the treasures of Han literature and spread worldwide in the form of Yuefu poems. The Yuefu poems (folk-ballads) embraced military odes, Xianghe ballads and Zaqu lyrics as well as the songs of the Han nationality and those of the ethnic minorities and the border regions featuring abundant contents, simple language and various genres, mostly represented by *War South of the City, Travel Through the East Gate, Travel of An Ill Woman* and *Enlistment at Fifteen*. These folk ballads reflected the emotions and heartfelt wishes of the lower-class people in society and were a focal point of literary history. These poems with five characters per line imitating the Yuefu poems appeared in the Eastern Han dynasty, mostly exemplified by some chapters in *The 19 Ancient Poems*. The Han prose was also fairly characteristic, mostly discussing current affairs freely and with literary grace, making sensible accurate and concise analyses, chiefly represented by Jia Yi's *Ten Crimes of Qin, Public Security Policy* and *Statement on Political Affairs*; Chao Cuo's *Good Countermeasures, Statement on Military Affairs* and *On the Enhancement of the Food-Grain Price*; Liu Xiang's *Collection of Stories*, eulogised by Lu Xun to be the 'masterpieces of the Western Han', all of which had a tremendous impact on future prose and essays.

The Records of the Grand Historian written by Sima Qian of the Western Han was the first general history presented in a series of biographies. It was an unrivalled prose masterpiece not merely in Han times but also from throughout ancient literary history. *The History of the Han Dynasty* written by Ban Gu was an excellent historical prosaic work after *The Records of the Grand Historian* came to the world. It served as the precedent of China's dynastic history. *Seven Strategies* written by Liu Xin of the Western Han, based on *Abstract Contents* written by his father Liu Xiang, not only marked the starting point of Chinese bibliography but was also a valuable ancient literary history. In addition, the *History of the States of Wu and Yue in the Spring and Autumn Period*, a historical prosaic work by Zhao Ye of the Eastern Han and *Contention Between the States of Wu and Yue for Hegemony* written anonymously initiated the preparation of the local chronicles; Xun Yue wrote the annals named *Records of the Han Dynasty*.

Art reached a high degree of development in the Han era. Especially, realistic paintings and sculptures featured diverse techniques, vivid depiction, plain lines, conciseness and fluency. An enormous amount of works such as the silk paintings, frescos, lacquer paintings, stone-carved figures, portrait bricks and stone sculptures still remain at large on a broad range of topics in social life, for instance, strange birds and beasts, celestial beings, myths and legends, warfare, fishing and hunting, feasts, daily routine, carriages and horses going on a journey. Architectural art made great strides in the Han period. The imposing and magnificent buildings such as the Shanglin imperial park, Chang'an city and palace had a huge influence on the parks, cities, houses and buildings of later generations.

The performing arts of the Han were divided into Yayue (elegant music) and Sanyue (popular music). The former was the rigidly stereotyped official dance accompanied by music. The latter was the vivacious folk dance accompanied by music rich in colourful contents. It was also called 'acrobatics' encompassing acrobatic feats, song and dance, martial arts, music and traditional Chinese opera. The acrobatic art of the Han laid a solid foundation for the development of China's acrobatics in later generations.

Buddhism was introduced to the Central Plains in the late Western Han dynasty. Emperor Ming once dispatched Cai Yin on a pilgrimage to Dayuezhi, an important ancient ethnic minority in the history of China and the world, for Buddhist scriptures. Cai Yin and the monk from Dayuezhi took the Buddhist sculptures on the back of white horses and built in Luoyang the first Buddhist temple, namely, the White Horse Temple, in Chinese history. In the period of Emperor Huan and Emperor Ling of the late Eastern Han dynasty, An Shigao, a famous monk of the western regions and Zhu Shuo, a monk from India, came to Luoyang to translate the Buddhist scriptures. When Buddhism was first introduced to China, the rulers basically adopted an encouraging and tolerant attitude, hence the subsequent development and popularity of Buddhism in China.

Han culture had a profound, open and far-reaching influence. It did not just change the spiritual world and the way of thinking of the Chinese nation but also influenced the surrounding ethnic minority areas, East Asia, West Asia and even Continental Europe. Many surrounding ethnic minorities gradually accepted the material civilisation of the Han and were integrated with the culture of the Central Plains. Especially, facilitated by the Silk Road, the ethnic minorities in West China, Central Asia, West Asia and Europe had close economic and cultural ties with the Han and were deeply influenced by Han culture which had both a direct and indirect influence on East Asia and Southeast Asia. During the international transmission of the Han culture, foreign spiritual culture was also introduced and absorbed and further enriched and fueled the development of Han culture.

3. The period of the Wei, Jin, and Southern and Northern Dynasties: More contention over cultural links between past and present

The period of the Wei, Jin, and Southern and Northern dynasties was a period of social turmoil. The comparatively weakened feudal shackles of the ruling class and the southward migration of the northern working class quickened exchanges and development of the southern and northern economies, scientific and technological progress, invigorated the assimilation of foreign culture and furthered ideological emancipation. Historically, it is known as the 'transitional period of culture'.

(1) The rise of metaphysics and focus on reasoning

The study of Confucian classics declined increasingly in the latter stage of the Eastern Han dynasty. With the collapse of the Han, the dominant position of Confucianism was shaken and social critical thinking emerged. Some advocated the theories of Lao Tzu and Chuang Tzu and concentrated on the study of Taoist philosophy; others were keen on probing into the

School of Logicians and the Legalists and developed the philosophy of humanitarianism and rationality. Accordingly, metaphysical ideology came into being.

Metaphysics was a new ideological system integrating Confucianism and Taoism. Its classics chiefly included *Lao Tzu, Chuang Tzu* and *The Book of Changes* which were jointly called the 'three metaphysical masterpieces'. Metaphysical celebrities conducted philosophical discussions about metaphysical doctrines and mysticism. They avidly discussed such philosophical problems as the fundamental and the incidental, everything and nothing, and the Confucian ethical code and nature. The main ideology of metaphysics in the Cao Wei period cherished 'inactivity' and held that nature was fundamental and the Confucian ethical code was incidental. It advocated that the emperors should take no action but let things take their own course while officials should do something else instead. It reflected the requirements of distinguished, influential families to monopolise political power. After the Western Jin dynasty, some social celebrities skilled at making small talk became appendages of the Sima family and advocated the similarities between the Confucian ethical code and nature. By then, metaphysics had evolved to become a theory to safeguard the ruling order.

Wei-Jin metaphysics was an academic trend of thought different from the Confucianism of the Han era and a new philosophical thought arising from the decline of Confucianism. Focusing on probing into the inner being of the ideal personality, it began to recognise the essence of the universe beyond the dimensions of politics, morality and ethics. The metaphysicians zeroed in on discriminating between the philosophy of humanity and rationality, opposed the cumbersome annotations of the Han by means of fresh analysis and argumentation, and discarded the broken sentences and phrases in ancient writings through abstract philosophy as speculation. The trend of rational speculation yielded huge influence on the style of study in the Wei and Jin period and on Chinese philosophy. It was hence regarded as the 'second age of philosophy in China after the philosophers of the Zhou and Qin dynasties'. (Zong Baihua, *Roaming in Aesthetics*, Shanghai People's Publishing House, 1981)

(2) Multiple collisions assimilating 'as rivers flow to the sea'

The period of the Three Kingdoms, the Liang-Jin and Northern-Southern dynasties featured great political upheavals and was a great cultural melting pot after the Spring and Autumn, and Warring States period. The collision and blending of the cultures of different ethnic minorities with different degrees of development significantly enriched traditional Chinese culture and drove the development of numerous ethnic minorities within the borders. Some ethnic minorities were integrated into the Chinese nationality and others stepped into a stage of higher development. All other ethnic minorities and the Han nationality were integrated through 'natural assimilation'. Some social elites of ethnic minorities consciously adopted measures to stimulate Han nationalisation. For instance, when Tuo Bahong, Emperor Xiaowen of the Northern Wei dynasty, took over the reins of government, he promoted Han nationalization under the influence of his grandmother, Empress Dowager Feng. His efforts tremendously stimulated the rapid economic, cultural, social, political and military growth of the Xianbei, an ancient ethnic minority in China, alleviated national estrangement and brought about the 'resurgence during the reign of Emperor Xiaowen'.

In the period of the Wei, Jin and Southern and Northern Dynasties, Buddhist culture from India was the foreign culture that most influenced Chinese culture. It was predominantly introduced to China by people from the Western regions and India. Most of them knew Chinese and Sanskrit. It was they who translated the Buddhist classics of India into Chinese. From the Wei and Jin period onward, a myriad of Buddhist classics were translated into Chinese. With the circulation of Buddhism, the ideological, cultural, artistic, scientific and technological accomplishments of South and Central Asia were successively introduced to China, encouraged the development of philosophy, logic, phonology and art such as music, painting and sculpture, and greatly enriched the contents of traditional Chinese culture. The wide circulation of Buddhism in the Wei, Jin and Southern and Northern Dynasties fostered important material achievements. These accomplishments primarily included the building of temples and colossal stone cave temples. Among them, the Mo Kao Grotto at Dunhuang and Yungang Grottoes in Datong city are the most famous. Buddhist temples spread all over in the Southern dynasty. Hence, the verses were created by a later poet: 'The 480 temples in the Southern dynasty stood firmly in the misty rain.'

Compared with Buddhism, Taoism boasted more advantageous conditions for existence and development as a traditional Chinese religion. Different from other religions in the world, Taoism did not believe in fate, retribution, or advocate fighting against nature, and stressed the method of original inhalation of air and fitness, the drawing of magic figures to invoke or expel evil spirits, and Chinese alchemy to get rid of disease, remove impending ill fortune and prolong life. In the period of the Wei and Jin, Taoism absorbed elements of Buddhism on one hand and integrated with it on the other purposefully to complete its own system. Nevertheless, Taoist doctrines were less ordered or systematic and less complete than Buddhism. For this reason, its influence was ultimately less than that of Buddhism.

After a long period of six to seven hundred years, the disciples of Confucianism, Buddhism and Taoism finally began to choose reconciliation and consistency. It was reflected in their mutual attraction, incessant improvement, imitation and absorption of the classics, and mutual argumentation and application. Moreover, Taoism became gradually more systematic and theorized, and absorbed more 'nutrients' from Buddhism; Buddhism changed in content, began to add metaphysical elements to suit the interests of the feudal literati and officialdom (especially the Zen[1]), absorbed Confucian elements, such as filial piety, loyalty and even the cardinal guides and constant virtues into the doctrines of Buddhism, and gradually became the Chinese religion. With the formation of neo-Confucianism in the Song dynasty, traditional Confucianism absorbed some Confucian elements and became the official Confucianism. Just as *Anecdotes of the Bureaucrats of the Tang Dynasty* described, the format of the doctrines of the three schools was 'mutually contradictory at first but assimilated as rivers flow to the sea' and finally metamorphosed into a three-in-one ideology with Confucianism (neo-Confucianism) as the core.

(3) Literature and history unrestrained, painting and calligraphy rampant

In the Wei-Jin and Southern-Northern dynasties, literature and art were freed from the shackles of the cardinal guides and constant virtues of the Confucian school. Furthermore, literature was fully infused with a spirit of realism. The 'three Caos', namely, Cao Cao, Cao Pi and Cao Zhi and the 'seven poets' namely Kong Rong, Chen Lin, Wang Can, Xu Gan, Ruan Yu, Ying Yang and Liu Zhen of the Jian'an literary tradition, inherited the

---

[1] Zen is a school of Mahayana Buddhism that originated in China during the Tang dynasty as Chan Buddhism. The Zen school was strongly influenced by Taoism and developed as a distinguished school of Chinese Buddhism.

realistic tradition of the Yuefu folksongs of the Han, generally adopted the five-character per line format, enjoyed prestige for their vigorous writing styles, displayed vehement yet desolate masculinity, and formed the unique 'Jian'an style (strength of character)' in literary history. Additionally, 'style', namely strength of character, became an important concept in the history of Chinese literary criticism.

The pastoral poems of Tao Yuanming, a famous poet between the Jin and Song dynasties, were simple, cordial and lively. His *Peach Blossom Spring* conceived a romantic approach to the model of the ideal society. He was accordingly regarded as the 'ancestor of the recluse poets in ancient and modern society' (cited from *Grades of Poetry*). The scenic poems of Xie Lingyun expanded the theme of poetry, enriched the poetry manifestation technique and caused the decline of the ruling metaphysical poetry in the Jin period. The period of the Southern and Northern dynasties saw the appearance of two well known selected literary works: Prince Liang Zhaoming's *Literary Selections* and Xu Ling's *New Songs from the Jade Terrace* which created a new literary genre. Two other famous theoretical works on literature were born in that period: Liu Xie's *The Literary Mind and the Carving of Dragons* and Zhong Rong's *Grades of Poetry*. Before that, Cao Pi's *Comments on the Theories of Literature and Art of the Han Nationality* sparked literary criticism. All these illustrated that Chinese literature gradually shook off its dependence on the study of Confucian classics and entered the era of 'self-consciousness'.

In that period, the study of Confucian classics declined, official historians also 'lost their status' and the situation whereby the government controlled historiography was disturbed. All these factors facilitated the preparation of historical books by the erudite and the knowledgeable, and brought about the thriving of historiography. The historiography presented in a series of biographies and in an annalistic style also marked breakthroughs in new styles and genres, as witnessed by five official historical books such as Chen Shou's *The Record of the Three Kingdoms*, Fan Ye's *The History of the Late Han Dynasty*, Shen Yue's *The Book of the Song Dynasty*, Xiao Zixian's *The Book of the Nanqi Dynasty* and Wei Shou's *History of the Wei Dynasty* which each had their own characteristics and represented new breakthroughs in the genre. Chinese historiography began to blossom and constituted an important part of the traditional cultural structure, second only to the study of Confucian classics.

The calligraphy in the period of the Wei, Jin and Southern and Northern Dynasties reached its peak in Chinese history, especially in the Jin dynasty characteristic of numerous calligraphic works and prestigious calligraphers. Sun Guoting's *Theory of Calligraphy* of the Tang dynasty stated at the outset: 'Those who have been good at calligraphy since ancient times are exemplified by Zhong Yao and Zhang Zhi of the Kingdom of Wei during the Han era, and Wang Xizhi and Wang Xianzhi of the late Jin era for their excellent writing.' The four major calligraphers enumerated by Sun Guoting, namely, Zhong Yao, Zhang Zhi, Wang Xizhi and Wang Xianzhi, were reputed by the people of the time to be the 'four sages'. Zhong Yao and Wang Xizhi were also venerated as 'Masters Zhong and Wang'. They were also leading figures of calligraphy and represented a record level of Chinese calligraphy.

Research on poems, essays, calligraphy and painting attracted great attention in the Jin dynasties, and that on calligraphy was deeper and more detailed than on poems and essays. Numerous calligraphic critics such as Wei Heng, Suo Jing, Chenggong Sui, Wei Shuo, Wang Xizhi and Wang Min were most famous for their excellent calligraphic works and commentary, and for their distinctive theoretical perspectives. Profound theories on calligraphy further promoted calligraphic creation in the Jin dynasties. In the Wei, Jin and Southern and Northern Dynasties, calligraphy was used to write inscriptions, memorials to the emperors, records and to lavish praise. It also resulted in changes from writing inscriptions to that of writing notes and enjoyed as much favour among calligraphy fans of the scholar-official class as poems, painting and music. It even evolved to be part of people's cultural life.

Although the changes in painting in the Wei, Jin and Southern and Northern dynasties were not as conspicuous as those of calligraphy, the changed general mood of society and the continuous ideological uptrend made the paintings that were originally simple and clear more complex. Cao Buxing created Buddhist painting. His disciple Wei Xie made new contributions. As one of the marks of the maturity of painting, a series of eminent artists became known to the world, such as Gu Kaizhi, Dai Kui, Lu Tanwei and Zhang Sengyao in the south and Yang Zihua, Cao Zhongda and Tian Sengliang in the north. The artists were recorded in historical books as having a new identity and began to play an increasingly vital role in social life.

4. The Tang and Song dynasties: the pinnacle of cultural development

In the history of Chinese culture, the Tang and Song dynasties are eulogised as the two most brilliant eras. The grand unification of the flourishing Tang promoted the feudal economy and culture to new heights; after the separatist rule of the Five Dynasties and Ten Kingdoms[1], the Northern Song dynasty realised partial unification and reinvigorated the feudal economy and culture.

(1) Taoism and Buddhism equally revered, pursuit of Confucian inheritance theories

Confucianism, Buddhism and Taoism were equally revered in the Tang dynasty but in different sequences and at different stages of time. Since Lao Tzu, the founder of Taoism, was surnamed Li and the royal family of the Tang dynasty was also surnamed Li, Lao Tzu was respected as their earliest ancestor. The royal family called themselves the descendants of Lao Tzu and especially worshiped Taoism. Emperor Gaozu of the Tang dynasty issued an imperial edict to distinguish the precedence of the three doctrines, namely, Taoism, followed by Confucianism and then Buddhism. Emperor Gaozong of Tang conferred the title 'Emperor Taishang Xuanyuan' upon Lao Tzu. Emperor Xuanzong of the Tang included Lao Tzu within the scope of the imperial competitive examination and conferred 'Holy Founder and Emperor Xuanyuan' and then 'Holy Founder of the Golden Imperial Palace and Emperor Xuanyuan' upon him. In the up to 300 years of the Tang dynasty, the Tang emperors worshiped Taoism as the 'royal doctrine' (or 'royal religion') and fueled the striking development of Taoism in terms of dogma, doctrine and the rite of setting up altars for prayers.

The Tang dynasty saw further development of China's Buddhist culture. Numerous Buddhist sects appeared in the Tang, for instance, the Tiantai sect, the Huayan school, the Dharma character school, the Zen, the Shingon Buddhism, the Pure-land school, the East Asian Mādhyamaka and the Ritsu. Famous monks Xuanzang and Yijing merit special mention amid Sino-Indian exchanges in Buddhist culture. Thanks to the painstaking

---

[1] The Five Dynasties and Ten Kingdoms period was an era of political upheaval in the Central Plains and beyond in 10th-century imperial China. The Five Dynasties included the Later Liang (June 1, 907-23), Later Tang (923-36), Later Jin (936-47), Later Han (947-51 or 979) and Later Zhou (951-60) in Northern China. The Ten Kingdoms referred to Wu (907-37), Wuyue (907-78), Min (909-45), Southern Han (917-71), Chu (907-51), Northern Han (951-79), Jingnan (also known as Nanping) (924-63), Former Shu (907-25), Later Shu (934-65) and Southern Tang (937-75).

preaching by eminent monks in the Tang dynasty and the vigorous advocacy of the emperor at that time, Buddhism prospered during a time when the Tang dynasty flourished. The world-renowned Vairocana Buddha stood 17.14m high and was a masterpiece of that period. In the late Tang dynasty, paying one's respects to Buddha was in fashion for a time. Several emperors then were firm believers in Buddhism and attached more priority to Buddhism than Taoism and Confucianism. All these factors caused believers in Confucianism during the late Tang to propose opposition to Buddhism.

Fierce conflicts befell Buddhism and Taoism in the Tang dynasty. After the 'anti-Buddhism campaigns' in the reigns of Emperor Taiwu of the Northern Wei dynasty and Emperor Wu of the Northern Zhou dynasty, another campaign broke out in the period of Emperor Wuzong of the Tang in which the monks were forced to pursue a secular life and Buddhism suffered another heavy blow. Emperor Xuanzong of Tang succeeded to the throne and ordered the restoration of Buddhist temples and support for the development of Buddhism.

Confucianism was dwarfed by Taoism and Buddhism in the Tang dynasty. Only two points should be mentioned about Confucianism during the Tang: first was the annotations to the five classics chiefly modified by the early Tang government and the other was the so-called 'Mid-Tang Dynasty Revival of Confucianism' initiated by Han Yu and Li Ao. Han Yu prepared the pedigree of Confucianist inheritance which was called 'Confucian orthodoxy' by Zhu Xi of the Song dynasty. Inspired by the 'Confucian orthodoxy' theory, the Confucian scholars of the Song continued to carry the torch of 'preaching' and created a new type of Confucianism, namely, neo-Confucianism.

(2) Emergence of neo-Confucianism and renaissance of Confucianism

Neo-Confucianism was a dominant Confucian school of philosophy of the Song dynasty. Based on the school of Zisi-Mencius, it was a new Confucian school permeated with Buddhist and Taoist thinking. The neo-Confucianism of the Song originated directly from the 'three gentlemen of the early Song dynasty', namely, Hu Yuan, Sun Fu and Shi Jie. It did not value annotated studies of ancient texts but argumentation and ushered in the creation by the neo-Confucianists of their own theoretical system with reference to the Confucian classics.

The real founders of neo-Confucianism were Zhou Dunyi and Zhang Zai. In accordance with the Confucian classics *The Book of Changes* and *Doctrine of the Mean,* and with reference to the Taoist doctrines and the *Diagram of the Infinite* passed on by Taoist disciple Chen Tuan in the Five Dynasties, Zhou Dunyi proposed the theory of the origin of the universe. In building the basic framework of neo-Confucianism, Zhang Zai living in the same period firstly distinguished between the 'nature of the world' and 'temperament' and publicised the topics of 'upholding heavenly principles' and 'exterminating desire'; secondly, he brought forward the idea of 'the separation and relationship between the truth and all things on the earth'[1] which became the foundation of the future theory of Cheng and Zhu with the 'truth' being the universe itself; thirdly, he came up with the epistemology that 'it is said that only after exhaustive enquiry into the wonder of things can one realise the changes in things' and that 'only by thoroughly exploring logic is the intrinsic character revealed' which became a key source of Cheng and Zhu's theory of 'studying the nature of things'.

Neo-Confucianism was formed by Cheng Hao and Cheng Yi. They were two brothers who took 'reason' or 'heavenly principles' as the pinnacle of philosophy and as ubiquitous, neither dying nor being born. They regarded it as the origin of the world and the supreme principle of social life. The appearance of their theories marked the formation of neo-Confucianism.

Zhu Xi epitomised the neo-Confucianism in Song times. He inherited and carried forward the ideas of the Cheng brothers, absorbed Zhang Zai's theories on 'vigour' and established the intact, exquisite, objective and idealistic ideology. Lu Jiuyuan, a master of neo-Confucianism and a contemporary of Zhu Xi, founded the 'heart-mind' school, a branch of the neo-Confucian school in the Song and Ming dynasties, and made significant contributions to the development of neo-Confucianism. He integrated Confucianism with Zen-Buddhist thinking, inherited Cheng Hao's view that 'heaven is the truth and the mind' and held the view that the 'mind' was the origin of the universe. Neo-Confucianism matured when it was moved ahead by Zhu Xi and Lu Jiuyuan.

---

[1] It means 'the universe changes based on the same rules and the separation of everything has its own law of development'.

(3) Tang poetry and Song Ci (poems) shining like the glittering milky way

Tang poetry was a brilliant part of the history of Chinese literature. *The Entire Tang Poems* prepared by a Qing citizen collected a total of more than 48,900 poems written by more than 2,300 poets, later supplemented by *Additional Works to The Entire Tang Poems* which added more than 2,000 Tang poems. The large population of poets, the huge number of poems, the abundant contents and the diverse styles and schools far surpassed those of any previous dynasty. Moreover, the poetry of that time is regarded to have 'surpassed anything that came before or since'.

Tang poetry progressed generally in the early, flourishing, middle and late Tang periods:

Wang Bo, Yang Jiong, Lu Zhaolin and Luo Binwang, jointly regarded as the 'four great poets of the early Tang dynasty', were opposed to the downcast, vulgar 'Shangguan style'. They brought forward the literary standpoint slighting 'superficially gaudy and inane contents' and highlighting 'strength of character' and contributed to the creation of the seven-character pattern, and the development of the five-character-per-line rhyming poetry and pentasyllabic quatrains. The Tang poetic style began to change from then on. For this, Du Fu wrote poems in praise of 'Wang Bo, Yang Jiong, Lu Zhaolin and Luo Binwang creating poems in the popular genre of their times, but some modernists criticise them frivolously. When people of this calibre lose their lives and fame, the poems of these poets will still be passed on eternally.'

Li Bai and Du Fu were most famous among the flourishing Tang poets. Li Bai was another great romantic poet after Qu Yuan. He was revered as a 'poetic genius' by later generations. His romantic poetic style, deep patriotism mirrored in his poems and outstanding artistic accomplishments had a substantial effect on later generations and have always been respected and imitated by later generations. The realist poet Du Fu, just as famous as Li Bai, was respected as a 'poet sage'. Amid his homeless, miserable and destitute life drifting from place to place, he keenly sensed the degeneration of the ruling class and the bitterness of ordinary people. He realistically reflected the social realities in his poems which were called the 'history of poetry'.

The middle Tang dynasty witnessed the new Yuefu poetry campaigns advocated by Bai Juyi and Yuan Zhen culminating in the 'revival' of Tang poetry. The celebrated poets in that period included Liu Zongyuan, Meng Jiao, Han Yu, Lu Lun, Li He, Li Yi, Liu Yuxi, Jia Dao, Zhang Ji, Wei Yingwu, Zhang Hu, Du Qiuniang, Zhang Ji, Dai Shulun and Gu Kuang. They created numerous poems that won universal acclaim. For instance, Meng Jiao's *Travelers' Song* was a poem whose recital was almost compulsory for children with an enlightened education. It was composed of the verses: 'The loving mother held threads in her hand, to sew clothes for the wanderer. Making the clothes with thick stitches, she feared he would return late. Who can understand a parent's love? Gratitude should be shown to them for their love and care for their children since childhood.' Furthermore, Jia Dao's verse 'the monk knocked at the door in the moonlight' served as the reference for poetic creation by men of letters.

A strong sorrowful atmosphere prevailed in poetic circles during the late Tang dynasty devoid of the poetic atmosphere in the flourishing Tang and the pattern in the middle Tang. Nevertheless, that period also witnessed the contribution of masterpieces by some outstanding poets such as Du Mu and Li Shangyin. The two poets were jointly celebrated as the 'Lesser Li (Bai) and Du (Fu)'. Moreover, Pi Rixiu, Nie Yizhong and Du Xunhe inherited the realistic traditions of Bai Juyi's new Yuefu style and contributed numerous fine verses reflecting people's suffering.

The literature of the Song dynasty encompassed the genres of Song Ci poetry, verse, prose, story-tellers' scripts and traditional Chinese opera scripts. Among them, Song Ci poetry attained the highest achievements followed respectively by verse, prose and story-tellers' scripts.

Poetic creation prospered and flourished in unprecedented quantities in the Song dynasty. *The Full Collection of the Song Dynasty* being compiled by Peking University was initially estimated to include the works of no less than 9,000 poets. The number quadrupled that of *The Entire Tang Poems*. Another feature of the Song dynasty was high-yield poets. Lu You, one of them, said: 'I've created about 10,000 poems in six decades' with more than 9,300 verses remaining in the world. Additionally, Yang Wanli allegedly created more than 20,000 verses although, unfortunately, only a small number of them remain. The prevailing atmosphere was quite different in the Song and Tang dynasties and the poets were very innovative. Therefore, the 'Song style' was formed in stark contrast with the 'Tang style'. Most often, the former attached more priority to 'reasoning in the poems' and added touches of argumentation rather than temperament and fun.

The most typical literary genre of the Song dynasty was the Song Ci poem. The Song Ci poems and Tang poetry were habitually linked in the history of Chinese literature. The Song Ci poetry was shortened from melodic Ci, a genre of poetry originating from the Yuefu in the Han and Wei dynasties, influenced by exotic music and boasting a unique system for singing with the accompaniment of music. Originating among the people, it emerged in the late Tang, went through the Five Dynasties and thrived in the Song. The Song dynasty featured a multitude of eminent Ci poets who contributed an enormous amount of Ci poems. *The Whole Ci Poetry of the Song Dynasty* compiled by contemporary Tang Guizhang recorded more than 19,900 Ci poems written by more than 1,330 Ci poets. The *Flower Lyrics* compiled by Zhao Chongzuo in the Later Shu period marked the emergence of the first school, namely, the School of Huajian Ci Poems in the 1,000 years of history of Ci poetry. It was a collection of the excellent works of a group of important Ci poets in the late Tang and the Five Dynasties, laid the foundation for 'Ci' to become the normal form of an emerging poetic genre and exhibited the 'unique style' and the aesthetic value of Ci poetry.

Ouyang Xiu achieved huge artistic accomplishments in prose, poems and Ci poetry. His historical verses were connected with reality and, proceeding from feelings, they started something by creating Ci poetry which reflected reality. Liu Yong was a Ci poet who exerted a considerable influence on Ci poems in the Northern Song dynasty and created plentiful new Yuefu poems (also called '*Man Ci*' meaning 'slow Ci') suitable for singing. He was good at adding folk slang and adages into Ci poems and his work was imbued with a strong taste of citizenry and enjoyed the favour of grassroots people. Ye Mengde of the Southern Song dynasty made the following comment about him: "He can write songs in his own Liu style for the townsmen that reflect their practical daily lives." Another master of Ci poem creation, Su Shi, broke through traditional barriers, made bold innovations in style, theme, conception and technique, and immensely extended the artistic conception and expressive force of Ci poems so that they could go beyond the 'flower world' into the 'man's world'. Su Shi was consequently hailed as a representative of the bold and unconstrained school of Song Ci poetry and occupies a special position in the history of China's poetry and Ci poems.

During the Southern Song period, the attitude of Ci poems took on an altogether new aspect amid the vehement anti-Jin (dynasty going down in the years from 1115 through 1234) atmosphere and the wave of patriotism. Themes reflecting the contradictions and social realities of the times and voicing the lofty sentiments of patriotism and heroism became the mainstream of Ci poems in that period. The giants of Ci poetry such as Lu You and Xin Qiji marked the pinnacle of Song Ci poetry development. Furthermore, Li Qingzhao, a Ci poetess of the Song dynasty, also enjoyed a high reputation. Her early Ci poems mostly described her leisurely life while later counterparts carried her lament for her life experience, which showed her missing the Central Plains. Later generations regarded her as the authentic origin of the graceful and restrained school of Chinese poetic genres.

(4) History compilation system established, historians emerge

Based on the prosperous historiography of the Sui and Tang dynasties, the historiography of the Song dynasty embraced new development. It was marked by an improved system of historiography, the appearance of many famous historians and was characterised by historical records of diverse genres.

The Song dynasty smiled at the appearance of prestigious historians and their masterpieces of historiography, including Sima Guang and his *History As A Mirror*, Ma Ruilin and his *General Examination of Literature*, Wang Yinglin and his *Sea of Jade*, *Record of Tales* and *Textual Research on The History of Art and Literature of the Han Dynasty*, and Li Tao's *A Continuation of History As A Mirror*. More new history styles and historical records arose in the Song dynasty compared with those in previous dynasties. It was also an important symbol of the evolution of historical research on the Song dynasty. For instance, Yuan Shu's *A Record of Historical Events for Management Consultancy* initiated the writing style of recording historical events; the life chronicle formally took shape in the Song dynasty. Additionally, history and philosophy also developed much in Song times. For example, Lü Zuqian and Chen Liang of the Jinhua school and Chen Fuliang and Ye Shi of the Yongjia school all brought forward their unique philosophy of history and exerted momentous influence on the development of Chinese historiography.

5. Multicultural clashes and fusion during the Liao, Xia, Jin and Yuan dynasties

Since its early founding, the Song dynasty was confronted with the nomadic people of the Liao and Western Xia regime (1038-1227). The conflicts and integration of the nomadic culture and the farming culture generated a double cultural effect. On the one hand, the Han people were passively beaten and miserable sentiments permeated every cultural dimension. On the other hand, such nomadic nationalities as the Qidan, Tangut, Qiang and Nüzhen absorbed abundant nutrients from the Han culture. In the 13th century, Genghis Khan (1162-1227) of the Mongol Empire launched attacks on the territories of the Han. It led to drastic political, military and ethnic conflicts and meanwhile drove profound and lasting cultural integration among all the ethnic minorities.

(1) Territorial expansion by military force and state rule in accordance with Confucianism

In the late 12th and early 13th centuries, Temujin established the unified Mongolian country and was elected to be the Khan, conferred with the honorific title 'Genghis Khan', and referred to as the first founder of the Yuan dynasty (1206-1368) in the historical records. In 1260, Kublai (grandson of Genghis Khan and the fifth emperor of the Yuan dynasty) succeeded to the throne. Referring to the meaning of 'the beginning of the vast heaven' in *The Book of Changes*, he defined the dynasty title as Yuan in 1271 and conquered the Southern Song dynasty in 1276. The Yuan dynasty was the first unified feudal dynasty founded by ethnic minorities in Chinese history.

The unification of the Yuan dynasty further expanded China's territory. Tibet was officially included under China's administrative jurisdiction, Taiwan and Penghu were included in China's territory and a province was established in Yunnan. The grand unification pattern invigorated the mutual economic complementarities and mutual cultural exchanges between all China's ethnic minorities. To cement the autocracy, Kublai followed the Han model and applied Confucian policies in terms of system installation, ideology, school education and the establishment of a team of officials. In politics, he established the systems and institutions based on traditional centralisation of authority and rule of the people by Han officials. In terms of culture, he appointed Confucian officials, resumed the imperial examination system, worshiped Confucius and made neo-Confucianism the official, dominant ideological orthodoxy.

Stimulated by such policies, the social status of Confucian culture was further heightened. The imperial Yuan court conferred the title of 'the Greatest Sage, Teacher and Lord Wenxuan' upon Confucius and other lofty titles upon such celebrated Confucian scholars as Mencius and exempted Confucian scholars avid to read more from all sorts of forced labour. For this reason, universal education for the populace in the Yuan dynasty surpassed that in past dynasties. More than 400 academies of classical learning and more than 24,400 schools at most were set up in prefectures and counties. Certainly, Confucian scholars in the Yuan dynasty were discriminated against, to some extent. That was the reason for the sequence of 'Confucian scholars being ranked ninth prior to the tenth ranking of beggars' in the social strata of that time. Nevertheless, 'Confucian scholars' here did not refer to Confucian officials but to private tutors offering enlightenment education.

(2) Religious freedom and cultural innovation

As to religion and culture, the Yuan dynasty adopted relatively flexible, diversified policies, respected the culture and religion of all ethnic minorities and encouraged cultural exchanges and integration in all areas.

The Yuan dynasty was the only one of its kind in feudal history that explicitly proposed religious freedom and treated all religious sects equally. Although all the emperors of the Yuan dynasty attached priority to a certain religion, they did not interfere with the development of other religions. Almost all the major religions in the world had their own arenas and disciples in China, especially Buddhism and Taoism that boasted far-reaching influence. Buddhist disciples publicly participated in political activities and Phagspa (a Tibetan lama who founded the Phagspa script in Yuan times) was imperially worshiped as the teacher of the state.

Cultural compatibility in the Yuan dynasty provided a sound environment for the growth of Chinese culture. Yuan verse came into being in those circumstances and was regarded as 'a major issue in the history of the theatre and literature of China'. It ranked alongside Tang poetry and Song Ci poetry.

The Yuan verses included Zaju and Chinese Sanqu poetry. The former was poetic drama set to music and the latter was a type of verse with tonal patterns modeled on tunes drawn from folk music. In their resistance against class oppression and national oppression, people badly needed literary forms that were strongly militaristic and characteristic of the masses. The Zaju reflected the social realities in those years and won wide acclaim among the people. It is said that no less than 500 operas were created (at least 160 were handed down) and dozens of theatres were built in many cities in the Yuan dynasty. Guan Hanqing, Bai Pu, Ma Zhiyuan and Zheng Guangzu were reputed to be the 'Four Great Writers of Yuan Verses' and pushed the growth of Yuan verses to their peak. Guan Hanqing's masterpiece *Snow in Midsummer* and a series of dramas on the upright official Bao Zheng, such as *Inspiring Butterflies, Righteous Capital Punishment of Lu Zhailang* and *Selling Rice in Chenzhou*, portrayed the gloomy and resentful emotions of the Chinese people in the 13th century.

The Sanqu arising in the Yuan dynasty first originated in the verses and the ballads during the Jin dynasty and were created by the poets and literati to express their interest and show their talent at the very beginning. Later, it became the literary genre adopted by poets with great concentration. According to the statistics, more than 200 Sanqu poets in the Yuan dynasty were recorded to have contributed more than 4,300 poems including more than 3,850 short lyrics and more than 450 divertimentos.

(3) Rapidly gaining momentum and turning outward to the world

Apart from the exchanges and integration of China's ethnic minorities, cultural exchanges between China and the West and reached new heights in the Yuan dynasty and transport and communications between the Orient and the West became much busier. The sea route reached out to the African coast and the land route directly to Western Europe. It was historically described that: 'A journey of a thousand li was just like stepping onto your front porch; a journey of 10,000 li was like visiting the neighbourhood.' After Kublai succeeded to the throne, the vassal states such as the Golden Horde and II-Khanate of the Yuan dynasty became gradually independent but still kept in close political, economic and cultural contact with the Yuan dynasty and merchants, priests and ambassadors came and went frequently.

Favourable trade policies, smooth trade routes, a rich and populous country and beautiful legends were highly attractive to the Western and Arab world. Shangdu, Dadu, Hangzhou, Quanzhou and Guangzhou had an aura of international metropolises. The Port of Quanzhou was the largest international seaport for foreign trade. Travelers, businessmen, priests, government envoys and craftsmen came to China by land and by sea. Some of them stayed in China for a long time and others even served as government officials. The records of these foreign friends returning home enabled Westerners to comprehensively know about China and the Orient for the first time, as exemplified by Marco Polo's *The Travels of Marco Polo*. From then on, China in the East became the dream lingering in the minds of Westerners. According to historical records, the number of countries and territories trading with the Yuan dynasty via 'the Silk Road' increased from 50 or more to over 140.

China developed frequent, close economic and cultural exchanges with Korea and Japan in the Yuan dynasty. After succeeding to the throne, Kublai married his daughter to a Korean and established mutual friendship with Korea. The merchants, scholars and monks of the two countries had an enormous amount of books transported to each other's territory. Neo-Confucianism was introduced to Korea and became the course taught in the imperial college in feudal China. Kublai went on two punitive expeditions against Japan and carried out commercial, trade and cultural exchanges with it after an armistice. Neo-Confucianism and Zen theory were integrated and became the ideological weapon of the ruling class of Japan for a protracted period of time.

When foreign cultures were introduced to China, Chinese culture was also transmitted to the outside world. Gunpowder and typography were among the Four Great Inventions of ancient China, alongside calendars, mathematics, chinaware, tea, silk, painting and the abacus which spread globally and contributed to the brilliant world culture.

6. The Ming and Qing dynasties: Seeking revival amid cultural decline

Autocratic rule in China went to extremes in the Ming and Qing dynasties. In the cultural domain, development trends in ideology and culture were rigorously controlled. Nevertheless, with the influence of social conditions, new trends of thought continuously flooded in. The new and old, Chinese and foreign cultures clashed, which ushered in the germination of a new culture.

(1) Rise of 'literary inquisition', Confucianism still revered

The emperors of the Ming and Qing dynasties were paradoxes, giving priority to Confucianism on one hand and going in for literary inquisition in a big way on the other. For instance, Emperor Zhu Yuanzhang (the founding emperor of the Ming dynasty) cruelly injured or killed a great number of Confucian scholars for faults in their writing and literary inquisition prevailed in the Qing dynasty resulting from verses like: 'Since a refreshing breeze does not know even a single word, why does it leaf through a book?'. The rulers implemented a cultural terror policy. Wrongdoing brought detriment on Chinese culture no less than that of 'burning books and burying the literati in pits' committed by the First Emperor of Qin. Nonetheless, the overview of all the cases concerning literary inquisition in the Ming and Qing dynasties shows that it did not negate the content of Confucianism but was an allergic reaction to the writings of some men of letters. It was believed that such writings somewhat satirised and alluded to the political rulers of the time. From another perspective, Confucian scholars were taken seriously. Most of the cabinet ministers of the Ming dynasty had a background of being successful candidates in the highest imperial examinations or civilians rather than coming from the royal family or the consort clan. Most of them were elite Confucian scholars. The emperors of the Qing dynasty followed suit. They were taught Chinese by learned men when they were crown princes and put Confucian scholars in an important position when they became emperor, especially Qian Long who launched literary inquisition on the throne, developed a liking for the Han Chinese, wrote poems diligently, left behind about 42,613 poems of all genres, designated special people to compile *The Complete Library in the Four Branches of Literature* and contributed to sorting out and summarising China's historical and cultural heritage. Although the Ming and Qing dynasties implemented a policy of cultural autocracy, the thread of traditional Chinese culture was not broken in these two periods.

(2) Magnificent spectacle of cultural integration

Despite the depressing cultural autocracy in the Ming and Qing dynasties, it was the conclusive era of traditional Chinese culture.

First, historiography underwent greater development. It was a new trend in the Ming dynasty that famous historical records were officially and privately compiled, taking on the following four major characteristics: first, private writing proliferated and a string of historians such as Zheng Xiao, Wang Shizhen, Jiao Zhan and Hu Yinglin gained renown. Second, numerous historical works were created, including more than 200 officially compiled books and an unknown quantity of private works. As to the collected works, up to 5,000 individual works were collected in the *Qianqingtang Books*. Third, history books were written in various genres, such as *The Memoir of the Ming Dynasty*, *The History of the Yuan*

Dynasty, The Major Events of the Ming Dynasty, Records of the Ming Dynasty, The History of the Ming Dynasty, The Ming History Scripts, History As A Mirror (Continued), The Chronicle of the Ming Dynasty and *Comprehensive Research on the History from the Yellow Emperor to the Ming Dynasty*. Some renowned Qing dynasty scholars like Gu Yanwu, Wang Fuzhi and Huang Zongxi were closely connected with the reality of fighting and recorded many figures and events in the Ming and Qing dynasties. Moreover, research chronicles hit an unprecedented peak and some relevant masters like Zhang Xuecheng (1738-1801, a historian and thinker of the Qing dynasty) rose to fame.

Second, the rulers of the Ming and Qing dynasties personally led and arranged for the compilation of ancient books and records on culture including *The Yongle Canon, The Collection of Ancient and Modern Books, Kangxi Dictionary* and *The Complete Library in the Four Branches of Literature*. *The Yongle Canon* was recognised as the earliest and largest encyclopedia in the world; the *Kangxi Dictionary* was the world's earliest dictionary with the most characters; *The Complete Library in the Four Branches of Literature* was a series of books with the most pages in the world up to now.

Third, monumental works on science and technology were published. For instance, Li Shizhen's *Compendium of Material Medicine* was one of the world's leading works in those years; Pan Jixun's *A Survey of River Defense Works* was a monograph on controlling the Yellow river; Xu Guangqi's *Pandect on Agriculture* was the most complete work on agriculture; Song Yingxing's *Exploitation of the Works of Nature* was a technichal encyclopedia renowned at home and abroad. Besides, *Travels of Xu Xiake*, a geographical and geological masterpiece and Fang Yizhi's monograph on natural philosophy *Basic Knowledge of Physics* all represented the pinnacle of scientific accomplishment in those years.

(3) Rise of schools of thought and cultural revival

Neo-Confucianism was upheld in the early Ming dynasty. However, as the social situation evolved, it was exposed to criticism and challenges. For instance, the theory of 'attaining innate knowledge' broke the dominant neo-Confucianism advocated by Wang Yangming, rebelled against the orthodox ruling thought and became the philosophical pillar of humanistic thinking. The 'School of the Mind' witnessed the peak development of subjective idealism in ancient China. Its gigantic social influence shook the ideological foundation of the agrarian society and offered theoretical conditions for the burgeoning enlightenment in the Ming and Qing dynasties.

Early Qing dynasty scholars paid more attention to knowledge for humanistic pragmatism, pushed back against the indulgence in empty talk about disposition of neo-Confucianism and Yangmingism, examined the trajectory of the ups and downs of all dynasties and came up with all sorts of plans for political transformation and social reinvigoration. Accordingly, academic thinking in the early Qing dynasty exhibited the ethos of pragmatism and gave impetus to the emergence of realistic textual research. Three such major thinkers - Huang Zongyi, Gu Yanwu and Wang Fuzhi - as well as Fang Yizhi, Tang Zhen, Yan Yuan, Dai Zhen and Jiao Xun, debated about neo-Confucianism, the orthodox culture in late feudal society, from different perspectives. Some of them directly criticised the despotism and the academic culture that thrived in the Qing dynasty. The later period witnessed the appearance of the Wu school composed primarily of Hui Dong and his father, Duan Yucai, Wang Yinzhi and Wang Niansun, the Wan school headed by Dai Zhen, the Tongcheng school led by Yao Nai and the Huxiang school founded by Zeng Guofan. They presented a new look for Confucianism. Hence Liang Qichao called the Qing dynasty the era of 'China's cultural revival'.

Legendary novels attained a high level of artistic accomplishment in the Ming dynasty. A multitude of lengthy novels, short stories and novels were written in the style of story-tellers' script, such as *The Romance of Various States*, *The Romance of the Northern Song Dynasty*, *The History of the Sui Dynasty* and *The Romance of Heroes and Martyrs*. *The Romance of the Three Kingdoms* and *The Water Margin* (or *Outlaws of the Marshes*) created in the late Ming dynasty were further improved and extensively circulated in the Ming dynasty. The newly created legendary novels were mostly represented by *Pilgrimage to the West*, *The Investiture of the Gods*, *The Golden Lotus* and the 'Three Words, Two Beats' volumes of stories.

The heyday of Chinese classical novels was in the Qing dynasty. Among them, Pu Songling's *Strange Tales from Make-Do Studio*, Wu Jingzi's *The Scholars* and Cao Xueqin's *Dream of the Red Chamber* were most well known. The profound traditional culture and the strong competence in generalizing about and precisely expressing life in late feudal society contained in *Dream of the Red Chamber* helped it reach the peak of China's classic novels.

7. Transformation of modern and contemporary culture

The First Opium Wars broke out in 1840 and pushed Chinese culture to a new historic stage where change and rebirth coexisted in the form of blood and fire.

(1) Internal and external pressure and the Cultural Revolution

Modern and contemporary culture refers to the culture from the First Opium War in 1840 to the eve of the 'May 4th Movement' in 1919, namely, the culture in the democratic revolution of the old type. Chinese culture at that stage began with its self-revolution amid the dual pressures of the impact of foreign culture and the upheaval of native culture.

First was the literary revolution. The new literary tendency prospered during the periods of Emperor Daoguang and Emperor Xianfeng in the Qing dynasty. It theoretically proposed the idea that literature should serve practical political struggles and was required to create content reflecting the reality of political society, eulogise the people's and heroes' brave resistance against foreign invaders and expose social conflict. The new, progressive literary trend of poetic prose was formed, for instance, the 'liberal school' represented by Gong Zizhen, Wei Yuan and Lin Zexu. Before and after the reign of Emperor Tongzhi and Emperor Guangxu, the capitalist reform and revolutionary movements sprang up accordingly. The brilliant 'poetry revolution', 'revolution in novelists' circles', 'novel revolution' and 'using modern Chinese instead of classical Chinese' in literature as well as the 'rebuking novels' exposing the social darkness in those years were launched and produced. Concurrently, a group of poets concerned about the fate of the nation represented by Liu Yazi and Qiu Jin sang loudly about the national-democratic revolution and formed a new literary trend in modern literature.

Second was the 'revolution in historical circles'. It was aimed at criticising and transforming the old feudal history and establishing a new chapter of history. The external reason for the rise of the revolution of historical circles was the introduction of Western historiography and historical evolutionism. The difference between 'the history of the emperors' and 'the history of civilians', and between the advantages and disadvantages of Chinese and Western history made the historians at that time aware that the old history of China must be transformed. The historical monographs, namely, *The Discussion About Chinese History* and *The New History* formally sounded the horn of China's modern bourgeois historical revolution. Zhang Taiyan advocated taking the theory of evolution as a guide, advocated 'applying the Confucian concept of passing through' and further advocated 'applying the concept of historical study'. Xia Zengyou's *Ancient Chinese History* implemented the viewpoint of historical evolutionism and stressed the tendency of historical development. Wang Guowei applied the 'double evidence for existence', namely, to do textual research by means of verifying ancient literature and archaeological remains that had been excavated, traced the credible history of the Chinese nation back more than 4,000 years and became the founder of modern archaeology.

Third was the moral revolution. During the period of Wuxu political reform, also called the 'Hundred Days' Reform', the supporters of constitutional reform and modernisation angrily denounced feudal ethics and rites, and focused their denunciation on the 'three cardinal guides' of the 'principles of feudal moral conduct' of traditional ethics. In the early 20th century, the revolutionaries proposed the slogan of 'revolution against the three cardinal guides' and some of them even created *Articles on the Wrong Guiding Principles* to that end. The new tide of moral revolution was formed during the May 4th movement. It still primarily criticised the 'three cardinal guides' and the three virtues, namely, loyalty, filial piety and restraint directly derived therefrom. The 'five constant virtues' (namely, benevolence, righteousness, propriety, knowledge and sincerity) among the 'principles of feudal moral conduct' of traditional morality were not merely exempted from impact in the modern moral revolution but also conversely advocated by many. As a result, they became part of the new virtues. 'Benevolence' was given the top priority among the 'five constant virtues'.

(2) The eastward transmission of Western science and enlightenment

The eastward transmission of Western science and enlightenment germinated in the Ming dynasty. *The Essence of the Universe* compiled by Matteo Ricci in 1605 was called 'the outset of the introduction of Western sciences into China' by the compiler of *The Complete Library in the Four Branches of Literature*. Nonetheless, it was circulated among only a few scholar officials rather than being widely popularised. Moreover, the transmission was interrupted due to the prohibition of religion by Emperor Yongzheng and changes in the Vatican's policy of preaching about religion.

Nonetheless, small-scale eastward transmission of Western sciences was not completely discontinued.

In the mid 19th century, driven by the Opium War and the invasion by the Anglo-French allied forces, the Qing government recalled a painful the Qing government recalled a painful experience and was determined to 'learn Western skills to fend off Western aggression'. From 1860, it began to launch the Westernisation movement on the principle of 'Chinese learning as the fundamental structure and Western learning for its utility'. However, it neglected and even collided with Western academic culture. After the Sino-Japanese War of 1894-1895, such thinkers as Liang Qichao, Kang Youwei and Tan Sitong argued that the Qing government should learn science and technology as well as social and political reforms from the West. Especially in the Republican period, some intellectuals directly advocated 'wholesale Westernisation' which triggered the debate during the 'May 4th movement' on which way China should go. The wave of eastward transmission of Western sciences has lasted even until now.

The eastward transmission of Western sciences brought various new academic accomplishments from Western countries to China, profoundly influenced the development of all the sciences, fueled the development of some previously neglected disciplines or non-existent sciences in China, completely shattered the basic framework of traditional Chinese learning composed of 'classics, historical records, philosophical writings and miscellaneous works' and impacted traditional learning. Some gradually declined while others absorbed Western learning and made improvements. By the period of the Republic of China, the entire Western academic architecture had been roughly formed.

The tide of eastward transmission of Western sciences hit its peak before and after the May 4th movement. Learning from the West, the Chinese people's outlook on the world, historical development, politics, the economy, society and nature changed a lot. During this process, many elements of traditional Chinese ideology and culture were re-estimated and re-evaluated in accordance with Western criteria. The thinking of some ancient philosophers of all schools was reproduced. Confucianism and some folk customs and culture were subject to strong criticism.

The introduction to Western political ideology, the parliamentary system, the democratic system, the new concept of country, anarchism and socialist ideology all had a tremendous influence on China's political development in the late Qing dynasty. The initiation of the Hundred Days' Reform, the promotion of the new policies of the late Qing dynasty, the attempts of the constitutionalism movements, the outbreak of the Revolution of 1911, the implementation of the parliamentary system in the early Republican period, the May 4th movement, the Federalist movement and the unification campaign after the northern expedition as well as the later socialist revolutions were all substantially influenced by such Western thinking.

The eastward transmission of Western sciences had an impact on society in that the advantages of the Western sciences gradually surpassed those of their Chinese counterparts and the Qing government had to abolish stereotyped writing and the imperial examination system. Under that influence, the top-ranking scholar-official strata in traditional society lost their access to officialdom which was the natural outlet for good scholars and the function of their traditional cultural knowledge was weakened. Concurrently, with the introduction of the trade-war mentality of the West in the late Qing dynasty, the social status of businessmen was enhanced and the collapse of the traditional social order was expedited. For that reason, a group of intellectuals hurled themselves into industry and the development of national industry. The economic structure of China's traditional agrarian society was consequently changed.

The greatest influence of the eastward transmission of Western sciences was the introduction of Marxism, the most advanced social reform ideology, into China. It presented socialism, a brand new development path, to the Chinese people.

(3) The New Culture movement, a new start

During the process of China's cultural march from tradition to modern times, the New Culture movement (around the time of the May 4th movement in 1919) was a critical stage. It enabled the culture to develop from the material and institutional level to the conceptual level. People like Cai Yuanpei, Chen Duxiu and Lu Xun played a decisive role in it. They vigorously advocated democracy, scientific knowledge, new morality and new culture, and overhauled traditional Chinese culture.

An important part of the May 4th New Culture movement was to oppose the old literature and advocate new literature, to object to classical Chinese and call for the vernacular, and to launch a literary revolution. Hu Shi, one of the leading proponents of the literary revolution, came up with the viewpoint of 'literary evolution', published *Literary Reform* and made an eight-point proposal on literary revolution. Chen Duxiu published *On Literary Revolution* and officially waved the banner of 'literary revolution'. The literary revolution effectively stimulated the development of ideological emancipation and efficiently collaborated with the anti-imperialist and anti-feudal struggles in the May 4th movement. It laid the theoretical foundation for modern literature and was nominated as a genuinely great revolution in the history of Chinese literature.

The eight vernacular poems published by Hu Shi comprised the first group of its kind in China's poetic movement. In addition, Liu Bannong, Shen Yinmo, Chen Duxiu, Lu Xun, Zhou Zuoren and Li Dazhao were all devoted to creating vernacular free verses. Guo Moruo, who authored *Odes to the Goddess*, represented the highest achievements in the period of new poetry creation. That period also saw achievements in prose. Lu Xun was good at writing essays and prose, and successively published *The Hot Wind, Vigour of Combat Against Feudalism and Flunkeys of Imperialism, Tomb* and the prose collection *Wild Grass*. His *Diary of a Madman*, *Kong Yiji* and *Medicine* were erected as a monument to the history of new literature (prompted by the May 4th movement) and had an enormous influence on writers around the world, including in China.

Modern Chinese culture is an extension and development of ancient Chinese culture but not a direct extension and development, rather in a collision with Western culture, it borrowed elements of Western culture, changed them and internalised them, and only then did these elements enter China's cultural domain. In the Ming and Qing dynasties in the 17th century, the ancient traditional culture gave birth to vestiges of the new culture. However, before it could take root, it was stifled by obstinate feudal modes of production and feudal politics. Nevertheless, Western capitalism progressed rapidly, included China into the global capitalist system by the mid-19th century and ushered in China's modernisation. Amid the transition from the old to the new, modern Chinese culture became complex and diverse. But ultimately a new socialist culture prevailed.

Chapter 3

Basic Tendency of Fine Traditional Chinese Culture

Against the backdrop of world multipolarisation and economic globalisation, the basic tendency of fine traditional Chinese culture was to stand fast to its roots and achieve modernisation. China's cultural revival is due to socialism and China's socialism owes its Chinese characteristics to Chinese culture. The cultural revival in the new century is the cultural bedrock for China to realise its dream. The Chinese dream will be more brilliant and charismatic against the background of cultural revival.

1. China's cultural development strategy against the backdrop of globalisation

As Karl Marx said, in the era of large-scale industry the bourgeoisie expanded the market so that the production and consumption of a country became global. So it is with material production and spiritual production. If economic globalisation began when the bourgeoisie expanded the market, the source of the world's multipolarisation evolved from the evolution of the world pattern after the Second World War (1939-1945). Culture played a focal role in the background of globalisation and cultural development strategy had a lot to do with it.

(1) Economic globalisation and cultural diversification

Following the dramatic changes in Eastern Europe after the revolutions of 1989 and the dissolution of the Soviet Union after the Second World War, the bipolar structure based on the Yalta system came to an end and there was a transition to a multipolar world order.

In conjunction with world multipolarisation, there was a trend for economic globalisation to gather speed. With economic development, global economic contacts became more frequent and reciprocity and mutual benefit were more intimate. For instance, an absolute majority of more than 10,000 airliners produced by Boeing were not produced independently by Boeing nor supplied by domestic companies in the United States. They were instead made in cooperation with numerous companies worldwide, with clients from more than 100 countries and territories. The Chinese aviation industry participates in the manufacture of Boeing airplanes of all types. In the present world, the economic cooperation between countries and between enterprises, just like the interconnection between Boeing and its parts manufacturing companies, depends more on shared interests. That dependence was just like a 'butterfly effect' in the analysis of US meteorologist Edward Lorenz: "A butterfly in the tropical rain forest in the Amazon River Basin in South America flaps its wings and sets off a tornado in the US state of Texas two weeks later." The financial disturbance in Thailand in 1997 rapidly swept through Southeast Asia and then throughout the world. In 2008, the great international financial storm triggered by the American subprime mortgage crisis went viral worldwide. The world economy suffered a heavy blow and could not easily recover from it. Countries stood and fell together.

In conjuction with economic globalisation, multicultural exchanges, integration and confrontation have become increasingly frequent. Cross-cultural communication, propagation and permeation have reached an unprecedentedly high level. During the process of cultural diversification, cultural conflicts and symbiosis have become pronounced. What will China do when the US's Hollywood blockbusters, Japanese anime, South Korea's romantic dramas and India's Bollywood movies become popular globally and usurp a large market share? It has become a problem of common concern among numerous men of insight.

(2) Cultural development and strategic advance

Cultural development strategy generally refers to the objectives, countermeasures and modes of implementation regarding a country's cultural development. It is the overall development plan guiding the whole issue concerning cultural development. Amid the application of Marxism in China, from establishing the strategic position of culture in the new democratic revolution and the basic strategic framework of socialist cultural construction to promoting the overall development and prosperity of socialist culture, views on the way forward for new cultural development have become increasingly mature.

The new democratic revolution theory established the strategic position of culture in the new democratic society. The cultural programme shares equal ranking with the political programme and the economic programme among the 'three major programmes' of the new democracy. In 1942, Mao Zedong addressed a speech at the Yan'an forum on literature and art, systematically expounded the Marxist literary theory for the first time, put forward the idea that the aim of art is to serve the people, primarily the workers, peasants and soldiers, and further pinpointed the service orientation of cultural development.

After the founding of the People's Republic of China (PRC), faced with social disruption and cultural desolation, the corrosion of feudal culture and the permeation of bourgeois culture, the Communist Party of China (CPC) determined the orientation for cultural development compatible with the new democratic economic foundation and the guidance of Marxism-Leninism and continued to develop the new democratic culture under the framework of the 'three major programmes' related to new democracy.

In the period of exploring the means of construction and after China's socialist development strategy was initially formed at the Eighth National People's Congress (NPC) of the CPC, the policies of 'letting a hundred flowers bloom and a hundred schools of thoughts contend' and 'making the past serve the present and foreign things serve China, getting rid of the stale and bringing forth the fresh' were proposed and laid a scientific theoretical foundation for the later construction of a cultural development strategy to promote socialist culture.

Since the third plenary session of the 11th CPC Central Committee, the basic strategic framework to build China's socialist culture was outlined to meet the requirements of the 'three-step' development strategy in China's modernisation drive. It advocated that culture should 'serve the people and socialism' and came up with a cultural development strategy based on 'three-orientations', namely 'oriented toward modernisation, oriented toward the world and oriented toward the future'. The 'three-pronged' economic, political and cultural strategic model was proposed at the 15th NPC and extended to become the 'four-pronged' overall design at the 17th NPC and the 'five-pronged' one at the 18th NPC. Culture became the soul of the centre of adjustment.

Seventy-two years after Mao Zedong delivered his *Speech at the Yan'an Forum on Literature and Art*, Xi Jinping underscored in his important speech at the Yan'an forum on literature and art in October 2014 that artistic creation should persistently concentrate on the people and come up with more outstanding and up-to-date work. Xi Jinping pointed out in a series of important speeches on culture that efforts should be made to adhere to the path of socialist cultural development with Chinese characteristics, to carry forward superior socialist culture, to stimulate the great development and prosperity of socialist culture, to constantly enrich people's spiritual world, to strengthen people's mental strength and to strive to build a strong country with a socialist culture.

(3) Opportunities and challenges for a strong cultural country

Although China has become a big country with economic growth and cultural resources, it is neither a big country in terms of cultural production nor a strong cultural country. The construction of a strong country with a socialist culture is exposed to both opportunities and challenges.

Building China into a strong country with socialist culture is chiefly exposed to the following golden opportunities:

First, peace and development are the theme of the time and make for a peaceful international atmosphere for China to build its socialist culture. The cardinal point to judge the theme of the present era is that it has been possible to avoid world wars for quite a long period of time and a peaceful environment can probably prevail for quite a long time to come. Although unstable and uncertain factors affecting world peace and development are on the rise, fundamentally speaking, the basic pattern and development direction of the world and the basic trend of the overall stable international situation and local unrest have not changed. In the trend of the times of seeking peace, development and cooperation, China's construction into a strong country with a socialist culture can be guaranteed by a reliable peaceful environment.

Second, cross-cultural and multinational cultural transmission, exchanges and cooperation provide a broad platform for China to strengthen its socialist culture. Practice shows that the mutual collision, impact and integration of different cultures constitute the driving force for the constant progress of world culture. During the development of traditional Chinese culture, the cultural integration of the Han nationality and the ethnic minorities has followed a similar pattern; amid the development of world culture, the integration of Chinese culture and other cultures follows quite a similar path. The cultures of different peoples share many values, for instance, the respect for life. In the 20th century, Zhang Hua, a student of the Fourth Military Medical University, lost his life saving an old farmer who fell into a manure pit. His death triggered great discussion on 'how to measure the value of life'. Some held the idea that it was an unworthy 'sacrifice' like exchanging gold for stone. A consensus on the value of life is reached through great debate. The American blockbuster *Saving Private Ryan* with the Normandy Landing in 1944 as the background tells the story that the survival of young private Ryan was guaranteed at the cost of eight lives to spare his mother from the fate that all her sons might die in the war. In another instance, disaster films show human feelings, with *Tangshan Earthquake* showing family affection and *Titanic* describing love on a new path. An additional example is China's *The Butterfly Lovers* and Britain's *Romeo and Juliet*, both odes to love created in different approaches and with a difference of 1,000 years, moving the audience to tears.

Third, the abundant cultural resources of the Chinese nation comprise an inexhaustible treasure trove for China to build itself into a strong country with a socialist culture. Many of them have become world renowned and more are waiting to be discovered. The ideology of Confucius is eternal after thousands of years. Now 'Confucius Institutes' at home and abroad are having a considerable impact on the global popularisation of Chinese culture. The thoughts and wisdom of Sun Tzu in *Master Sun's Art of War*, a military classic, have been applied by some countries in military strategy, political governance, operating management and sports competition. At the thought of the *Pilgrimage to the West*, one of China's 'Four Great Classical Novels', Chinese audiences will remember the scene that everybody watched on TV (shot in 1986) leaving no one in the street. It has been replayed more than 3,000 times so far and an application has been submitted for the world record of rebroadcasting and audience rating. To many Westerners, it was nothing but a story of a Chinese traveling to the West in the company of two pets and a servant. After thinking about it meticulously, they sense its spiritual appeal.

Building China into a strong country with a socialist culture is primarily confronted with the following problems:

First, the powerful position of Western culture poses China with the harsh task of safeguarding its cultural security. Ideological struggle has become more complicated in the modern world. To safeguard China's cultural security should be cautionary words to warn the whole of China. The United States adheres to power politics and implements cultural imperialism under the pretext of the globalisation process. If the US considering itself to be the 'military police of the world' were to implement Americanisation, the world would head toward unipolarity. It would be a catastrophe for the human race.

Second, the lack of cultural openness restricts the international influence of Chinese culture. Today, China has become the world's second largest economy. Nevertheless, its relatively backward cultural construction is mismatched with its great power status. In the competition of the international cultural industry, the powerful cultural countries occupy the international market for culture and make high profits. But they also concurrently try their utmost to export their political and cultural ideas and have a profound effect on the culture of all countries. In this regard, China should actively respond and try to boost its cultural openness.

Third, citizens' beliefs and moral tendency have gone downhill amid cultural diversity. With the in-depth development of reform and opening up, the ethos has changed a lot and disturbances often arise in the cultural and ideological spheres. Some bad anti-Marxist and anti-socialist ideologies appear and disappear now and then and pose challenges to mainstream socialist ideology. Some people regarded the impact on and transformation of the old, backward traditional moral concepts in the reform and opening up to be the negation of the entire moral system. They applied the market rules prevailing in the economic sector to social life and misunderstood the moral principles regulating people's behaviour. The 2-year-old Little Yueyue was killed by two passing cars successively without any rescue from passers-by in Foshan, Guangdong. Yao Jiaxin, an undergraduate of Xi'an, Shaanxi, ran over a passer-by and stabbed the victim several times in a fight to the death. Many similar issues have tortured the social conscience and citizens' conscientiousness and aroused the attention of the country and even the whole world to the morality of Chinese nationals.

What's more, as to the inheritance of Chinese culture, the Confucian classics have been marginalised and cultural faults have arisen. Some authoritative scholars have pointed out that some professors in the department of Chinese language and literature do not reach a sufficient standard in ancient Chinese; some doctors of liberal arts speak fluent English but cannot read the original text in ancient Chinese; even the intellectual elites cannot read the Confucian classics. That situation indicates that the roots of national traditional culture are breaking. Therefore, we need to rapidly realise the modernisation of Chinese culture and strengthen traditional cultural protection.

2. Stick to the roots and march towards modernisation

Chinese culture is the 'roots' and 'soul' of the Chinese nation. The modernisation of Chinese culture must be based on its roots, advance with the times on the basis of inheriting fine traditional Chinese culture and highlight the characteristics of the era during the creative transformation and creative development.

(1) Socialism revives culture

After the Opium Wars broke out, the important measure of imperialist cultural invasion was preaching. A group of priests from religions such as Western Catholicism, Christianity and Tsarist Russia's Eastern Orthodoxy played an ignominious role in the invasion under the cover of religion. At the same time, the imperialists moulded public opinion for their invasion of China, widely propagated the 'theory of superior and inferior races' and denigrated the Chinese nation as an 'inferior nation'. They cooked up the 'Yellow Peril', namely, the 'China threat theory'. *The Yellow Peril*, an oil painting given by German Kaiser Wilhelm II to the Czar, was a typical reflection of this. Imperialist military aggression against, political control over, economic plundering of and cultural permeation into China encountered strong resistance from the Chinese people and evoked their cultural awakening.

The Westernisation movement followed the principle of 'Chinese learning as the fundamental structure and western learning for utility', attached high priority to learning Western science and technology, set up new-style schools, officially dispatched overseas students and marked the launch of modern education. The new knowledge learnt in the movement broadened people's horizons and created conditions for the transformation from traditional Chinese culture to modern culture. The movement impacted the traditional idea of 'emphasising the fundamental and repressing the nonessential', changed the general mood of society and stimulated the transformation of values to suit modern times. Nevertheless, due to its own limitations, it could not fulfill the duty of fundamentally realising the self-improvement and prosperity of the country.

The Hundred Days' Reform (11 June-21 September 1898) promoted learning from the West to a record high. The reformists advocated 'wholesale Westernisation' and held the view that we should learn not merely Western science and technology but also their political systems, ideology and culture. Although the movement was crippled due to the 'Wuxu Coup'[1], its banner of 'national salvation', political improvement programmes and enlightenment of imagination accelerated the awakening of the Chinese nation.

The Revolution of 1911 held the banner of the Three People's Principles (nationalism, democracy and the people's livelihood) up high, demarcated revolution and reform in the debate between the revolutionaries and the reformists, spread democratic and revolutionary thinking, promoted ideological emancipation and social reform, and brought new positive changes in China's economic life, ethos, ideology and culture. Yet, Yuan Shih-kai appropriated the achievements of the Revolution of 1911 and implemented warlord autocracy which caused the restorative trend to run wild for a time.

The New Culture Movement (around the time of the May 4th movement in 1919) came up with the basic slogans of democracy and science and aroused the trend of anti-feudal ideological emancipation. Although it criticised Confucianism, it did not negate all the traditional culture of China. The May 4th movement, which broke out after the October Revolution (1917), became the starting point of the new democratic revolution.

The CPC established in 1921 ushered in a new path of the Chinese revolution in a brand new way and constantly renewed the process of Chinese socialism thanks to the application of Marxism in China and relevant practical achievements. One of the contents of the application of Marxism in China was to integrate the fundamentals of Marxism with the fine historical traditions and culture of China.

---

[1] The 'Wuxu Coup', an epoch-making historical event in modern China, refers to a bloody coup inside the Qing government in 1896 launched by the conservative forces headed by the Empress Dowager Cixi against the reformists headed by Emperor Guangxu, ending up with the failure of the reform, the killing of six reformists – Tan Sitong, Kang Guangren, Lin Xu, Yang Shenxiu, Yang Rui and Liu Guangdi – the exile of reformists Kang Youwei and Liang Qichao, the Emperor Guangxu's loss of personal freedom and the resumption of power by conservative forces.

In formulating the new-democracy cultural platform, the CPC placed top priority on 'national' culture among national, scientific and popular culture. The national style, national form, Chinese style and power it stressed were closely related with traditional Chinese culture. In the new period of socialist construction, reform and opening up, the contents of the socialist cultural platform with Chinese characteristics became increasingly enriched and developed. The newly-designed cultural development strategy also saw its establishment and constant improvement. Scientific and cultural modernisation constituted a vital part of the 'four modernisations' proposed in the 1960s. A series of guidelines, policies and principles for cultural construction, such as the 'double hundred' guiding principles (letting a hundred flowers bloom and a hundred schools of thought contend), the 'two serves' (culture should serve the people and serve socialism) direction and the 'three orientations' ('Education should be oriented toward modernisation, toward the world and toward the future' proposed by Deng Xiaoping), added splendour to Chinese culture and reinvigorated Chinese culture in socialist China.

(2) The Chinese characteristics manifested in culture

The great socialist course with Chinese characteristics encompasses abundant contents such as the socialist path, the socialist theoretical system and the socialist system with Chinese characteristics. Among them, the socialist path with Chinese characteristics is the way to reach the end, with the socialist theoretical system being the guide to action and the socialist system being the fundamental guarantee. The three vital elements are unified into the great socialist practice with Chinese characteristics.

The proposals of humanistic pragmatism and giving wealth to people advocated by Chinese culture were put into practical application in the socialist economic growth with Chinese characteristics. For instance, the establishment of the basic economic system with public ownership remaining dominant and allowing diverse forms of ownership to develop alongside it, and the distribution system with distribution according to work playing the dominant role and allowing the co-existence of multiple distribution forms pooling all the social forces to focus on economic growth and further cement China's economic foundations.

The political progress of socialism with Chinese characteristics reinvigorated the democratic spirit of being 'people oriented', the rule-of-law thought of 'running the country according to law' and the state concept of 'grand unification' of the Chinese nation adhered to by Chinese culture. The Scientific Outlook on Development referred to the concept of 'people foremost' initially put forward in *Guan Zi*, a book on the words and actions of Guan Zhong and his school, endowed it with the new contents of the times and proposed that the core of the Scientific Outlook on Development was being people oriented.

In the prosperous socialist culture with Chinese characteristics, the reforming, educating and cultivating functions of the 'transformation of all living things' followed by Chinese culture, the strategies of 'trying peaceful means before resorting to force' and attaining both political and military achievements as well as the measures and tools for 'writing to convey truth' manifested the abundant deposits, mighty force and great strides of Chinese culture in modern times. For example, the dominant position of Marxist ideology should be upheld, the citizens with 'four haves' (have revolutionary ideals, sound moral integrity, good education and a strong sense of discipline) should be cultivated and socialist core values should be advocated and practiced. Socialist core values advocated at the 18th NPC of the CPC include: prosperity, democracy, civility, harmony, freedom, equality, justice, rule of law, patriotism, dedication, integrity and friendship. All these reflect elements of fine traditional Chinese culture and the traditional origin of modern Chinese culture.

In building a harmonious socialist society with Chinese characteristics, the advocacy in Chinese culture relating to interpersonal relationships and forgiveness, for instance, 'harmony and peacefulness are prized', 'a favourable climate is less important than favourable geographical conditions which are less important than human conditions' and 'the benevolent love of others' are carried forward in the new era. It is the overall requirement to build a harmonious socialist society featuring 'democracy and the rule of law, fairness and justice, integrity and friendship, vigour, stability, order and harmony between man and nature'. And it is also the refining of China's traditional ideal for the 'perfect society' in reality.

During the building of socialist ecological civilisation with Chinese characteristics, the natural harmony of the 'unity of heaven and man' and the essence of the idea of ecological harmony that 'people are my brothers and all things are my kind' upheld by Chinese culture are inherited in modern times. It requires establishing the concept of ecological civilisation featuring respect for, compliance with and protection of, nature, building a resource-conserving and environment-friendly society, striving to present a gorgeous China and to realise permanent development of the Chinese nation. It has also pointed out the direction of future building of the socialist ecological civilisation.

(3) Cultural modernisation needs further endeavours

To become the endless impetus for the life, growth, unity and advancement of the Chinese nation against the backdrop of cultural diversity of the international community, the modernisation of Chinese culture must be realised. To that end, arduous efforts should be made in the following four respects.

First, the roots of fine traditional Chinese culture should be upheld during cultural inheritance. To keep to one's roots is the premise of the modernisation of Chinese culture. In terms of the development of natural science and social science, countries around the world may, to a certain extent, accomplish the same goals. Cultural modernisation may also be achieved correspondingly, however, by using different approaches. The 'different' here refers to the 'difference' in culture. Under the backdrop of world cultural diversity and amid the exchanges, conflicts and mutual influence of world culture, powerful cultures will gain the upper hand with their present strength and the nations that are weak in defending their culture will lose their own battlefields and even be assimilated by stronger culture. For this reason, to realise the modernisation of Chinese culture, efforts should be made to hold fast to the roots and the spiritual core of fine traditional Chinese culture, to carry forward the national culture, to maintain the individuality of traditional Chinese culture and to continue the legend and the amazing glamour of Chinese culture.

Second, it is necessary to absorb the merits of fine cultures around the world for cultural reference. Any culture that is favourable for reform and opening up, productivity development and the grand prosperity and development of socialist culture, whether it is Western or traditional or both, is the culture we will pursue. Otherwise, it is what we should discard. Lu Xun once commented that "it is easier for literature with a regional style to become popular worldwide". It used to be deduced and frequently quoted that 'the more national it is, the more global it is'. However, this does not mean that a nation's national and regional culture can grow in isolation without learning from others' advantages. Conversely, they should draw on the strong points of others and develop their own features.

Third, to address cultural conflicts is to fight against cultural hegemony. At present, there is no denying that Western culture is leading the diverse world culture. But it doesn't mean its domination. Cultural hegemony is the manifestation of extreme cultural conflicts. Some advanced Western countries depending on their strong overall national strength have dumped their values and behavioural norms on the whole world via diverse cultural products in the ideological domain and attempted to act as the 'military police' of world culture. That has severely hindered the progress of world culture. If we want to realise cultural elevation based on economic elevation, we must firmly fight against cultural hegemony.

Fourth, efforts should be made to expand the influence of Chinese culture worldwide during cultural exchanges. It is an urgent task to spread Chinese culture to the whole world. To improve its weak influence on the world, Chinese culture should, based on absorbing the fine cultural achievements of the world, advance with the times and go through constant reform and innovation to augment its influence on the world. Learning from the successful experiences of Germany's Goethe Institut and Spain's Instituto Cervantes, China should persistently set up Confucius Institutes and Confucius Classrooms throughout the world to popularise not just the Han Chinese but also fine Chinese culture.

3. Cultural revival and fulfilling the Chinese dream

China once created an ancient civilisation with a long history, but it gradually declined from its heyday after the Opium Wars. It was the CPC that led the Chinese people to attain national revival. Amid the trend of modernisation, China urgently hopes to realise cultural revival and fulfill the Chinese dream through the modernisation of Chinese culture.

(1) Revitalisation of the Chinese nation through cultural revival

In a certain sense, national revitalisation is the cultural revival which serves as the barometer of the former. Globally, the Renaissance and the Enlightenment that successively took place in Europe boasted touches of cultural revival. The Renaissance re-explored the essence of classical European culture, inspired a new vision of human thinking and expanded a new realm of human perception. The Enlightenment further proposed to establish the capitalist political system and advocated such political principles as 'Liberty, Equality, Fraternity'. They exerted direct, far-reaching influence on the American War of Independence (1775-1783) and the French Revolution (1789-1799) and fueled the economic growth, political progress and cultural prosperity of Europe.

The Meiji Restoration of Japan in the 1860s ushered in Japan's modernisation. The Japanese government conducted political reforms, adopted a policy of 'industry breeding and business incubation' to invigorate its economy, advocated 'civilisation and enlightenment' and made Japan the first industrial country in Asia and a world power.

Where is China's 'cultural revival'?

In modern history, China's social reforms such as the Westernisation movement and the Hundred Days' Reform, its learning from European and Japanese models and trials to transplant the European Renaissance in China, registered the achievements of modern Western civilisation although they failed in succession. The learning from the West in the Westernisation movement only learned the symptoms rather than the fundamentals of Western countries. The Hundred Days' Reform was elevated to the level of political reform but still failed to fundamentally eradicate the base of feudal society. Sun Yat-sen was the earliest to shout the slogan 'to revitalise the Chinese nation'. But the Revolution of 1911 learning from the West led by him failed because Yuan Shih-kai stole the fruits of the revolution.

It was not until the early 20th century that advanced elements in China became aware that ultimately, to realise modernisation, comprehensive cultural and social transformation must be carried out to expedite cultural development and social reform.

The New Culture Movement brought forward the slogans of 'democracy' and 'science', advocated new culture and banished all blind faith. But it attached most importance to the Western model, implemented wholesale Westernisation and generated side effects through its excessive criticism of traditional culture. For instance, Hu Shi and others suggested that Chinese history should start from the later period of the Zhou dynasty and even the period of Confucius rather than the Xia dynasty; Qian Xuantong advocated 'doing away with Chinese characters'. Their advocacy of such things was all wrong. Some people even preached the adoption of national nihilism, discarding the 5,000-year-old Chinese civilisation, and accepting the 'three struggles' civilisation of the West, namely, competition, struggle and war. By contrast, they advocated ignoring and forgetting China's 'three peaces' civilisation, namely, family togetherness, social harmony and international peace. That was especially detrimental for China's cultural revival.

The erroneous 'Cultural Revolution' not merely harmed culture itself, but also hurt intellectuals. The negative impact of the decade-long cultural havoc has not been uprooted even until now.

After the reform and opening up, some people were eager for quick success and instant benefits and anxiously pursued quick realisation of economic benefits, which led to cultural marginalisation. China aspired to become powerful, especially a country of powerful culture. Nevertheless, cultural development is a millennium programme of lasting importance, just like a tree that takes as long as a hundred years to grow. It is a slow process and cannot be accomplished at a stroke. The pragmatism prevailing in those years gave rise to some after-effects which prompted people to reconsider the negative influence of materialism and the trend toward economic dominance on declining ethical beliefs.

China's cultural revival in the new century constitutes a focal part of the great rejuvenation of the Chinese nation and is an adaptation of its overall objective.

(2) Cultural revival, a dream of 100 years

The proposal of the 'Chinese dream' made by Xi Jinping visiting the 'Road to Revival' exhibition at the National Museum has vividly, aptly and pertinently sketched the contours of the wonderful aspirations of the Chinese people to pursue the great national rejuvenation, national prosperity and strength, and happiness in their personal lives, and aroused the national affections, responsibilities and sense of urgency of millions upon millions Chinese. It is not like water without a source or a tree without roots. Instead it boasts a profound cultural background. China's cultural revival has created favourable conditions for the realisation of the Chinese dream and has provided cultural support to that end.

Culture is the soul for realising the Chinese dream. Chinese culture once influenced the surrounding countries and beyond to the whole world. China's reputation as an ancient civilisation originated from worldwide recognition of China's great culture. The decline of modern China was caused by seclusion and cultural backwardness. Therefore, the rejuvenation of the Chinese nation was also instrumental in achieving China's cultural revival through the opening-up process.

Culture is the soft power to realise the Chinese dream. The Renaissance and the Enlightenment in developed Western countries created the modern civilisation that has lasted until now and dominated the world for hundreds of years. New types of culture have led to the germination and development of new forms of society, and have been proved in the practice of the development of human society. Culture has a gigantic role to play in terms of soft power. Ji Xianlin's idea that 'the 21st century is the century of China' has been widely accepted. Only when the cultural revival of the Chinese nation is realised can the great rejuvenation of the Chinese nation be really achieved.

In the uptrend of world culture, the rise of China's economy via a different model of modernisation from that of the West has captured world attention and aroused the interest of Westerners in Chinese culture. They have explored the core of Chinese culture, sought the common ground between Western and Chinese culture, and hunted for an effective remedy to the ideological crisis in the Western world. It has also strengthened our self-confidence in Chinese culture. The functions and power of culture are just like the 'thunder amid silence' as depicted by Lu Xun. The profound influence of culture seems to occur without sound or movement but bursts out with breathtaking explosive force after profound accumulation.

(3) The 'three selfs' of culture and the fulfillment of the Chinese dream

The 'Chinese path', 'China model' and 'China's rise' are tightly correlated with cultural self-consciousness, cultural self-confidence and cultural self-improvement. The realisation of the Chinese dream for great national rejuvenation cannot be achieved without the great prosperity and expansion of socialist culture. Special efforts should be made to enhance cultural self-consciousness, cultural self-confidence and cultural self-improvement.

First, efforts should be made to boost cultural self-consciousness. This refers to cultural awareness and awakening, and encompasses recognition of the position and functions of culture, mastering the rules of cultural development and the responsibilities for cultural construction. The awakening of a nation primarily hinges on its cultural awakening. From keeping records by tying knots, totem worship, myths and legends in ancient times to the present radio, television, internet and mobile new media, each step of the Chinese nation to aspire for and pursue civilisation and progress has been based on cultural awakening. To boost cultural self-consciousness, we must deeply identify with the significance, position and functions of culture, positively take responsibility for cultural construction, development and progress, know about the history and development trends of our national culture, master the ideological quintessence and source of wisdom of traditional culture, and continuously improve our cultural and spiritual qualities. In the face of the conflicts interwoven between national culture and foreign culture, and between traditional culture and modern culture, we must discern the false from the genuine, clearly differentiate right from wrong, safeguard national cultural safety and expand the national strategic interests.

Second, work should be done to strengthen cultural self-confidence. It highly affirms the value of our own culture and strengthens belief in its vigour and vitality. Speaking of ancient China, Chinese all take pride in the Confucianism of Confucius, the cultural and military achievements of wise and enlightened past emperors such as Emperor Taizong Li Shimin of the Tang and Emperor Taizu Zhao Kuangyin of the Song, the magnificent Great Wall and the zigzagging legendary Silk Road. The fine traditions fostered in the socialist revolution, construction and reform and opening up, the ethos concentrating on patriotism and the spirit of the time focusing on reform and innovation have been carried forward relentlessly in modern times. To strengthen cultural self-confidence, we should respect and be proud of our fine traditional Chinese culture and persistently believe in the vitality and prospects of Chinese culture; not only rationally view, scientifically analyze, inherit and protect our own historical traditions and culture but also tolerate, learn from and absorb world history and culture, exotic and ethnic culture, and the accomplishments of modern civilisation, always stand fast to the cultural position of the Chinese nation, focus on the development and affairs of the Chinese nation and apply culture in developing China and Chinese culture in cultural opening. Since values are deeply ingrained in culture, the self-confidence in values is the centralised reflection of cultural self-confidence. The strengthening of cultural self-confidence is reflected in the self-confidence in socialist core values for the time being.

Third, cultural self-improvement must be realised. To boost cultural self-consciousness and strengthen self-confidence is to realise cultural self-improvement. This means we should follow the path of cultural development with Chinese characteristics and build national, scientific, and public advanced socialist culture geared to the needs of modernisation, the world and the future in a move to tap into the strong appeal, influence, creativity and competitiveness of Chinese culture and develop China into a great country with a socialist culture with Chinese characteristics. Cultural self-improvement provides strong cultural support and soft power for the realisation of the Chinese dream and is the centrepiece of the strategy of building China into a powerful cultural country as proposed by the CPC central committee. To that end, we should correctly master the path, orientation and soul of culture, blaze a new trail for the cultural system, collaboratively promote cultural creation, transmission, undertaking, industries and talent growth, and continuously boost the level of cultural productivity.

Chapter 4

The Unique Creation of Fine Traditional Chinese Culture

Since 2006, the second Saturday each June has been designated a special Chinese festival, namely, 'Cultural Heritage Day'. It was initiated to make people aware of and protect traditional culture and to instil in people a sense of pride and mission for their brilliant 5,000-year-old civilisation and the exceptionally abundant cultural heritage of China. The present culture is cumulatively sourced from traditional culture and is the re-creation and re-development of fine traditional culture. We should inherit the fine culture, especially the fine traditional culture whose unique creation was the valuable legacy bequeathed by our ancestors to later generations.

1. A unique historic fate has nourished unique humanistic feelings

The Chinese nation has gone through 5,000 years. This long history saw the rise and fall of 25 dynasties. Although the emperors succeeded to the throne in turns, the 'basis of the country', namely, the yellow-skinned and black-haired nationals, has never changed and the ancient Chinese and contemporary Chinese are still closely linked by their bloodline. In the mind of each Chinese, 'all the people of the world are brothers' and came from the same family 500 years ago, no, 5,000 years ago. The historical deposits of 5,000 years have vested in each Chinese a unique historical destiny: to pass on the precious heritage of their ancestors, just like Sisyphus in Greek mythology who pushed the rolling stone up the mountain.

(1) The endless thread of culture

Western countries have always held more or less biased views on Chinese civilisation due to lack of knowledge, inadequate emotional identification, hearsay or parroting what others say without enough empirical knowledge about China. Therefore, to some scholars, the East and China are just something that has been conjured up in the imagination of Westerners. The 'Clash of Civilisations' and 'the end of history' theories of Huntington and Francis Fukuyama thought that only Western Christian civilisation was the ultimate exemplary form of civilisation and that human society would eventually evolve in that form; hence, other civilisations were simply sections of the development chain; they would head for the same civilisation and the Chinese civilisation would be no exception.

The 'Clash of Civilisations' theory is obviously based on the stance and perspective of Western countries. It neglects the inherent logic and endless, exuberant vitality of other civilisations including the Chinese civilisation for their own development. The Chinese civilisation is the only form of civilisation worldwide that has lasted uninterrupted for thousands of years. The three other major civilisations among the four civilisations in the world were all conquered by alien races. Nevertheless, despite the replacement of 25 dynasties and the baptism and reconstruction of modernism, the core values and ideologies of the Chinese culture have not been lost. Even today we can see the wisdom, characters and morals left by our ancestors. Their legacy is still supporting us to push the wheel of civilisation ahead.

(2) An agrarian civilisation with a unique moral character

Many scholars have pointed out that the Chinese civilisation is a typical agrarian civilisation markedly different from other nomadic civilisations. This has fostered the continuity of the Chinese civilisation and the unyielding personality of the Chinese nation.

People in an agrarian society are attached to their native land and unwilling to leave it, unlike the hordes accustomed to migration. With a stronger concept of homeland in mind, they stress the stability of family structure and even the whole society. The land left by forefathers for generations has nourished the same personal and social character. They attach priority to the systems and guidance left by their ancestors which developed a powerful social inertia. It is the 'super stable structure' of the traditional society featuring on the one hand greater inertia, slow self-updating and very stubborn resistance against modern society and, on the other hand, conservation, continuity and non-severance of the interdependent humanistic feelings in traditional culture.

The realistic pursuit of an agrarian civilisation is not a visionary unknown future but to realise goals in life stably and step by step. *The Book of Rites - Great Learning* reads: 'In ancient times, those who wanted to propagate their virtues worldwide had to do a good job of governing their own countries first; those who wanted to govern their countries well had to put family affairs in order; those who wanted to put family affairs in order had to cultivate their moral character; those who wanted to cultivate their moral character had to have a righteous heart; those who wanted to have a righteous heart had to have sincere thoughts; those who wanted to have sincere thoughts had to investigate the nature of things. The nature of things had to be investigated for knowledge to be acquired. After the acquisition of knowledge, people developed sincere thoughts; sincere people had a righteous heart; those who had a righteous heart cultivated their moral character; those who cultivated their moral character put their family affairs in order; those who put their family affairs in order governed their countries well and those who could govern their countries well propagated their virtues to the world.'

In the sequence of investigation into the nature of things, cherishing sincere thoughts and a righteous heart, cultivating moral character, putting family affairs in order, governing the country and running the world, the Chinese set up a complete, orderly chain for personal struggle, followed the prescribed order and dared not to exceed or slight it. This came to pass with an agrarian civilisation that stressed accumulation. The agrarian civilisation was well aware of how hard it was to accumulate wealth and fostered restraint and tolerance in the personal and national character. That was also the typical national character of Chinese civilisation.

An agrarian civilisation attaches priority to collaboration and harmony. Farming, water conservancy and mutual exchange of products needed as the means of production cannot be completed by toiling on land alone but is conducted by collaboration and division of labour in an orderly group comprising more hands and families. Harmony was more profoundly recognised in agrarian society. Only when individuals lived in a harmonious family in a harmonious society could the huge community operate synergistically and in good order, and could the most fundamental material production proceed normally.

An agrarian civilisation features significant inclusiveness and assimilation. For thousands of years, China developed in a basic pattern of 'changing the barbarians in accordance with the ancient Chinese model'.

The 'change' does not refer to simply conquering by force but the cultural centripetal force and inclusiveness. It is widely known that ancient China in the Xia-Shang-Zhou period was just an outlying place on the Central Plains surrounded by the barbarian tribes we called 'Eastern barbarians', 'Western tribes', 'Northern minorities' and 'Southern aboriginal tribesmen'. These intrepid nomadic minorities were at least not weaker than ancient China in terms of military achievements. So the emphasis of 'changing the barbarians in accordance with the ancient Chinese model' prevailed in civil administration and cultural assimilation. We can see that the Yuan dynasty was the one established when the so-called 'barbarians' conquered ancient China and was finally integrated into the big family of the Chinese nation; similarly, the Qing dynasty also widely absorbed and learned from the ancient Chinese civilisation after conquering it by force. Just as Engels said, it was not rare but normal in history for the conquerors to be conquered by the conquered, and that was the salutary influence of culture. 'All nations live side by side in perfect harmony' reflects the spirit of compatibility and inclusiveness.

(3) Historical destiny bred unique humanistic feelings

It is precisely the unique historical destiny of the Chinese nation that shaped the brilliant and longstanding Chinese culture and it is the brilliant and longstanding culture that bred unique humanistic feelings. Such humanistic feelings encompass the unique Chinese approach to handling the relationship between people and themselves, between different people and between people, society and country.

As to the relationship between people and their ego, the Chinese people pay attention to innermost harmony. Material things are irrelevant, particularly high position and great wealth. Confucius stated in *The Analects of Confucius - Narrations* that: 'Pleasure lies in simple food, drinking water and a bent arm for head support. It is like floating clouds to pursue ill-gotten high positions and great wealth.' This means that a simple life actually consists of infinite circumstances and sentiments, and the pursuit of wealth and rank by whatever possible means indeed lacks the understanding and experience of life. Confucius and Hui's cheerfulness shows the contentment in leading a humble but virtuous life and the inner concentration of the men. Although the Confucian school had no lack of sentiments of going into society, Confucius most admired a life full of humanistic feelings as in his verses: 'The clothes for spring have been made in the early spring; five or six adults and six or seven children swam in the Qishui river, did a rain dance in the wind and returned chanting'. Contentment is the cardinal point for seeking a happy life and the value and harmony of life should also be realised on the basis of a magnanimous mind, generous feelings, a sober mind, enough confidence, clear positioning and good state of mind. Only with all these elements can the lofty personal qualities and the harmonious microenvironment of man himself be achieved.

Chinese people cherish harmony and peace in getting along with others. The principle of 'prizing harmony and peace' shows the wisdom of the Chinese people to get on with others. Chinese society highly values human relations, namely, ethical relations between people. The so-called five cardinal relationships are those between a monarch and his subjects, between father and son, between man and wife, among brothers and among friends, which are the basic interpersonal structures and relationships in society. 'Benevolence' is the top priority, the fundamental code of ethics, personality state and philosophical proposition in the interpersonal structural relationship in traditional Chinese society. The ancient Chinese called those of high morality, ambition and devotion to dreams as people of lofty ideals, the lenient and people-nourishing policies as benevolent policies, the learning that benefited the world as benevolent learning, honesty and faithfulness, and kindness and goodness as benevolent affections. It can be said that 'benevolence' was the logical starting point of Chinese ideology on which a whole set of social norms and criteria of moral evaluation was set up. Ethics played a pivotal part in ancient Chinese ideology and 'benevolence' advocated by the Confucian school has been the general principle persistently upheld in Chinese society.

As for interpersonal relationships, traditional culture requires us to show respect for seniority, courtesy and affection between man and wife, filial piety between mother and son and brotherly love. It also requires us to 'extend affection' based on 'affection for kinsmen'. There is a famous quotation from *Mencius - King Hui of Liang Vol.1*: 'Care for the elderly of our own and others; love for children of our own and others; if so, the governance of the country can be easily handled.' *The Book of Songs* has the verses: 'Set a good example to your wife and then your brothers and do a good job of managing the family and the country.' That means of governance should be promoted in every respect. Therefore, widespread benevolence is enough to pacify the world. Otherwise, even one's wife and children will not be well controlled. The ancient wise kings were far superior to the general population just because they were proficient in getting things done! That means showing consideration to others. Furthermore, friendship is based on 'sincerity' and 'faithfulness', lenience and tolerance. And an ideal society can be shaped only by guaranteeing fairness and justice, harmony in diversity, good reason, restraint and flexibility.

In terms of the relationship between individuals and the collective, and particularly with regard to ethnic minorities, the Chinese people regard the interests of the family and the state as the most important. Traditional Chinese culture attaches importance to addressing the relationship between individuals and small collectives, and between individuals and big collectives. What's more, a noble spirit also plays a vital part in personal cultivation. As to a noble spirit, Mencius told us: 'The noble spirit is massive and fearless, cultivated by righteousness without damaging it and pervasive in heaven and earth. It must be born in the marriage of justice and the right path. Without these, it would be weak and feeble. It is born in the accumulation of justice rather than a rightful action for a while. Any guilty action will weaken it.'

The noble spirit of a gentleman seemed more extraordinary when the nation was in peril. Wen Tianxiang spoke outright in the *Song of the Guerrilla*: 'The enemy has seven filthy spirits and I have one. What is there for me to fear in fighting against their seven filthy spirits with my noble spirit? In particular, it is the magnanimous spirit of fearlessness and the uprightness of the world. Throughout the ages, when the country was in critical danger, many martyrs pursued justice and righteousness at the cost of their lives.' Gu Yanwu noted in his *Daily Understanding*: 'Sometimes, a country is subjugated; sometimes, the nation perishes. If the regime of a country is changed, it is the replacement of a dynasty by another; if righteousness and justice are lost and the people are tyrannised or eaten by their counterparts, the nation perishes... For this reason, safeguarding the nation should come before that for the country. It is the duty of the monarch and the officials to safeguard the regime and it is the responsibility of ordinary men to safeguard the whole nation.' It is the principle that 'all men share a common responsibility for the events of the nation' upheld by the Chinese people. It was just the unfortunate destiny and the tortuous history of China that fostered the deep feelings of the traditional Chinese culture for the nation.

2. The unique fundamental realities of China cultivated its unique cultural genes

What are China's fundamental realities? Lu Xun once incisively argued about Chinese myths: 'There are chiefly two reasons why Chinese myths have been sporadically handed down: The first is that the aboriginal Chinese ancestors initially lived in the fertile Yellow river basin, however, frequently plagued by floods. They had to work very hard for a living. They paid more attention to practical production rather than imaginary tales. Consequently, rare classic articles were handed down. The second rests in the emergence of Confucianism that civilised people with articles for realistic application, such as self-cultivation, good management of family affairs and rule of China, and despised the mention of supernatural beings and absurd ancient stories. For these reasons, Chinese myths could not be carried forward but, more seriously, tended to perish.' Although he talked about the reasons why Chinese myths were not presented in a more serious light, Lu Xun actually narrated the fundamental realities of ancient China at that time. In those years, numerous countrymen living alongside the Yellow river suffered from a bad environment, lived by farming and jointly coped with flooding of the Yellow river year after year. The farming culture of thousands of years forged the cultural genes exclusive to the Chinese people.

(1) The collective consciousness generates 'genes'

In modern society, 'genes' appear in all aspects of our life, such as genetic engineering of crops, gene therapeutic agents, genetic weapons and hotly disputed genetically modified food (GMF). 'Genes' have become the most familiar strangers. Tracing them back to their source, 'genes' in terms of their biological meaning were discovered more than 150 years ago. As early as the mid 19th century, celebrated Austrian scholar Gregor Johann Mendel discovered the existence of genes in his experiment on hybrid peas. Although it was more the result of logical deduction, it could not be denied that genes had captured people's attention as the basic genetic unit. Moreover, the research on genes was not limited to biology circles and theorists in social organisms easily translated it to all the fields of social sciences. To scholars of social culture, the society and organic matter shared similar structural features and organic matter boasted the traits of genes so that the character of later generations resembled that of their predecessors; that was why similar phenomena in social life existed widely in different areas and times. For instance, the systems coming down in one continuous line, consistent taste, the unfailing arts and authentic customs also originated from a social gene, a custom gene and even a cultural gene. It is an easy deduction and cultural genes have been endowed with proper meaning in the research on social culture.

The concept of a 'cultural gene' came to light in the 1950s and was named after an American anthropologist. As a matter of fact, it is not rare to talk about the elements of inheritance from a cultural perspective. For instance, the 'mythemes' in mythology, the 'motif' in folklore and the 'collective unconsciousness' in social psychology more or less relate the unchanged core of cultural circulation. Nevertheless, the most famous concept of a 'cultural gene' was the 'meme' put forward in *The Selfish Gene* by British scholar Clinton Richard Dawkins in 1976. Although it was just a concept created by Dawkins himself, 'meme' refers to the basic unit of cultural inheritance, namely, the cultural gene.

In a certain sense, the cultural gene is a collective consciousness for a kind of behaviour identified, accepted and formed by a nation or a group of people. The collective consciousness is usually manifested in collective unconsciousness. Since the identification and acceptance of a certain kind of behaviour is the result of long-term unconscious influence, it is always reflected in involuntary compliance and unconditional acceptance. The collective consciousness of a nation can usually be traced back to the experiences of the ancients in their collective life. The harsh natural environment in ancient times forced human beings to live a collective life and take collective actions and it meant the death of individuals leaving the collective. That life experience was deeply ingrained in the minds of human beings, gradually developed to become the collective unconsciousness and sub-consciousness of human beings and became their instinctive behaviour.

(2) Cultural genes carry tradition

We have reached universal consensus on the inheritable cultural core. Going through the vicissitudes, we can still see numerous antiquities, possibly including customs, moral evaluation, language expression and a certain phenomenon of spiritual culture. Nonetheless, cultural genes are different from biological genes whose stability is much greater than that of cultural genes. With the passage of time, cultural genes constantly change and only keep relatively limited stability. Not all traditional culture will be maintained as cultural genes and evolve to become present cultural traditions. Cultural genes and biological genes equally boast selectivity and variability. As to biological genes, we often talk about 'the survival of the fittest'. Through rounds of elimination, the fittest are left and the backward are eliminated to ensure the sound development of the population. Likewise, most of the residual cultural genes are generally what is left of outstanding cultural elements after what has been eliminated by society and the times. Concurrently, society and the times reshape and rebuild cultural genes and develop new cultural genomes suitable for social development.

After selection and development for thousands of years and reconstruction and integration in new times, many outstanding genes of Chinese culture have been inherited and pervade the daily conduct norms, code of ethics, aesthetic forms and ways of thinking. They inherit the genes of fine traditional Chinese culture, reflect the ideals and faith established by the Chinese people after exploration, trial and hardship, and bear our beautiful visions of ourselves in modern times.

Cultural genes can play a vital role in all aspects of culture. From the most superficial material culture, we can see many fixed cultural symbols in the minutiae of living, catering and clothing; the middle-layer spiritual culture including customs, etiquette, religion, art, systems and laws, and the deepest-seated world outlook, values and ethics. These are permeated with consistent cultural factors.

Another relevant concept of cultural genes is 'cultural tradition'. It is both different from and connected with 'traditional culture'. They differ because cultural tradition chiefly highlights tradition, namely, the continuity of culture while traditional culture centres on culture and stresses the inherited cultural spirit. Cultural genes are related with cultural traditions and traditional culture. On the one hand, cultural tradition is the combination, awakening and revival of cultural genes; on the other hand, cultural genes are a carrier of traditional culture. Traditional culture is inherited through cultural genes and reinvigorated in new time and space.

(3) Cultural genes mold the Chinese heart

The glorious history and tortuous destiny of the Chinese nation have bred fine cultural genes. These genes have not influenced the physiological structure but have molded a Chinese heart that houses the greatest pith of Chinese culture, namely, benevolence, 'people-oriented', integrity, justice, harmony, concord and great unity.

'Kindheartedness', meaning leniency and kindness, is the soul of Chinese culture. *Huai Nan Zi - On Cultivation* said: 'Emperor Yao pursued filial piety, benevolence and kindness and treated his subjects as his own children.' That is to say, kindheartedness can be dated back to the oldest ancestors in China. It has historically evolved to be a natural instinct of Chinese people. Just as Mencius said, people have 'four senses', namely, the sense of compassion, the sense of shame, the sense of reverence and the sense of right and wrong. They respectively correspond to benevolence, righteousness, etiquette and wisdom which are intrinsic rather than extrinsic. Therefore, Confucius took kindheartedness as the fundamental of being and strived to practice kindheartedness. In *The Analects of Confucius*, 'benevolence' appears 109 times. The cardinal point of kindheartedness is 'to love others' out of innermost kindness.

Being 'people oriented' is magnified kindheartedness. It means the current political rulers release benevolence to the people in society. Modern Chinese are fairly familiar with the TV play *Prime Minister Liu Yong* which relates a story about Liu Yong, Prime Minister of Emperor Qianlong, fighting against influential officials and pleading for the people. The lyrics of the theme song read: The ordinary people serve as the steelyard measuring the rights and wrongs between heaven and earth. Mencius said: "People are the most important, followed by the state and the monarch." This means that the ordinary people are always placed in the top position compared with the country and the emperor. In addition, 'people-oriented' thinking goes back a long way and was well established in ancient China, and the rulers recognised the power of the people. As *Hanshi Anecdotes* described: 'The people will get along peacefully with emperors who consider them as most important and assist them in becoming more powerful. Otherwise, the country will be thrown into peril and perish in short order.' The people are fairly mighty, just like 'the water that bears the boat is the same water that swallows it up'. Only when people's power is given more priority can long governance be secured.

As to 'integrity', China is known worldwide as 'a state of ceremonies'. Integrity has always been a traditional virtue of the Chinese nation. More than 2,000 years ago, Confucius advocated 'honouring your word and taking resolute action'. Besides, China's language system also includes a multitude of idioms eulogising integrity, such as 'a word carries weight', 'a promise will be kept' and 'a real man never goes back on his word and what has been done cannot be withdrawn'. In the long Chinese history going back thousands of years, many figures and stories about integrity have been extensively read. The word integrity has been ingrained in the heart of the Chinese people and the core of traditional Chinese culture.

'Justice' has always been upheld by the Chinese nation and innumerable articles on traditional Chinese culture have talked about 'justice'. *Mencius - Gao Tzu Part I* narrates: 'I want to live on and I want to safeguard justice. If the two elements cannot be achieved concurrently, I will pursue justice at the cost of my life." *Xuncius - Non-Prime Ministers* says: 'People with integrity, vigour, wisdom and justice are most valuable in the world.' *The Analects of Confucius - Living in a Benevolent Environment* mentions: 'The mind of the noble man is conversant with righteousness and that of the mean man with gain.' *The Commentary of Zuo - The First Year of Duke Yin* holds the view: 'The wages of sin are death. Just wait and see.' Tan Sitong expressed in his *Inscriptions on a Prison Wall*: 'I will smile at my death with devotion to righteousness that inspires reverence! What will be left is my great spirit as mighty as the towering mountain!' All these reflect the unbreakable will of the Chinese nation to pursue justice. At the military parade at the 70th anniversary of the victory of the Chinese people in the War of Resistance Against Japanese Aggression and the Global War Against Fascism, Xi Jinping elaborated on the course of hard struggle and special contributions of the Chinese people in fighting for human justice and world peace in the great anti-Japanese war. He solemnly declared: "Let's bear in mind the great truth inspired by history: Justice will most certainly triumph! Peace will most certainly triumph! People will most certainly triumph!" His speech revealed the distinctive cultural genes for the Chinese nation to uphold justice.

'Harmony and concord' is another important concept in traditional Chinese culture and the cultural gene pervading in China. The chapter on military strategy and tactics of Guan Zi writes: 'If people are managed and helped according to the rules of development of things and society, they can live in peaceful co-existence. Insofar as people live in a favourable environment and abide by the rules of development in human society, the society and people can co-exist in a sound structure and help each other. Concord evolves to become harmony, which can consequently organise people. Well organised people living in harmony cannot be destroyed by external factors.' *Words and Deeds of Emperor Shun* records: 'Poetry expresses the will and songs extend the language of poetry. Songs are sung slowly to highlight the meaning of poems. High and low voices coordinate with long verses. Musical instruments are used to mediate the singing.' 'Harmony and concord' is an ideal state of society and the highest state for the people, nature and society to get along well.

'Great unity' is both a political ideal and a value belief. Since ancient times, the Chinese nation has been unswervingly pursuing the ideal of 'great unity' and faith. Confucius and Mencius of the Confucian school, Lao Tzu and Chuang Tzu of the Taoist school and even Hung-Siu-tshuen and Sun Yat-sen in modern times had their own aspirations for and persistence in the 'society of great unity'. The metamorphoses of 'the whole world as one community' and 'the world of universal harmony' in *The Book of Rites* and 'the nirvana' featuring 'ultimate peace', 'great fairness', 'utmost benevolence' and 'superb governance' depicted by Kang Youwei all reflect the longing of the Chinese nation for a politically and morally ideal society living in great unity. The unremitting pursuit for 'a society in great unity' has also become an unchanged cultural gene of the Chinese people.

3. Unique cultural paradigm fostered by unique path of development

It is widely known that China is now pursuing a path of socialist development with Chinese characteristics. As a matter of fact, that is not only true of today but also ancient China followed a unique path of development. The most unique thing is that it has survived through its own efforts of self-reliance. In investigating the rise of some great Western powers in modern times or beyond, we can find that almost all the countries except China thrived and became powerful by means of launching wars against, annexing and plundering other countries. China, however powerful, never assaulted other countries but most of the time made peace with rulers of ethnic minorities in the border areas by intermarriage or compensation trade.

(1) The cultural paradigm of a unique style

American philosopher Thomas Kuhn proposed the 'paradigm' concept in *The Structure of Scientific Revolutions* in 1962. It originally referred to a set of beliefs, values and technology shared by community members. To him, the so-called scientific revolution is actually a paradigm shift, replacing one theory with another and one explanation with another. The so-called paradigm is the method for people to think about questions and recognise the world in a period of time.

Later, the 'paradigm' concept was extended from the field of philosophical science to social normalisation and formed a series of sets of different domains and disciplines including the paradigm of management, economy, ideology and culture. The paradigm of culture interpreted in this concept comprises the basic logic, method, characteristics and content of culture in a stage or period.

The paradigm of Chinese culture is one with national characteristics. It is the sentiments of Chinese culture and the Chinese aesthetic strategies comprising the spirit of the times and Chinese national genes. It is a channel of transmission and a mode of expression of Chinese style and the spiritual appeals and value orientations featuring strong Chinese threads and Chinese visions, having a particularly direct and important impact on cultural and artistic creation. The channels of transmission and modes of expression of culture differ a lot in different historical periods, which generate different culture paradigms. For instance, the Fu of the Han, the poetry of the Tang, the Ci poetry of the Song, the Yuan verses and fiction of the Ming and Qing were the most reasonable ways and best choice of the Chinese people to express their cultural sentiments and aesthetic values in different historical periods.

(2) Cultural paradigms differ in history and in modern times

A review of the historical thread of Chinese culture clearly shows that each period was represented by a typically exclusive cultural paradigm.

First of all, the cultural paradigm of the ancient society dating back thousands of years is that of traditional culture represented by Confucianism. With its influence on traditional Chinese society, that cultural paradigm fostered a 'superstable' social structure. The political pattern of a 'country in the world' grew at a quickened tempo. Uniformity and cultural consistency became normal and conventional. With splitting and the entry of heterogeneous culture, the powerful restoring function of the system began to work. The pattern of a 'country in the world' was practically woven by the imperialist system and the civil service organisation. Central and local power formed an effective, subtle relationship, considering both legitimate central rule and the particularities of different areas in the vast expanse of China. The rule boasted ingrained Confucian characteristics, especially, as Mr Hsu Cho-yun said, the politics of the empire adhered to Confucianism in appearance while being legalist in nature in the hope of realising Confucian ideals with the backing of the legalist system. Although the system had to be established with legalist tactics, the Confucian criteria for intrinsic evaluation still prevailed in society. The Confucian culture served as the standard for selection and promotion of civil officials. Most of the ruling classes were elites from the Confucian school. After the Song dynasty, Confucianism waned day by day and fell into the long process of expounding the classics. A complete moral system which had a huge impact on future generations was set up. After the Song and the Ming, the ruling class gave up the humanistic care advocated by the Confucian school and the cultural paradigm and value system of the entire society descended into specious stereotyped writing. It is self-evident that from its sudden rise to its final decay, the cultural paradigm of the whole ancient society was in the hands of Confucianism and the Confucian school. Even exotic Buddhism and the indigenous Taoist school were more or less assimilated and influenced by Confucianism.

The second cultural paradigm in China arose in modern times, especially before and after the Opium War. The opening process embraced powerful Western weapons and the pervasive heterogeneous Western culture. With the effect of social Darwinism, Chinese nationals re-conceived progress. The broken dream of the 'celestial empire' cast light on the Chinese people that only a modernisation drive could enable China's rejuvenation and there was an urgency to introduce Western learning. Chinese nationals tended to spare no efforts for technological, political, economic and cultural development. Although cultural inertia and cultural self-consciousness still seized people in the entanglement about the 'Yi-Xia distinction' (the distinction between barbarians and Chinese or between culturalism and ethnicity), 'the utilisation of Western technology in a Chinese form', how to 'learn from the West to curb Western aggression' and how to 'learn from the West for self-improvement', an enormous amount of Chinese nationals advocated completely discarding tradition and embracing Western values. Especially, when the state was reduced to being a semi-colonial and semi-feudal society, a complete break with old traditions was deemed to be necessary and urgent, and 'new culture' became the mainstream social awareness. Nonetheless, different torches were carried by different parties. Constitutionalists, reformers, reformists, revolutionaries, westernisationists and people of the Chinese quintessence school advocated different things. Although democracy and science have become a social consensus, cultural reform was always attached to a political wave, different political factions had their own plans and what they advocated in terms of culture naturally differed a great deal. They thought the study of Chinese ancient civilisation should not be abandoned and that fundamental Chinese culture must be held up high amid learning from the stronger West, although such perseverance was not scientifically measured, good and bad people were mixed up, including all sorts of dross and dregs of society. Others were excessively radical, advocated wholesale Westernisation and totally abandoning Chinese traditions. Just as Professor Lin Yusheng of the Department of History of the University of Wisconsin-Madison USA said in his book *Crisis of the Chinese Consciousness*: 'The anti-traditionalism was fairly fierce so that we are well justified in taking it as wholesale anti-traditionalism. As far as the social and cultural vicissitudes we know are concerned, the anti-idolisation required for thorough destruction of past ideologies presented an unprecedented historical phenomenon in many respects'. All in all, with 'the change of the political regime', culture and ideology both took on a chaotic outlook. All the factions stuck to their arguments with none of them giving way to the others. There were all manner of culture clashes, confronting one another and changing the current situation into a huge experimental melting pot. Thus, the modern cultural paradigm was reduced to a binary state, with either Chinese learning triumphing over Western learning or vice versa. The zero-sum game brought the consideration and resolution of the issues into a binary framework and fostered people's world outlook, values and code of behaviour in those years.

(3) Modern China and a new paradigm

In fact, the so-called cultural paradigm does not have a uniform standard but is only accepted or rejected in the binary framework of Chinese learning and Western learning. In essence, it has not developed a cultural system influencing all Chinese nationals. That problem was not thoroughly resolved until the founding of the CPC. With the founding of a unified and strong new China, a new cultural paradigm was finally established, or rather, stood out in the chaotic cultural system. With the influence of Marxist materialist dialectics and historical materialism, and with the application of Marxist theory in China, a whole set of new ideologies such as Mao Zedong Thought and Deng Xiaoping Theory came into being, were applied in the cultural domain and eventually formed the cultural paradigm in modern China.

Guided by classic Marxist theory, the cultural paradigm of modern China started from the prevailing status quo and historical phases of development, fueled cultural reform in social revolution and finally established the foundation for the cultural revival of the Chinese nation. Overcoming the past binary cultural outlook, it completely freed itself from the struggle between the focuses of culture and the plight of cultural selection and realised the scientific and complete transfer of the cultural paradigm.

The establishment of a new cultural paradigm could not be accomplished at a stroke. Undergoing a new democratic revolution, socialist revolution and socialist construction with Chinese characteristics, history finally saw the formation of the scientific cultural paradigm with Chinese characteristics in conformity with universal truth of Marxism. Different from the cultural paradigm of ancient China and the Western countries, it is in accordance with China's reality and constitutes a reasonable cultural statement that answers the requirements of globalisation and modernisation. The cultural concept has gone through the baptism of modern times and the collision and game-playing between Chinese and Western culture. Nevertheless, it is a brand new mentality and approach. Just as Qu Qiubai described: "The foundation of the new culture hinges on two sorts of culture, namely, Oriental culture and Western culture, which were in confrontation historically but complementary in early modern times." That is to say, the socialist cultural paradigm with Chinese characteristics necessitates careful treatment of the difference and opposition between Chinese culture and Western culture. It is not a matter of black or white. Chinese culture should have a global vision, play its role in the world arena and display its attitude and character in its integration into the progress of world civilisation.

This new cultural paradigm does not feature a nihilistic attitude towards liberalism with regard to national culture, overcomes blind adherence to nationalism, and really establishes a new sort of culture that perfectly integrates China with the world, tradition with modernity and inheritance with innovation.

Chapter 5

The Value Proposition of Fine Traditional Chinese Culture

For thousands of years, the great Chinese nation has created glorious and profound traditional Chinese culture with a rather long history. Especially, the political ambition 'to be the first to worry about the troubles across the land and the last to enjoy universal happiness', the patriotism that 'even humble people are always mindful of their duty to think about national concerns' and that 'if our interests can be achieved at the cost of our own lives, none will avoid it for the sake of their own safety', the awe-inspiring righteousness that 'neither riches nor honour can lead one astray, neither poverty nor lowly conditions can make one swerve from principle and neither threats nor force can bend one', the contention that 'men are mortal but my loyalty may leave a page in the annals' and 'spare no effort in performing one's duty to the end of one's days' and the self-cultivation for diligence and improvement have influenced and nourished generations of Chinese people. Even to this day, they still have their great existential value and guiding significance.

1. Political ambition intrinsic in fine traditional Chinese culture

Political ambition, also called political ideology refers to people's objectives in state governance and their own official careers. Confucianism, as the mainstream ideology of traditional Chinese society, in the course of valuing the upgrading of individuals' lives, always stresses the value and importance of individuals for the clan and society, and the strong expectations for and involvement with political and social affairs. It should be pointed out that the latent, profound worries about society and diligent work for society nurtured in Confucianism, despite the influence of Buddhism and Taoism upholding 'being above worldly considerations' and 'being free and unfettered', did not fade away or die out. Instead, they were tenaciously rooted in the long river of traditional culture and became an immortal impetus to push history ahead.

(1) Unselfishly return to propriety and the path of benevolent government

The Spring and Autumn period witnessed the deterioration of social order and upheavals. Confucius was devoted to rescuing people from the turbulent times in which they cared for nothing but lust and treacherous ministers ran amuck in the hope of rectifying social order through resuming the *Rites of Zhou* (a Confucian text on bureacracy and organisational theory). For this, Confucius advocated 'exercising government by means of virtue', 'rule by rites' and 'rule by virtue'. In the Warring States period, in the face of more chaotic social realities, Mencius advocated implementing 'benevolent government' and Xuncius, namely, Xun Kuang, stressed worshiping ceremonies, respecting the worthy, attaching importance to law and loving the ordinary people. Broadly speaking, the Confucian 'rule by virtue' or 'benevolent government' advocated 'unification' and clear and bright politics, emphasised making a distinction between superiors and subordinates and dominance hierarchy, and upheld respecting the worthy, benevolent emperors and righteous ministers, tax reduction and social well-being. It was the ideal society envisaged by Confucianism and their practical political view and lifelong advocacy although they knew 'it was impossible'.

Qu Yuan once chanted: 'I was endowed with so many good inherent qualities and I also attached much attention to cultivating my morality'. In the course of ceaselessly enhancing his self-learning, he also positively pushed political reform and stressed 'appointing virtuous and able officials and strictly abiding by laws and regulations' in the hope that measures could be taken to appoint capable officials and make clear, ordered laws at home and unite with external forces to fight against the Qin dynasty and reinvigorate the State of Chu. He also hoped to realise his political ambitions and ideals for the 'unification of China'. Confronted with defamation by a minority of partisans, for instance, 'the jealous maidservants around you fabricated rumours that I enchanted charm by flattery' and in the face of King Huai of Chu's suspicion and changeable temperament, Qu Yuan was exiled twice in succession. Despite internal torment, he never hesitated, retreated or gave up. In the end, on the occasion that Bai Qi, a general of

Qin, occupied Yingdu and the State of Chu was about to fall, he resolutely threw himself into the Miluo river in Hunan province with stones around his body and drowned himself, and safeguarded his independent personality and 'ideal politics' at the expense of his own life. In the *Records of the Grand Historian - Qu Yuan and Jia Sheng Biographies*, Sima Qian praised him by saying that 'his morals could outshine the sun and the moon'.

(2) Taking overall responsibility and maintaining one's own integrity

In traditional culture, almost all able men cherished political ambitions of supporting the country and helping people. Especially, the wise emperors and ministers took national and personal prosperity as the goal of their lifelong hard work.

The class of scholar officials in ancient China were both the creators of culture and knowledge, and participants in political life. Moreover, they were the main followers, developers, proponents and practitioners of traditional Chinese politics and culture. In ancient Chinese culture, political culture seemed more advanced.

An absolute majority of the scholar officials in ancient China had grand political ambitions. When out of power, 'they chanted loudly with great emotion and their morals could be shown at the beginning of their career'; before being appointed to an important position, they were often conceited: 'If I were employed, I would succeed in a couple of months or three years.' They took ruling the world and leaving a good reputation as their life goals and regarded it as a burning shame that 'their names were unknown even until the end of their lives'. Once they prospered, they would show their lofty aspirations, try to sweep away obstacles for the king, and spare no effort in performing their duties until their death. Meanwhile, the scholar officials declared that they 'paid attention to maintaining their integrity when they were less prosperous'. They were 'neither subjects of the emperor nor friends of feudal princes'; they 'were their own masters'; they 'read books to entertain themselves' and lived a reclusive life 'picking chrysanthemums beneath the eastern fence and leisurely appreciating the southern mountains'.

The scholar officials cherished meritorious thoughts of 'serving the royal court with their civilian and military skills' but often lived in seclusion and refused to become officials. The two entirely different attitudes were taken not merely by people of the same social strata but also by the same people. In the last years of the Eastern Han dynasty, Zhuge Liang 'tilled the soil by himself in Nanyang, barely managed to survive in the troubled times and did not seek fame among the dukes'; meanwhile, he aimed high and 'compared himself to Guan Zhong and Yue Yi'. However, when he hurled himself into society, he spared no efforts in 'weeding out the crafty villains and helping to restore the Han royal family. Ambitious Li Misu, 'proud of being the emperor's right-hand man' in the Tang dynasty won recognition from Emperor Xuanzong of Tang. But he was hated by the powerful minister Yang Guozhong who was jealous of him and he 'hid himself in a famous mountain and lived a secluded and reclusive life'. Nevertheless, in the An Lushan rebellion, he put himself forward boldly, but concurrently declared himself 'to be a recluse and refused to be an officer' and announced that he would 'return to live in the mountains after the rebellion in the capital was squashed'. After the An Lushan rebellion was suppressed, Li Fuguo became jealous of him. So he 'was willing to hide himself in Hengshan mountain in Hunan to avert disasters. An imperial edict was issued to grant him a third grade official's salary, hermit gown and treatment room'. It was a typical case of living a secluded life to avert disasters.

With the decline of the imperial examination system in the late Qing dynasty, the scholar official class vanished but the scholar official spirit survived. The mentality of 'remembering to worry about the country even when in a low social position' and 'serving the country worthily' still linger in the minds of intellectuals today.

(3) The universal community and pursuit of great harmony

Pre-Qin Confucianism started from the basis of a doctrine of benevolence and built a picture of a beautiful society. In the Qin and Han dynasties, it evolved into an ideology of 'great unity'. *The Commonwealth State* reads: When the great way prevails, the world is equally shared by all. Worthy and able men are selected as office holders. Mutual confidence is bred and good neighbourliness developed. Hence, people do not take only their own parents as parents, nor do they treat only their own children as children. Provisions are made for the aged until their death, adults are given employment, and the young can grow up. Widows and widowers, orphans, the old and childless as well as the sick and the disabled are all well taken care of. Men have their proper roles, women their homes. While they hate to see wealth lying about on the ground, they do not necessarily keep it for their own use. While they hate not to exert their own effort, they do not necessarily devote it for their own purposes. Thus evil scheming is repressed, and robbers, thieves and other lawless elements fail to materialise so that outer doors do not have to be shut. This is called 'the Age of Great Harmony'. It can be said that it was the peak and ultimate political ideal pursued unswervingly by the Chinese nation for thousands of years. With the calling of this ultimate political ideal, generations of Chinese took responsibility for society and the nation, took up the positions of the fallen, rose to fight one after another and went around campaigning for the great cause. While boosting their own value, they also promoted social progress.

Confucius and Mencius traveled through all the kingdoms and paid formal visits to the feudal princes; Qu Yuan explored the way out persistently; people suppressing conspiratorial cliques heroically went to help save the country from danger until their deaths in the late Han dynasty; the six martyrs in the Hundred Days' Reform met their death calmly. It can be easily seen that although traditional Chinese scholar officials cherished the concepts of insular loyalty to the monarch and filial piety to their parents due to historical limitations, there is no denying that political ambitions and ideals connected with the common people and taking the family-country as the most important element have influenced and encouraged generations of Chinese people to make successive and persistent contributions to building a richer, more democratic and more civilised China.

2. Fine traditional Chinese culture fosters feelings of dedication to serving one's country

An important characteristic of ancient China was the serious residue of the patriarchal clan system and the blood relationship, and family (clan) organisations became the main national structure. Hence, a patriarchal society featuring 'clan and country isomorphism (two different elements sharing a similar structure)' with typical Chinese characteristics came into being. 'Clan and country isomorphism' is in essence the identity of family, clan and country in terms of structure. Family is the epitome of country and country is the amplification of family. It means the close ties of individuals, family and country in terms of rights and obligations. Hegel held the view that: China was purely established in moral combination and the characteristic of country was the objective 'filial piety to the family'. There is no denying that the political structure model featuring 'clan and country isomorphism' of traditional China realised two-way interaction between restriction of political rights and moral constraints based on blood relationship. It was good for enhancing the centrifugal force and cohesion of the Chinese nation and the lasting political stability of Chinese society.

(1) If it is good for the country, no need for fame and fortune

The obsession with and sentimental attachment to family in traditional Chinese culture cannot be compared to any other country. Family and state, family and state integration, are the sincerest emotional sustenance of the Chinese people and doing a good job of managing state affairs has also become their lofty ideal and pursuit. 'As long as it is good for the country, the Chinese are willing to do it at the cost of their lives and will not back down for fear of a scourge on them.' High-ranking officials must undertake responsibilities for the country. Ordinary civilians, in the face of family and national crises, bear in mind that 'everyone is responsible for the rise and fall of the country', and are willing to come out boldly and die a heroic death.

In the Spring and Autumn and Warring States periods, Ziyuan (younger brother of Emperor Wen of Chu), prime minister of Chu, led his troops to attack the State of Zheng. Withdrawing the troops, he lived in the royal palace and attempted to force himself on the wife of the deceased Emperor Wen of Chu. The ministers of Chu manoeuvred to have him removed and appointed Dou Guwutu as prime minister. At the sight of the weak, impoverished country, Dou Guwutu donated all his family property to save the country from crisis. It is the origin of the literary quotation of 'sacrificing one's wealth to save the state' (*The Commentary of Zuo - The 30th Year of Duke Zhuang's Rule*).

The demise of the Western Jin dynasty raised the heavy curtain of history on up to 400 years of south-north confrontation in China. At a critical moment determining the rise and fall of the country and the whole nation, a large group of scholars rose to the challenge and stepped onto the road of serving the country worthily, protecting the homeland and helping the common people. Eminent General Zu Ti on the northern expedition was one of the representatives. When he served as the deputy governor of Sizhou, Zu Ti, together with his friend Liu Kun, 'rose up upon hearing the crow of a rooster and practiced with their swords', and were determined to serve the country worthily. After the fall of Luoyang, Zu Ti was forced to lead hundreds of clans on a southward migration to Jinhkou (now Zhenjiang in Jiangsu province) and suggested Eastern General Sima Rui (later Emperor Yuan of Jin) lead the troops on a northward expedition to recover the Central Plains. Under extremely difficult conditions, Zu Ti, after eight years of bitter fighting, established a large expanse of base area south of the Yellow river. When he was about to follow up a victory, cross north of the Yellow river and fulfill the great cause of reunification, conflicts broke out inside the Eastern Jin regime and the northern expedition was contained. Zu Ti died of worry and indignation, and the northern expedition failed on the verge of victory. Nevertheless, he refused to yield, disregarded his own safety and served his country galantly. His righteousness and ambition have always been eulogised and admired by later generations.

(2) Serve the country with supreme loyalty and even at the cost of hundreds of lives

'I have not used the feather arrow at my waist for long; the feathers have faded away. I can still cross the desert and fight on the battlefield; why do the scholar officials weep uselessly? I will serve the country even at the cost of my life; my hair has turned white never to be blackened; I can only remember the berth of my boat; I lie on the bed listening to the wild geese fall on the water in autumn; a year comes to pass; but my ambitions have not been fulfilled.' It is *Berth at Night*, a poem by Lu You, a noted patriotic poet of the Southern Song dynasty (1127-1279). The verse 'I will serve the country even at the cost of my life' shows Lu You's unshakable patriotism and ambition to serve the country. In his lifetime, Lu You always hoped for a chance to kill the enemy, serve the country, and take part in the northern expedition to the Central Plains and retake the lost land. Even to the point of his death, his ambition did not die. In his poem *To My Son*, he told his descendants: 'I surely know that after death everything becomes void; yet, failing to see my country unified still makes me sad. When the emperor's northern army does win back the Central Plains; in your ancestral sacrifices, don't forget to tell your sire!' It was the last poem of the poet reflecting his greatest pity and last expectation. More importantly, it was the summary and crystallisation of his concern for the country and his determination to serve the country.

The Northern Song dynasty fell in the Jingkang Calamity in 1127. Chinese history entered another era of south-north confrontation and national conflicts. A great number of patriots and heroic figures rose to the occasion and jointly uttered the strong heroic and solemn voice of the times. Among them, Yue Fei, a famous general of the Southern Song dynasty in the war of resistance against Jin, was the quintessence of 'loyally serving the country'. It is said that when Yue Fei hurled himself into the army, his sensible and considerate mother engraved the four Chinese characters '精忠报国 (meaning 'serve the country worthily')' on his back. It became the lifelong ideal and pursuit of Yue Fei. The troops led by him, brave and battle-hardened, defeated their enemies time and again. The Jin troops were struck with fear at the mention of them and murmured profoundly: "It is easy to shake the mountain but impossibly difficult to shake the Yue troops."

Xin Qiji was a well known poet master and more famously a patriot and combat hero who strongly advocated fighting against Jin and recovering the lost land. His heroic and solemn poems were imbued with strong patriotism and fighting spirit. Their main theme was on 'fighting against Jin and recovering the lost land'. His poems constituted the strongest voice of the times. They also served as the battle cry for thousands of years to encourage future generations and boasted immortal vitality.

When the Chinese nation was repeatedly invaded, heavily mauled and threatened with extinction, it was precisely the generations of righteous patriots safeguarding the homeland and country, rising up and fighting with their selfless patriotism and their sentiment of serving the country that rescued the nation from disaster.

(3) Grieve first, rejoice later and be concerned for the world

Being concerned for the world is a fine element of traditional Chinese culture. The cultural celebrities of China's past dynasties bemoaned the state of the universe and pitied the fate of mankind.

Qu Yuan, inaugurator of the Songs of Chu, wrote *Lisao* (*Sorrow after Departure*) circulated for thousands of years to express his concerns for China being in dire straits. The verses 'breathe deep and long sighs, and bemoan one's harsh livelihood' revealed his concerns for ordinary people in the chaos caused by war. Du Fu, a celebrated poet of Tang, remained poor all his life. But he never forgot to care for the fate of his nation. Even when he lived the poorest life in his thatched cottage damaged by the autumn wind, he still hoped that 'I'd be happy and contented if tens of thousands of high and spacious houses could shelter the country's poor scholars, though I would be freezing to death in my dilapidated cottage."

Famed statesman, militarist and man of letters Fan Zhongyan in the Northern Song dynasty, accomplished with both the pen and the sword and distinguished for his political achievements, was worried about the common people, acted impartially and spoke forthrightly. Whether administering in court or demoted to garrison the frontiers, he was always concerned about national safety and people's suffering. In his *Notes of the Yueyang Tower*, he proposed: 'In high positions, officials should care about the common people; demoted, they should be concerned about the monarch and the people', 'be the first to worry about the troubles across the land and the last to enjoy universal happiness.' They were also the hallmarks of his lifetime. He earnestly practiced what he preached. Although he did not give material possessions to his descendants, he left them valuable family traditions and qualities. He had four sons. Thanks to their political integrity and professional competence, they were all high-ranking officials who won public acclaim. 'Grieve first and rejoice later', the ideology and sentiments of Fan Zhongyan, became words that resonated for thousands of years and were admired by later generations.

3. The awe-inspiring righteousness reflected in fine traditional Chinese culture

The 'spirit of the gentleman' or the 'scholar official spirit' as the main spirit of traditional Confucian culture refers to being upright and taking responsibility for the world. Confucius once said: 'Resolve and stiffness are close to benevolence.' (*The Analects of Confucius - Zilu)*.). Mencius further emphasised and elaborated on the philosophical meaning of 'uprightness' and held that 'righteousness is the greatest and most unbending virtue. Cultivated without any damage, it will prevail in the universe. It must be fostered together with justice and the right path; otherwise, it will be rather weak." *(Mencius - Gongsun Chou Vol.1)*

(1) Serve unyieldingly and stick steadfastly to the mission

To serve the state means to uphold integrity. Integrity indicates ambition and moral integrity. It is also a lofty, noble personality trait manifested in sticking to justice and remaining indomitable under huge pressure. Confucius said: 'In the cold season of the year, pines and cypresses wither.' *Mister Lü's Spring and Autumn Annals* records: 'Stones can be broken however with their hard texture unchanged; cinnabar can be ground however with its red colour unchanged.' In history, Boyi and Shuqi treating themselves as subjects of the Shang dynasty (17th century BC-11th century BC, conquered by the Zhou dynasty) refused to eat the millet of the Zhou dynasty (1046BC-256BC). Instead, they lived a secluded life in Shouyang mountain and finally starved to death there. Sima Qian nominated the *Biography of Boyi* as the first book among the 70 biographies in the *Records of the Grand Historian*, which showed his reverence and praise for this integrity.

Magnanimous, open and upright, Su Wu boasted the utmost dignity and honour all his life. In the first year (100BC) of the Tianhan period of Emperor Wu of Han, Su Wu was sent on a diplomatic mission to the Xiongnu, an ancient nationality in China. Implicated in his subordinates' rebellion, he was detained by the Xiongnu. In the face of repeated intimidation and bribery by the Xiongnu, Su Wu showed his inspiring awe by upholding justice and would rather die than surrender; afterwards, the Xiongnu had no choice but to exile him to be a shepherd in Beihai (the North Sea, now Baikal) and announced that they would release him to his homeland only when rams could be milked. Between hunger and the cold, and after much suffering in the North Sea desert, Su Wu held a sceptre made of bamboo granted to him by the emperor and did not put it down even when he slept at night so that the decorative tail hair on it fell out. After 19 years of bitter suffering and hardship, he was rescued by envoys of the Han dynasty and his subordinates and returned to the Han. He started out as a strong young man but returned white-haired and white-bearded. Despite being detained so long by the Xiongnu, being helpless to return to Han and huge suffering, he remained steadfast, faithful, unyielding and loyal to his motherland and nation. What a rare man of the highest integrity known at any time anywhere in the world.

(2) Upright and straightforward, not afraid to confront danger

Speaking of 'integrity', people naturally think of 'Bao Zheng' reputed as 'Justice Bao', the incarnation of honest and upright officials. When he was the magistrate of Kaifeng prefecture, it was the old practice that written complaints for lawsuits were not allowed to be directly submitted to government offices. However, Bao Zheng ordered the main entrance to be opened so that plaintiffs could state their disputes directly to him and minor officials would not dare to cheat him. Because of his resoluteness, noble relatives and eunuchs restrained themselves. There was a saying in the capital city that 'only the King of Hell and Bao Zheng would not take a bribe in the world,' meaning that there were only two people who would not take bribes, one being the King of Hell and the other being Bao Zheng.

In the Ming dynasty, the official Hai Rui, as famous as Bao Zheng, witnessed the substitution of Emperor Zhengde, Emperor Jiajing, Emperor Longqing and Emperor Wanli throughout his life. 'He was upright and called himself Gangfeng, meaning utmost uprightness. So he was known as Mr Gangfeng." (*History of Ming Dynasty - Biography of Hai Rui*) He was righteous, uncorrupted and hated injustice. Wherever he went, bullies and evildoers restrained themselves and didn't dare to act wildly against the law. Some powerful, wealthy and noble families successively painted the originally red gate black to hide their properties from his notice. In February of the 45th year (1566) of Emperor Jiajing in the Chinese lunar calendar, Hai Rui prepared his coffin and braved his death to submit *Memorial on Public Security* to Emperor Jiajing, Shizong of the Ming dynasty to criticise the emperor's defects of indulging in superstition, his extravagant lifestyle and ignorance of affairs of state. With his awe-inspiring righteousness and fearless bravery, Hai Rui exposed the hidden malpractice of the court and stated what other officials did not dare to say. His voice shook the court and his stories were widely read.

(3) Poor but with lofty ideals and immune to temptation

In the viewpoint of Mencius, a righteous man is immune to all temptations and threats with presence of mind in the face of disasters and with self-poise, and becomes a real man 'impervious to the temptations of wealth and high position, not shaken by poverty and not bent by power or force' (*Mencius - Duke Teng Wen Vol. 2*). Society was characterised by a healthy atmosphere of righteousness. The creative philosophical concept brought forward by Mencius profoundly influenced the traditional thinking of the Chinese nation for more than 2,000 years. Since then, righteousness and being uncorrupted have become the typical images and ideal personality traits of traditional intellectual officials.

Statesman and intellectual Wen Tianxiang in the late Song dynasty had a niche in history thanks to his uprightness. In its last years, the Southern Song dynasty waned and swayed in the midst of raging storms. Wen Tianxiang raised money in every possible way, racked his brains to rescue the country and ended up being captured. He was imprisoned in a dank dungeon and suffered all kinds of torture. The Yuan dynasty dispatched interrogators time and again to persuade him and promised to appoint him to high positions as long as he surrendered. Wen Tianxiang resolutely refused these temptations and wrote the heroic verses: 'Death comes to all men but my loyalty may leave a page in the annals'. In winter of the 19th year of Yuan (1282), he kowtowed to the south and fearlessly died a martyr.

4. Dedication demonstrated in fine traditional Chinese culture

The development of society and civilisation is often achieved at huge costs and even at the cost of individual happiness or valuable life. It is always the case everywhere in all ages.

(1) Sacrifice and selflessness

In the abundant Chinese fairy tales with a long history, dedication to pursuit of the truth and people's well-being appeared for the first time. The genesis mythology, ancestral mythology, flood myths or myths of heroes all without exception showed vehement and high-spirited dedication. Pan Gu, creator of the universe in Chinese mythology, became sun, moon, mountains and rivers to nourish all living things on earth after his death; Kua Fu ran after the sun and turned into a peach forest after his death; Yi shot down nine suns with his bow and arrows, and rescued people from fire and water; Shennong tasted a hundred grasses and brought benefits to posterity. Additionally, Yu the Great tamed the flood, which was an unfading legend of the Chinese nation. It is told that Yu the Great, during water control, laboured, ate and slept like others. Oblivious of himself and his own home, he 'refused to return home when passing it'. In the myths, people expressed their expectations and firm adherence to the cultural genes of the nation when initially creating the culture.

A quintessential selfless figure praised by Confucius was Qi Huangyang, a senior official in the State of Jin in the Spring and Autumn period. *Mister Lü's Spring and Autumn Annals - Selflessness* records two stories about him. Once, Duke Ping of Jin asked him to recommend a magistrate. Qi Huangyang recommended his enemy Xie Hu. Duke Ping of Jin asked Qi Huangyang in surprise: "Isn't Xie Hu your enemy?" Qi Huangyang responded: "You asked me who was qualified to be a county magistrate but not who my enemy was." Another time, Duke Ping of Jin asked Qi

Huangyang to recommend a judge for the imperial court. Qi Huangyang recommended his own son. Duke Ping of Jin felt strange again: "Isn't Qi Wu your son?" Qi Huangyang replied: "You asked me who was qualified to be a judge but not whether Qi Wu was my son." Later, the two men recommended by Qi Huangyang did an excellent job of carrying out their duties. Qi Huangyang's selflessness and high morality exemplified by 'his recommending worthy men, regardless of whether they were his enemies or his relatives' spread far and wide.

(2) Fear no hardships to benefit people around the world

Mo Zi, namely, Mo Di, and the Mohist school founded by him and active at the turn of the Spring and Autumn and Warring States periods were a vivid manifestation of heroic dedication. Mohist theory was centred on universal love. 'Universal' appeared many times in *Mo Zi*, which meant 'extensive' and 'comprehensive'. Universal love referred to gratuitous and selfless sacrifice of one party for another and asking for nothing in return. The Mohist school, a rigidly disciplined group, wore short garments and straw sandals, laboured together, took pride in bearing hardship and took pleasure in helping others. It is recorded that Mo Zi, during his travel to all corners of the world, helped those in distress, delivered selfless contributions, won the support and respect of the world's people, especially those of the lower class, and became famous for the 'prestigious doctrine' he bequeathed to the world. A story went around that, when Gongshu Ban made ingenious weapons to help the State of Chu invade the State of Song, Mo Zi came out boldly, opposed Gongshu Ban tit for tat and led his disciples and subordinates to help the State of Song resist the State of Chu. Finally, the State of Chu was forced to stop attacking the State of Song. The selfless 'chivalrous deeds' of the Mohist school made Mencius, who defamed the Mohist school due to the contention among different schools, admit that: "The universal love of Mo Zi advocated sacrificing oneself to save others and doing good for the world." (*Mencius - Selfless Dedication*) The spirit of selfless dedication to sacrificing oneself to save others upheld by the Mohist school was integrated with the spirit of scholar officials being concerned about the country and saving the country. It also became the most valuable spiritual wealth of the Chinese nation.

In the late Qing dynasty, there was a typical story about schools run by a beggar. Wu Xun, the beggar, lost his father at the age of 7, lived by begging and could not afford to go to school. After he was 14 years old, he left home and worked as a servant on several wages for odd jobs. Wu Xun argued about it only to be framed and beaten for 'blackmail'. Frothing at the mouth, he refused to eat or utter a single syllable and was confined to his bed due to illness for three days. Suffering a lot from illiteracy, he was determined to learn by begging. He turned to begging at 20. After begging for 38 years, he built three charity schools offering education to innumerable children from poverty-stricken families. The Qing court in Shandong granted him the title of 'Yi Xue Zheng (implying his selflessness for running charity schools) ', an imperial yellow jacket (a robe of the Qing dynasty) and a tablet reading '乐善好施 (given to doing charitable works)' and set up an honourific arch for him. Wu Xun's spirit was respected and imitated by later generations. After his death, Governor General Yuan Shuxun of Shandong province presented a memorial to the throne requesting that 'the Academia Historica should write his biography' and that a special hall should be built in his honour for his personal loyalty. He became the first beggar in history to be officially recorded and got the name of 'legendary beggar throughout the ages'.

(3) Be true to your convictions and vehemently save the country from danger

The Wuxu Reform in China, also known as the 'Hundred Days' Reform' in the late 19th century, was an experiment in political reform launched by men of insight represented by Kang Youwei, Liang Qichao and Tan Sitong to change the status quo in China. The reform began in June and ended on 21 September 1898. The conservatives headed by Empress Dowager Cixi staged a coup, imprisoned Emperor Guangxu, caught and killed the reformists, and brought the 103-day reform to an end. When the coup occurred, Tan Sitong, versed in both literature and military affairs, had the chance to escape safe and sound at first. But with no regard for his own safety, he tried by whatever means to positively devise a plan to rescue Emperor Guangxu. When the situation was irreversible, he flatly refused the suggestion of escape with the help of a Japanese envoy. He was determined to sacrifice his life for the reform and show his intrepid fighting spirit with his own blood. Just before his execution, he raised the cry: "I'm determined to kill the enemy. Though I could not turn the scales, it is a worthy death for me. What a pleasure!" He met his death bravely and showed no sign of fear, fully manifesting the heroic spirit and dedication of a patriot keeping loyal to the faith, and brave enough to assume responsibility and face death unflinchingly. His deeds could even move the gods to tears.

Qiu Jin, an excellent woman bravely sacrificing her life to overturn the despotic monarchy of the Qing dynasty and founding the Republic of China (1912-1949) called herself the 'Jianhu Lake Swordswoman'. She proactively threw herself into revolution, successively joined such revolutionary organizations as the Triad Society, Restoration League and Chinese Revolutionary League and contacted the leagues and parties to make plans to respond to the Pingxiang-Liuyang-Liling revolt to no avail. In 1907, she and Xu Xilin organised the Restoration League and planned simultaneous revolts in Zhejiang and Anhui on 6 July. However, their plan was leaked. Declining Wang Jinfa's advice for her to temporarily leave Shaoxing, she was unluckily arrested in Shaoxing Datong School. In the face of the enemy's coercion, bribery and cruel torture, she wrote down 'mournful winds and monotonous rains of the turbulent situation in autumn' and fearlessly died a martyr. From 16 to 20 August 1916, Sun Yat-sen paid a visit to Qiu Jin's tomb and said: "Before the restoration, Ms Qiu was the first Zhejiangese to join the Chinese Revolutionary League. Although she is dead, her verse 'mournful winds and monotonous rains of the turbulent situation in autumn' will be widely read and remembered."

5. The path of self-cultivation shown by fine traditional Chinese culture

Some scholar once pointed out that traditional Chinese culture was ethical culture. The mode of farming with land as the main means of production directly gave rise to the feudal patriarchal political system based on patriarchal kinship and clan and country isomorphism. The long existence of the political system and feudal patriarchal concept made China attach importance to ethical standards for a long time.

(1) The decrees of heaven are not unchanging and god helps men of virtue

In the Shang dynasty, people believed in supernatural beings, frequently held grand sacrificial ceremonies and placed more stress on supernatural beings than on rule of man. *The Book of Rites - Models* records: 'The Shang dynasty worshiped supernatural beings, led its people to venerate ghosts and gods, and implemented punishment before reward. It was a defect of its people to respect without closeness, live a dissolute and discontented life and try shamelessly to become preeminent.' The outstanding statements represented by the Duke of Zhou learned lessons from the fall of the Shang dynasty and concluded that 'the decrees of heaven are not unchanging' (*The Book of Songs - Emperor Wen of Zhou*). Concurrently, they came to the awareness that 'God is selfless and unbiased and always helps men of virtue' (*The Book of History - The Book of Zhou - Fate of Cai Zhong Part 19*) and thought that, to promote their longevity, the monarchs should cultivate their morality so as to 'match heaven with virtue'. For this reason, the rulers of Zhou respected supernatural beings but kept them at a distance. They attached more importance to earthly perceptions of human relations, moral rule and benevolent administration in the hope of strictly adhering to moral integrity themselves and matching heaven with virtue. Meanwhile, rituals and music were made according to political needs and cultural traditions to specify people's words and deeds so that everything was regulation-based and in order. Just as *The Book of Rites - Models* records: "The people of Zhou upheld the law, discipline and rituals, gave favours to others, respected supernatural beings but kept them at a distance, cherished humanity and showed loyalty." In the last years of the Spring and Autumn period, Confucius 'modelled on the theories and conduct of Emperor Yao and Emperor Shun and the systems applied by Emperor Wen of Zhou and Emperor Wu of Zhou' (*The Book of Rites - The Doctrine of the Mean*), inherited the thoughts and perceptions of previous dynasties, especially since the Zhou dynasty, proposed the core concept of 'benevolence' and deemed it as the core character and morals of intellectual officials. Based on inheriting Confucius's thoughts, Mencius upgraded the concept of 'benevolence' to the political level and advocated 'benevolent policy' and 'benevolent government'. On the basis of the doctrine of good human nature, he creatively came up with the 'four ends' theory and thought that: 'The sense of compassion is humanity; the sense of shame and hate is justice; the sense of reverence is propriety; the sense of right and wrong is wisdom. The four cardinal virtues, namely, humanity, justice, propriety and wisdom are not externalised but inherent' *(Mencius - Gao Tzu Part 1)*. Although Xuncius differed from Mencius in the theory of human nature, he advocated 'changing the congenital nature and establishing the moral idea'. His advocacy stressed acquired education and cultivation and reflected reverence for moral education. Pre-Qin Confucianism attached importance to and emphasised moral principles and laid solid theoretical foundations for moral reverence of future generations and their concept of 'morality foremost'. For a rather long period from then on, morality or personality became critical for political considerations, official selection and even public attitude.

Moreover, unlike the Western logic of binary separation, Confucianism regarded the human mind and body as a unified entity. As an integral whole, the mind and body are inseparable. It also stressed that the mind is the master of the body and that the body externalises the mind. Therefore, *Great Learning* says: 'Nurtured by morality, a person will be fit and happy.' *The Yi Commentary - Classical Chinese* believed that: 'Men of noble character used the neutral yellow colour to indicate that they understood the truth; sitting in the right position, they chose a stable way to conduct themselves in society; their intrinsic virtues flowed in their actions and were reflected in their undertakings." It shows that moral cultivation and health were complementary and morality could nourish, cultivate and adorn the human body. In this sense, with regard to the body, moral cultivation was always in the leading position. It was the internal cause and the core that influenced and determined people's outlook, bearing and appearance. Su Shi's lines 'knowledge makes a gentleman' echoed that idea. Although the rupture between the mind and the body occurred in Chinese ideological history and the mind suppressed the human body, the integration and co-existence of the mind and the body were always the mainstream. The mutual penetration, integration and transfer of the mind and the body constituted the main thread of the traditional Chinese outlook on the human body.

(2) Inner cultivation and exterior action, self-discipline to calm others

The Great Learning reads: 'The goal of education through great learning is to illustrate exemplary virtues, endear oneself to the people and aim at absolute perfection.' They were both the guiding principle and goal of Confucian education, and the objective and requirements for the moral cultivation of scholar officials. In the viewpoint of the Confucian school, the ultimate goal of the moral realm was to achieve absolute perfection. It was not merely the perfection of individual moral cultivation but also consideration for others. It aimed to fulfill oneself and others, to foster friendship among people, to let ordinary people live in peace and happiness, to rule the world and realise great harmony. After proposing the 'three guiding principles', *The Great Learning* put forward that the 'investigation of things', 'knowledge acquisition', 'sincerity', 'rectification of the heart', 'self-cultivation', 'good management of family affairs', 'sound management of state affairs' and 'ruling the world' became the 'eight rules' to implement the 'three guiding principles', namely, the specific steps to materialise 'absolute perfection'. In the interdependent system, self-cultivation was the core and key point of moral cultivation and played a decisive role. For this reason, 'the emperor and the common people were all centred on self-cultivation.'

Confucianism held the view that the final destiny of self-cultivation was to achieve a saintly personality, go into society, practice diligently, manage family affairs well and rule the world. Afterwards, Zhang Zai, uplifted the playful spirit of the moral subjects and expounded the lofty pursuit of 'setting one's mind on heaven and earth, standing fast to the people, taking over the duty of past sages and saints to continuously spread the immortal theories in danger of not being passed on, and creating the great undertaking of eternal peace for future generations.' It can be seen that the moral spirit of the Confucian school came down in one continuous line. It did not merely hinge on improved self-cultivation and the personal realm but more importantly on 'self-discipline and calming others with the former aimed at pacifying ordinary people' (*The Analects of Confucius - Yuan Xian's Questions*). Besides, it also aimed to finally realise the great harmony and supreme realm featuring inner cultivation and exterior action, good management of family and state affairs and rule of the world. The realm of absolute perfection illustrated the ideal goal and lofty pursuit of self-cultivation, which encouraged the spirit of Confucian scholars and defined their direction which constantly improved their self-cultivation and realised sublimation and transcendence in their lives.

(3) Internal self-examination, external action and the unity of knowledge and action

How to cultivate moral character? The ancient Chinese intellectuals represented by the Confucian school summarised many approaches and methods. Though expressed differently by different schools, generally speaking, these approaches and methods were internally inherent and consistent. That is to say, internal self-examination and external action represented the unity of knowledge and action.

Self-examination means self-criticism or self-reflection today. The aim was to reflect on one's own mentality and behaviour, inspect and analyse the good and bad, right and wrong of them, conduct self-criticism and self-correction, and constantly boost one's moral standard and realm of life. The Confucian school advocated self-control, self-examination, etiquette-controlled emotions and self-restraint, and stressed the self-assessment of moral subjects. It also emphasised that external moral concepts could play their role in identifying and internalising moral subjects. Confucius had begun to stress the important effect of self-examination on self-cultivation. He said: "Seeing another better than oneself, one tries to equal them. Seeing another worse than oneself, one tries to examine one's own behaviour." (*The Analects of Confucius - Living in a Benevolent Environment*)

In the opinion of Confucius, as long as a person often examined himself, he could get rid of his bad points and gradually become virtuous. Zeng Zi, a disciple of Confucius, said: 'I inspect myself many times a day and ask myself whether I give my advice and suggestions loyally, whether I get along or cooperate with my friends faithfully and whether I often review what the teacher has taught me.' (*The Analects of Confucius - On Learning*) This most familiar proposal suggested self-examination and self-exploration from the perspectives of handling affairs, conducting oneself and learning. Mencius came up with the idea of 'self-criticism'. Thinkers after the Song and Ming dynasties 'examined their thoughts and conduct' to enhance their self-inspection. It can be seen that people's awareness of self-cultivation through self-inspection was consistent in different historical periods. Despite their different names, they led to the same destination. They also shared the same goal, namely, to achieve benevolence through self-cultivation.

Morality is an issue of both knowledge and deeds. In addition to stressing self-examination, the Confucian school attached importance to moral practice, especially physical deeds. It held up the idea that all benevolence, kindness and virtue must be practiced painstakingly. So *The Doctrine of the Mean* reads: 'The learned are close to becoming wise; the strenuous doers are close to becoming benevolent; the people bearing in mind 'honour and disgrace' are close to becoming brave.' Zixia said: "The sages neglecting women's charms should be respected; they can do their utmost to serve their parents; they can devote themselves to serving the emperor; they get along faithfully with their friends and honour their words. Although such sages modestly say they have not read many books, I still believe they are knowledgeable." (*The Analects of Confucius - On Learning*) Confucius stated: "Initially, I believed others' behaviour after hearing their words; now, I also observe their behaviour after hearing their words." (*The Analects of Confucius - Gong Chang*) On this basis, Wang Yangming of the Ming dynasty called for 'the unity of knowledge and action'. The 'knowledge' here generally refers to the moral sense, views and values of people. 'Action' here means people's moral and practical actions. 'The unity of knowledge and action' indicates that 'knowledge is the idea of action and action is the practice of the idea; knowledge is the beginning of action and action is the realisation of the idea.' (*Sayings and Letters of Wang Yangming on Learning*) It must be admitted that Confucianism became the mainstream ideology of ancient China thanks to its advocacy of 'being diligent in action'. Hence, Zeng Gong of the Song dynasty said in his *A Letter to Wang Shenfu*: 'The intellectuals are cool-hearted and practice what the sages advocate. That is how Confucius and Mencius delivered their contributions to the world.'

Chapter 6

Distinctive Characteristics of Fine Traditional Chinese Culture

Traditional Chinese culture has been handed down and developed its own distinctive characteristics over a period of more than 5,000 years. These characteristics can be summarised as national character, tenacity, matter-of-fact spirit, inclusiveness and continuity. These 'five characteristics' reflect the Chinese style, the Chinese spirit and the Chinese boldness of vision.

1. National character: People are my brothers and all things are my kind, rooted in rites and morality

Traditional Chinese culture is a national culture reflecting the national features and style amid the evolution of Chinese civilisation. It is the culture created by our Chinese ancestors and inherited and developed by the Chinese nation for generations. Hence it boasts its own distinctive national character.

(1) The culture of family names and blood being thicker than water

Huaxia was the earliest nation in the world where family names appeared. No other nation can be mentioned in the same breath. The matriarchal clan society formed in the Neolithic Age about 10,000 years ago witnessed the appearance of family names to distinguish blood relationships. In Chinese, '姓' *xing* (family name), comprising the characters for '女' *nu* (woman) and '生' *sheng* (fertility or life)', signified women's fertility and referred to the matrilineal blood relationship. People of the same family name were not allowed to get married. Otherwise, it would affect fertility and propagation. *The Commentary of Zuo* reads: 'Couples of the same family name cannot reproduce for posterity.' *Views of the Noblemen of All*

States records: 'Couples of the same family name are not allowed to marry to avoid infertility after marriage.' After patriarchy replaced matriarchy, generally, the lateral radical '女' was not used to form new family names.

In the pre-Qin period, surnames and family names were different. Surnames were used by males and family names by females. Family names were applied to distinguish marriage and avoid the marriage of couples with the same family names. There was no distinction between high and low social status but they were simply code names for a big family or national minority. Surnames were adopted to distinguish between high or low social status. Only when people were surnamed after getting titles of nobility, official positions and manors could they become noblemen. Only noblemen had surnames while common people had only names without surnames. People with the same surnames and different family names could get married but those with different surnames and the same family names could not. After the Qin dynasty, surnames and family names were unified. Nevertheless, they still functioned to distinguish marriage to avoid inbreeding and optimise the nation. The Huaxia nationality boasted numerous family names. *The Book of Family Names*, a book for the educational enlightenment of later generations, collected a total of more than 500 family names. For this reason, the Chinese people were called '百姓' *baixing* (people with hundreds of family names).

The times of the Yellow Emperor, Emperor Zhuan Xu, Emperor Ku, Emperor Yao and Emperor Shun recorded in *Biographic Sketches of Five Emperors*, the prelude to the *Records of the Grand Historian*, reflected the general picture of a patriarchal clan society. Among them, 'abdication of the crown from Emperor Yao to Emperor Shun' reproduced the situation when the chief of the tribal alliance was recommended. From it, the Yellow Emperor was confirmed to be the common ancestor of the Chinese nation in the cultural sense and the Chinese people of the world were proud of being the descendants of the Yan Emperor and Yellow Emperor.

The political system in ancient China was a hereditary system. Since the Xia dynasty initiated a family-governed monarchic country during the 21st to the 16th century BC, the hereditary system extended for thousands of years and came to an end in the Revolution of 1911. However, the hereditary system in ancient China did not transcend dynasties and the emperors of any family name were likely to govern the monarchical country. Chinese history saw the rule of emperors with dozens of different family names.

Family names were not distinguished by lowliness or nobility, and any family name could be used by rulers, reflecting the awareness of equal competition since ancient times.

(2) Civil administration and cultural influence on Chinese people

The moderately prosperous society upheld rule by rites. The Xia, Shang and Zhou dynasties had their own distinctive characteristics. The Xia dynasty implemented 'rule by loyalty'. The corrupt practices of 'rule by loyalty' resulted in people being uncouth and unruly. For this reason, the Shang dynasty adopted 'rule by respect'. The defect of 'rule by respect' was that people worshiped spirits and gods. So the Zhou dynasty replaced it with 'civil administration'. The disadvantage of 'civil administration' was people's emotional barriers. That was remedied by re-applying 'rule by loyalty'. 'The ruling approaches of the three dynasties moved in circles.' 'Civilisation' reached its apogee of rule by rites in the Western Zhou dynasty, stressing superiors and inferiors, different social strata and elaborate formalities.

The Western Zhou dynasty distinguished class with 'rites' and regulated emotions with 'music'. The two perfectly complemented each other. The royal authority declined in the Eastern Zhou dynasty and gradually came to exist in name only. The princes vied for supremacy in the Spring and Autumn period and the Seven Powers in the Warring States period fought against each other. Takeover battles occurred now and then. On the occasion of the collapse of rites and music, Confucius assumed the duty of denying self and returning to propriety, integrated the rites of Zhou with folk customs, and founded the Confucian school which was advocated by feudal dynastic rule. Although the dynasties changed, the essence of rites and music was passed down from generation to generation. Therefore, the Chinese nation has always been called 'a state of ceremonies'.

Confucius attached priority to edification in rites and music and upheld elaborate formalities. Nonetheless, his educational objective was not simply to know and practice rites but 'benevolence', namely, the graded and differential love born of family ties. Confucius hoped to stimulate the qualitative enhancement of the inner heart through fastidiously implementing elaborate formalities to reach the realm of 'benevolence'.

The princes respectively established different political regimes in the Warring States period. The hundred schools of thought successively offered remedies for salvation of the world. The Legalist school, political strategists and military strategists had a direct impact on social change. 'Placing more importance on wars than on comity, discarding benevolence and reason in favour of fraud and deceit', the State of Qin fulfilled the great cause of reunification. Nonetheless, the Empire of Qin collapsed after a short reign of only 15 years after discarding comity and justice. As to the cause of the Qin's ruin, Jia Yi of the Western Han concluded that 'if justice was not implemented, the situation was different in offending and defending'. That was to say, state power could be seized by craftiness and armed force. But governing the people after state power was seized was different. The emperors had to comply with the aspirations of the people and act in a benevolent and just manner. From the Western Han dynasty, Chinese history returned to the path of benevolent government and rule by rites.

(3) Cultural backbone dates back to ancient times

The Han dynasty ruled China for more than 400 years, during which the dominant role of Confucian culture was established. The early Han dynasty pursued 'governance featuring clear and bright politics implemented by the Yellow Emperor and abandonment of all desires and worries from the mind advocated by the Taoist school' and implemented the rehabilitation of its people. Emperor Wu banned a hundred schools of thought, only worshiped Confucianism, applied law and discipline rites and tempered justice with mercy and virtue.

With exclusive reverence for Confucianism, *The Book of Songs*, *The Book of History*, *The Book of Rites*, *The Book of Music*, *The Book of Changes* and *The Spring and Autumn Annals* were collectively defined as the 'Six Classics' or 'Six Arts'. *The Book of Music* was not handed down, so this body of work is known as the 'Five Classics' – a name that has prevailed. In the Tang dynasty, three rituals and three biographies were added: *The Book of Zhou Rites, Ceremonial Etiquette, The Book of Rites, The Biography of Zuo (The Commentary of Zuo), The Biography of Gongyang* and *The Biography of Liang*. Together with *The Book of Changes, The Book of History* and *The Book of Songs*, they were collectively called the 'Nine Classics'. Emperor Wenzong of Tang ordered the classics to be carved in stone. So *The Classic of Filial Piety, The Analects of Confucius* and *Erya* were added. They were collectively called the 'Twelve Classics'. *Mencius* was added in the Song dynasty, the last one of the 'Thirteen Confucian Classics'. The scientific research and dissemination of the Confucian classics was called the 'study of Confucian classics'. It was the main channel for intellectuals to start an official career. The selection of officials on the basis of imperial examinations based on the study of Confucian classics sourced from the Han, originated in the Sui, was established in the Tang, was completed in the Song and prospered in the Ming and Qing, lasting a total of 1,300 years.

The *Records of the Grand Historian - Collected Biographies of the Eloquent* stresses that: '*The Book of Rites* aimed to restrain human desires, *The Book of Music* was written to temper the emotions, *The Book of History* provided references, *The Book of Songs* expressed people's aspirations, *The Book of Changes* exerted a subtle influence on people's character and *The Spring and Autumn Annals* demonstrated morality and justice. The 'three biographies' attached special importance to interpreting *The Spring and Autumn Annals*. *The Commentary of Zuo* put particular emphasis on narration and the demonstration of righteousness and immorality, etiquette and bad manners of the figures in the Spring and Autumn period. *The Biography of Gongyang* and *The Biography of Liang* placed special importance on reasoning, explaining sublime words with deep meaning and distinguishing between right and wrong. *The Classic of Filial Piety* expounded the ethics of faithfulness and piety advocated by Confucianism comprising the cultural system of filial piety. *The Analects of Confucius* recorded the words and deeds of Confucius and his advocacy of promoting kindheartedness through rites and music. *Erya*, the ancestor of Chinese dictionaries, was the key to interpreting the classics. *Mencius* recorded the words and deeds of Mencius and elucidated the essence of *The Book of Songs, The Book of History* and Confucian thoughts.

Confucianism is the backbone, but not the whole of the Chinese civilisation. Taoism ran parallel with Confucianism. Lao Tzu, named Li Er, founder of the Taoist school, stressed self-cultivation. The doctrines of the Taoist school integrated with the occult techniques of pursuing immortality gradually evolved into China's indigenous religion - Taoism. Taoism worshiped Lao Tzu as the founding father. The royal family Li of Tang took Lao Tzu as their ancestor and conferred the title of 'Emperor Taishang Xuanyuan' upon him. *Lao Tzu* was honoured as *Tao The King*. The Taoist classics were called 'Taoist scriptures'. The Taoist scriptures were compiled in all ages after the Tang. Numerous such books were published as being among the treasures of traditional Chinese culture. At the same time, Buddhism includes the spirit of 'leniency paramount', 'mercy most important' and 'delivering all living creatures from torment'. The spirit of peace in religion fostered the Chinese people's ideological pursuit of 'benevolence', 'the achievement of harmony', 'dying a hero's death', 'embracing universal education' and 'bringing peace and tranquility for future generations'. These aspirations were condensed into the essential ethics of 'loyalty, filial piety, kindheartedness, faithfulness and peace'. The ideology of enriching the country and increasing its military force as well as the rule by law of the Legalist culture and its viewpoint that 'everything, close or distant, noble or humble, should be judged by law' were strongly woven into the fabric of the country's politics, culture and morality, and generated far-reaching influence on modern legality.

2. Tenacity: Constant self-improvement with high aspirations and diligence

The Book of Changes states: 'A man of honour strives constantly for self-improvement.' This means that heaven runs resolutely, steadfast and beyond the control of any external force. Men of honour should model themselves on heaven and strive hard ceaselessly. 'Men of honour strive constantly for self-improvement' was the humanity and personality inspired by heaven representing a heroic and aggressive attitude towards life. Most of the last emperors of the Chinese dynasties perished due to their retroaction. Nevertheless, the Chinese nation revived like a phoenix rising from the ashes. Though old dynasties were replaced by new ones, traditional Chinese culture was passed down from generation to generation and continued in an endless succession. It has become more stately and stronger.

(1) Know what is impossible but dare to struggle against heaven and earth

The tenacity of traditional Chinese culture arose with the formation of the Chinese nation. The myths of heroes in the pre-historic culture ran through the tenaciously struggling national spirit, including the contention between man and nature and the wars between different primitive tribes.

The Goddess Mends the Sky relates that Goddess Nü Wa reorganised the perilous universe and created the conditions necessary for man's survival. That myth came from the matriarchal clan society. Nü Wa saved the human race with her miraculous power and showed her unparalleled contribution to mankind as a great goddess. Actually, it eulogises man's heroic and tenacious struggling spirit.

Hou Yi Shooting the Sun tells the story about Hou Yi shooting 10 suns, removing evil from people and killing vipers, beasts and ferocious birds with his miraculous skills and incredible bravery. This story reproduces scenes of fighting against the universe in a patriarchal clan society.

Gun and Yu Control the Flood narrates a tale where Gun steals magic soil from the Emperor of Heaven to control water, which is analogous to the ancient Greek myth of Prometheus stealing Apollo's kindling. Both of them benefit mankind with their intrepid spirit of self-sacrifice. After Gun dies, Yu succeeds to the throne and controls the flood. The story reflects the fighting spirit of human beings rising up to fight against floods one after another and not retreating until they succeed.

Jingwei Fills up the Sea represents how the willpower of a little bird can be compared favourably with Xing Tian, a legendary god in ancient China. The little bird seems like a drop in the ocean. Nevertheless, Jingwei's willpower to fill up the sea is higher than the sky and deeper than the sea, showing the strong wish and tenacious fighting spirit of human beings to conquer nature.

(2) Strive ambitiously and diligently to make the country prosperous

The tenacity of traditional Chinese culture in the Xia, Shang and Zhou dynasties where rule by rites evolved was more evident in all the ambitious and diligent efforts exerted to make the country prosperous. Yu the Great, Emperor Tang, Emperor Wen, Emperor Wu, Emperor Cheng and the Duke of Zhou were all elites sincerely honouring rites and morality and typical representatives of self-improvement.

Emperor Wu of Zhou conquered King Zhou, established the Western Zhou dynasty and died soon afterwards. The Duke of Zhou acted as regent and assisted the young prince Emperor Cheng. For fear that Emperor Cheng would not be conscious of the hardships of the time and the difficulties of holding power, crave comfort and pleasure, and neglect government affairs, he specially wrote *No Indulgence in Ease and Comfort* to inculcate Emperor Cheng. Emperor Cheng lived up to the inculcation of the Duke of Zhou and became the 'second generation of brilliant master'. The Duke of Zhou edified Emperor Cheng to make his every effort to make the country prosperous; Emperor Cheng admonished the officials of all ranks and descriptions, and put the emphasis on high ambitions and diligence so that they could maintain their spirit of persistent hard work and struggle to achieve a harmonious society and lasting political stability. Emperor Yongzheng of Qing, through a series of drastic reforms, rapidly turned around the situation of serious longstanding malpractice in the late period of Emperor Kangxi. He not only created abundant wealth for the country but also left future generations relatively clean and efficient taxation and administration systems. All his efforts laid a solid foundation for Emperor Qianlong to become a 'generous and lenient' wise king.

(3) Make determined efforts despite suffering setbacks

The tenacity of traditional Chinese culture is also reflected in the people of noble aspirations who suffered setbacks, made determined efforts, constantly strove to become stronger, released their gigantic energy and attained immortal fame after death. The Confucian school upheld the spirit of 'three immortals': 'The most important is moral composition, followed by meritorious service and expounding ideas in writing, which will become forever useful and immortal.' It emphasises the fact that people become immortal not because they pursue immortal reputation at a high cost but rather because they are not willing to degrade themselves and exert themselves after a string of heavy blows or extreme setbacks.

To save the Eastern Zhou society lost in ritual collapse, Confucius spared no efforts to preach his doctrine and spread the moral principles and concepts of governing a state with 'benevolence' as the core. He thought that the army might fight without a commander in chief but that even ordinary men should not lose their willpower. Gentlemen should not deviate from kindheartedness even during meal times and must act benevolently even drifting from place to place homeless and miserable at the most pressing moment. Although he was aware that his doctrines would not be fully understood or accepted, Confucius still adhered to his idea of 'seeing the gentlemen after his doctrines were not accepted' and strived hard all his life. He was not merely worshiped as an exemplary teacher for all ages for his transmission of the 'six arts' but also earned people's admiration for his indomitable perseverance.

With the aim of making the country prosperous and strengthening military forces, the vassal states in the Warring States period competed to implement political reforms. Li Li of the State of Wei was the first among the warring states to launch reform, which helped the state grow rapidly and dominate the Central Plains for more than a hundred years. Wu Qi, a famous political reformer and excellent military strategist, commander and military reformer, carried out reform in the State of Chu and Shang Yang conducted reform in the State of Qin. Although they both won the support of the emperors and registered abundant achievements, they encountered vehement opposition from the hereditary influential officials and lost their lives. Wu Qi was shot by showers of arrows and Shang Yang was torn asunder by five carts. Political reforms would inevitably damage the interests of the influential officials and the hereditary influential officials would certainly put up a desperate struggle and bring calamity to the reformers. There was definitely no leeway for reconciliation between them.

In *A Letter to Ren An*, Sima Qian said: 'Death befalls all men, whether heavier than Mount Tai (worthwhile sacrificing one's life for a noble cause) or lighter than a goose feather (worthless), because of their different pursuits in life.' He added: 'Many men of wealth and high rank end up in oblivion and only those preeminent elites can be frequently commended for their excellence. Emperor Wen of Zhou was imprisoned but deduced the eight trigrams to be hexagrams and wrote *The Book of Changes*; Confucius, worn out and unsuccessful all his life, created *The Spring and Autumn Annals*; Qu Yuan was sent into exile but completed *Sorrow after Departure*; blind Zuo Qiu wrote *Views of the Noblemen of All States*; Sun Tzu was crippled but completed *The Art of War*; Lǚ Buwei was banished to Shu, namely, Sichuan province, and his *Mister Lǚ's Spring and Autumn Annals* was handed down for generations; Han Fei was imprisoned in the State of Qin but wrote articles *Lobby on Difficulties* and *Lonely Indignation*; *The Book of Songs* was created by sages and men of virtue out of indignation.' Sima Qian encouraged himself to continue with the spirit of the outstanding elites who wrote books out of indignation. His work, *Records of the Grand Historian*, was praised as being 'the peak of poetic perfection in terms of its historical value and a masterpiece on a par with *Sorrow of Departure* with respect to its literary value. More than half of the works in the book were named after tragic heroic figures, over 120 of whom were quite famous. What the tragic figures exhibited was precisely the spirit of the Chinese nation to work hard and aim high.

3. Inclusiveness: Self-discipline, social commitment and kind-heartedness

According to the doctrine of yin and yang, all things are comprised of yin and yang, hardness and softness, which are both opposite and complementary to each other. They constitute the basic law of operation. The Chinese nation boasts the tenacious willpower to strive to be strong and an all-embracing mind.

(1) Inclusiveness of a hundred schools of thought

In Chinese history, traditional Chinese culture has brought the multi-ethnic culture and hundreds of millions of people closer together and fostered their shared Chinese culture. Amid the contention of a hundred schools of thought in the pre-Qin period, different ideological trends, values, concepts of state governance and attitudes towards life exchanged, confronted, collided with and learnt from each other. Their integration was formed based on multiple elements. Since Confucius, in the long historic development of Chinese feudal society, Confucianism underwent twists and turns unfailingly and finally became the basic value system of traditional Chinese culture and the foundation underlying all the efforts to build the ancient Chinese society. The Chinese culture of 'harmony' generated during the long integration of Confucianism, Buddhism and Taoism and its values lasted for more than 2,000 years.

Why was traditional Chinese culture able to last unfailingly after so many frustrations? Its compatibility cannot go unnoticed. In the development of Chinese culture, the backbone of the three major cultures, namely, Confucianism, Buddhism and Taoism, which adapted to and were compatible with one another, comprised the imposing and grand traditional culture. Since all sorts of culture in traditional Chinese culture were mutually inclusive, the cultural system of China has lasted for quite a long time until now without any interruption and has remained intact. It was just this sort of inclusive culture that has kept Chinese society in a state of 'grand unification' for more than 2,000 years.

(2) Adopt best practices from all quarters and coexist harmoniously with thousands of other countries

During more than 2,000 years of feudal Chinese society, China embraced people from all other countries and drew on others' successful experience with its own demeanour as a big country, its profound culture and a broad mind. In Chinese history, Chinese culture once covered the surrounding countries and fostered a cultural sphere of influence radiating over a vast territory. It did not conquer the surrounding countries through hegemony but these countries became appendages to it on their own initiative. The Chinese culture upholding 'concord and harmony', 'unity of heaven and man', 'universal peace' and 'harmony in diversity' continued for more than 2,000 years, showed its own inclusiveness and further indicated the glamour, value and significance of Chinese culture.

In modern times, China fell behind because it came to a standstill. The inclusiveness of traditional Chinese culture was assimilated by and suffered from Western cultural invasion. Nevertheless, the Chinese culture struggled with its indomitable vitality and aroused the cultural awakening of the Chinese nation. From breaking with the practice of 'bringing in everything' during the process of 'bringing things in', a new cultural model was formed featuring 'Chinese learning as the fundamental structure and Western learning for utility'.

The 21st century has seen the co-existence of diverse cultures. Developing and cultivating national spirit must, amid the mutual influence of diverse ideologies and cultures worldwide, give full play to the spirit of inclusiveness of traditional Chinese culture, make the best of both worlds and help one another forward. Chinese culture has always been all-embracing and broad-minded resulting in its long-lasting greatness. Cultural inclusiveness activates abundant, colourful and lively scenes within the ideology and culture of Chinese society. Externally, it is open to the outside world and constantly accepts the inspiration and nutrition of different cultures to reinvigorate its own development. Just as Ji Xianlin stated: "China should both 'bring' and 'send'. That is to say, it should 'bring' something good to itself from overseas and 'send' something good of itself overseas. It is the combination of 'bringing in' and 'sending out'. As long as it is good for cultural development and construction, China should unhesitatingly bring it upon itself to promote China's cultural construction and foster the national spirit featuring lofty morals and nobility of character.

(3) Communication, combination and advancing in unison

The culture of all nations in the world gradually developed in the exchanges, mutual absorption, integration and even conflicts among different cultures. The political, economic, scientific and technological exchanges and collisions between different nations were diverse and colourful and brought cultural advancement through interaction.

In the history of the world, Zhang Qian was sent on a diplomatic mission, opened up the world-renowned 'Silk Road' and brought the East and the West into increasingly frequent cultural exchanges. The formidable armada used for Zheng He's journey to the West passed along the Silk Road, sowed the seeds of peace, showed friendship, understanding and respect to the countries along the route, and brought China to the world.

In the flourishing period of the Tang, Xuan Zang went on a pilgrimage to the west for Buddhist scriptures and gave a new explanation for Buddhism. The diplomats to the Tang dispatched from Japan learned Chinese culture, with traces of traditional Chinese culture left even to this day. Jian Zhen braved danger, took a sea-voyage eastward to Japan, taught Buddhist theories, spread Chinese culture, stimulated the enhancement of Japanese Buddhism, medical science, architecture and sculpture, and won the respect of the Chinese and Japanese people and the Buddhist circles.

In the 13th century, Italian traveler and merchant Marco Polo gave an oral account of a myriad of stories about China. According to his account, his inmate Rustichello da Pisa wrote the famous *The Travels of Marco Polo*. The book described what he saw and heard in the wealthiest countries in the East, which aroused the Europeans' vehement longing for the East and exerted huge influence on the development of the new sea route.

Matteo Ricci, a Roman Catholic missionary from Italy who came to live in China during the period of Emperor Wanli of Ming, was the first Western scholar to read Chinese literature and study the Chinese classics. He spread Western scientific and technological knowledge on astronomy, mathematics and geography to China and ushered in the ethos that the Chinese scholar officials studied Western learning in the late Ming dynasty. In 1607, Matteo Ricci and Xu Guangqi cooperated and published a translation of the first six chapters of *Elements of Geometry* written by Euclid. Their works not merely contributed to Chinese-Western exchanges but also significantly influenced the recognition of Japan and the Korean peninsula for Western civilisation.

The interaction of traditional Chinese culture has continued until modern times. It is precisely this interaction that has enabled the Chinese culture to go through innovation, integration, regeneration, transformation and modernisation. The cultural exchanges, cooperation and interaction of all nations expedited cultural development and progress of their own and of the whole world.

4. Matter-of-fact spirit: studying the nature of things for humanistic pragmatism

An overview of the spirit of the traditional culture of ancient China indicates that pragmatism boasts a long tradition in China. The so-called 'studying the nature of things' is to explore the theories of things from a practical point of view so as to acquire knowledge and wisdom and apply them in 'self-cultivation, good management of family affairs and rule of the state'. This utilitarianism refers to the material gain of individuals and the whole society. For instance, the ancients pursued 'serving the emperor after learning cultural and military knowledge' or 'assisting the emperors in fulfilling the great cause of reunification and being recognised posthumously'.

(1) Scrupulously abide by one's duty and come down to earth

In traditional Chinese culture, abiding by one's duty has been regarded as one of the virtues of a gentleman. Zisi, a successor of the Confucian school, once said: "Gentlemen should do whatever they can in their positions rather than go beyond their duties; those in high and rich positions should do whatever they can and those in low and poor positions should do likewise; people in high positions should not bully those in low positions and those in low positions should abide by their duties and give up any inordinate ambition; people should not blame everyone and everything but not themselves." It stressed that gentlemen should take delight in their positions and environment to do whatever they can without coveting anything inordinate. Lie Yukou, one of the representatives of the Taoist school, interpreted that the Chinese people 'abided by their duty' from another perspective through the story 'The Foolish Old Man Who Removed the Mountains'. The story goes: The Foolish Old Man, almost in his 90s, was determined to dig up the mountains and carve out a way. His family and neighbours all came to help him chiseling stones and carrying earth day after day and year after year. Facing a Wise Old Man who derided him for being 'foolish', the Foolish Old Man responded fully at ease: "I will die. But I have sons who will have their own sons and innumerable descendants. Nevertheless, the mountains will not rise. Why should we fear they are not leveled?" Afterwards, the Emperor of Heaven was deeply moved by the spirit of the Foolish Old Man and dispatched some celestial beings to remove the mountains. The fable reveals that as long as people boast firm confidence and tenacious perseverance in removing mountains and filling up the seas, abide by their own duties and keep their resolve, they can surely register successful careers.

To abide by one's duty, people should come down to earth, correctly recognise their environment and positions, bear in mind their responsibilities and duties, and do their share of work. China's geography is of a closed structure. In traditional society where geographical obstacles could not be overcome, the best way out for the Chinese nation was to abide by its own duty and come down to earth. Although the Yellow river flooded repeatedly, the Chinese people did not slack off but still lived their lives there. Since the Chinese upheld a matter-of-fact spirit, did not seek expansion and stressed 'people's stability', they were able to manage the territory quite well. As a matter of fact, if farmers had not ploughed in a down-to-earth manner, no cereals would have grown from the soil by themselves. Therefore, only by 'hard toil and sweat' all year round could bumper harvests be achieved. In this sense, the 'concurrent farming and reading' upheld in ancient China was a typical case of abiding by duties and coming down to earth.

(2) The matter-of-fact spirit, practical actions, and emphasis on practical results

The first value of Confucius was to prioritise human events and slight supernatural beings. Xuncius upheld the idea that 'deeds were better than words'. Wang Chong wrote *Discourses Weighed in the Balance* and propagated his empiricism 'combating sham'. The learned Han Yu of the Tang dynasty took the utilitarianism advocated by the Confucian school as the weapon to criticise Confucianism. Although the neo-Confucianism in the Song and Ming dynasties constructed the detached, metaphysical 'truth', Cheng Yi, Zhu Xi, Lu Jiuyuan and Wang Shouren all repeatedly stressed personally and diligently practicing moral empiricism. The basic trend of empiricism in the Ming and Qing dynasties was humanistic pragmatism. It renewed the gist of primitive Confucianism. Additionally, stimulated by Western learning, the learning style of China against neo-Confucianism featuring 'impractical discussion' and 'discussion of ideological guidelines', and advocating 'emphasising practical learning to avoid empty talk' and 'saving

China through empirical learning', developed and became the important ethos of enlightenment in the late Ming and early Qing dynasties. Some prestigious representatives, such as Xu Guangqi who 'studied celestial beings with lifelong learning only for practical application', while others like Luo Qinshun, Wang Tingxiang and Wu Tinghan, advocated empirical learning in the stance of materialist philosophy.

At first glance, Taoism is a doctrine of nihilism or impractical metaphysics. In fact, it pursues a longer utility. That is to say, it advocates reducing people's energy consumption in pursuing ephemeral utility so as to lengthen realistic survival. So the Taoist school developed Taoism for health maintenance, prolonged life and even immortality. Buddhism stresses leniency, merit accumulation and good deeds with no strings attached. However, it aspires to the afterlife and yearns for the other shore. It pursues not this life but the afterlife, endows all benevolent deeds with 'merits' and adds longer realistic significance to practical good deeds.

(3) Humanistic pragmatism and unification of ontology and function

Since it attached importance to pragmatism, traditional Chinese culture developed the following characteristics: unification of church and state, the mutual function of instrumental reasoning and value reasoning, and the interconnection of metaphysics and physics. Not merely learning but also literature and art emphasised pragmatism, ways to manage state affairs, how to secure official positions, how to handle interpersonal relations and how to deal with the relationship between man and nature. Since pragmatism was stressed, all sorts of cultural functions could be transformed. The so-called 'river regulation according to *Evolution of Chinese Geography*, the observation of changes in line with *The Great Plan*, case handling in accordance with *The Spring and Autumn Annals* and admonition with the help of *The Book of Songs*' and the fact that 'articles were written to serve the times and songs and poems were created for things' emphasised expanding the function of literature from merry-making to intervening in reality.

'Ontology' in the 'unification of ontology and function' is the theoretical basis system where 'function' refers to the process of application and practice, namely, approaches and methods. The unification of ontology and function is the organic combination of theory and practice. Modern scholars proposed 'Chinese learning as the fundamental structure and Western learning for utility' not because 'Chinese learning' lacked practical content but because the practical content in 'Chinese learning' was outdated. Actually, 'Chinese learning as the fundamental structure and for utility' was inseparable like people's body and soul. The 'ontology' determined the 'function'. If any of them were replaced, they would not accord with each other and cultural nationality would finally be lost.

There is no denying that China's Great Wall stands erect from ancient times, the doctrines of Confucius and Mencius have been handed down without any trace of decline and the self-sufficient agricultural economy can continue thanks to the solid foundation laid by the matter-of-fact spirit.

5. Continuity: Pursue reform to add or subtract for an orderly inheritance

Confucius devoted his whole life to renewing the system of rites and music of the Western Zhou dynasty. Confucius and his Confucian school appeared at the outset to directly inherit the fine culture of the previous generations in the Shang and Zhou dynasties. Judged from the fact that Confucius's spirit of 'believing in and loving antiquity' and 'pursuing antiquity out of love' and his longing and praise for the culture of the Xia, Shang and Zhou dynasties, especially that of the Zhou, the scholar officials in Shandong represented by Confucius and Mencius indeed took the responsibility for inheriting the culture and tradition of previous generations.

(1) Trace back to its source and bear ancestry in mind

Confucius and almost all other Chinese had a fairly good tradition - bearing their ancestry in mind. They bore in mind not only wise individuals of previous generations but also the fine traditions and fine family traditions left by them, the meritorious feats they delivered and their unfinished wishes.

The research on the culture of Chinese family names reveals an interesting phenomenon, namely, that our ancestors established the system of Chinese characters for genealogy for future generations or dozens of generations. This system comprises the Chinese characters indicating seniority in the family or clan and is often called 'clique'. It is a rule of naming in line with ethics. *The Genealogical Studies* records: The system of Chinese characters for genealogy originated in the Song dynasty. Emperor Taizu of Song Zhao Kuangyin listed 13 'stipulated characters', namely, '德 *de* (virtue)', '惟 *wei* (only)', '从 *cong* (follow), '世 *shi* (world)', '令 *ling* (order)', '子 *zi* (son)', '伯 *bo* (senior)', '师 *shi* (teacher)', '希 *xi* (hope)', '与 *yu* (give)', '孟 *meng* (the first month of a season or eldest brother)', '由 *you* (reason)' and '宜 *yi* (appropriate)'. Together with '匡 *kuang* (correct)', the 14 characters comprised the names of his descendants. It was most probably the earliest system of Chinese characters for genealogy in China. That practice became popular among the people and one of the essentials for the ancestral temple of all ethnic nationalities. That is to say, people established and continued different 'cliques' according to the past achievements of their ancestors with the same family name. Some even arranged the clique names of their descendants in the form of songs. Although this system had something to do with the feudal patriarchal clan, it was gorgeous and colourful from a literary perspective. It represented people's best wishes for self-cultivation, good management of family affairs, peaceful life, orderly management of state affairs, good luck, good health and prosperity.

Not just the blood relationship but the family tradition and moral standing of the family have all been passed on from one generation to another. The Yang family in the Eastern Han dynasty had a 'Four Knows Hall', the ancestral temple of the family. This title was sourced from the allusion of Yang Zhen, a celebrity of the Eastern Han when he served as the feudal governor of Jingzhou. Once, a person came to bribe him with gold late at night. Yang Zhen flatly refused and sternly criticised him. He was unwilling to give up and said smilingly to Yang Zhen: "It's in the small hours of the morning and we are in your house. No one else will know about it. Please keep it!" Yang Zhen responded sternly: "Heaven knows about it. The earth knows about it. You know about it and I know about it. Why did you say nobody knows about it?" At that, the giver offered an apology and left in shame. Yang Zhen later named his ancestral hall the 'Four Knows'. Today, descendants of the Yang family still take pride in the 'Four Knows Hall' and admonish their children to hold fast to the sharp sense of integrity of their ancestor and live as honest men acting worthily in accordance with heaven, earth, their ancestors and their own conscience.

(2) Protection, utilisation, inheritance and development

Intangible cultural heritage in modern times is handed down faithfully from generation to generation. From 2006 to 2014, the State Council of the PRC successively approved the naming of four groups of national-level intangible cultural heritage totaling 1,517 items. The provinces, cities and autonomous regions named up to thousands of items of province-level intangible cultural heritage. The prerequisite for determining the intangible cultural heritage items was recorded inheritance of them. For instance, Chen-style shadow boxing, one of the first group of items nominated as national-level intangible cultural heritage, was passed on for more than 400 years in a clear sequence from generation to generation.

Among this intangible cultural heritage, a large part of the items in some fields, for instance, oral literature, folk painting, performing arts, manual skills and folk knowledge, were generally handed down, continued and developed through oral teaching that inspired true understanding among the inheritors. In these fields, the inheritors were vital bearers and passers of intangible cultural heritage. Definitely, their inheritance was not merely single-track extension or displacement of the original elements. They attenuated, increased and effectively passed on culture through accumulation of innovative culture.

In reality, in any period of Chinese cultural development, something 'in a direct line of succession' can be found. It is the deep cultural spirit, which is the symbol of a nation to show its intrinsic vital characteristics distinct from other nations. A nation differs from other nations not only in materials for basic necessities of life or economic model and political system, but chiefly in a certain collective deep cultural spirit. If a nation loses this cultural spirit, even though the descendants of this nation still multiply to sustain their biological existence (as a race), they would vanish as a matter of fact. For this reason, the continuity of culture and traditions are very significant with regard to a nation's survival or extinction.

(3) Pursue reform to remove or supplement, and make innovative expansion

How to pass on traditional culture? The ancients found the most effective way for us. It can be summarised as 'pursuing reform to remove or supplement'. In modern society, it means removing the dregs and absorbing the quintessence, making innovative expansion and vigorously carrying forward traditional culture.

No culture in history was handed down unchanged. The traditions were mostly handled, that is to say, with elements removed or supplemented by the inheritors according to the requirements of the times. Confucius's requirement of 'denying self and returning to propriety' did not mean restoring a specific cultural form or ritual or cultural system but reflected the deep cultural spirit of all the ancient cultural forms. In fact, the core of the traditional Chinese culture upheld by Confucius, namely, the spirit of 'benevolence' could be traced back to the ancient culture and traditions represented by Emperor Yao, Emperor Shun, Emperor Yu, Emperor Tang, Emperor Wen and Emperor Wu. However, to a large extent, it encompassed supplementation and innovation by Confucius himself. Additionally, Confucius's successors like Mencius, Dong Zhongshu, Confucian scholars of the Tang stressing 'Confucian orthodoxy' and masters of neo-Confucianism of the Song all broke new paths for the development of inherited traditional culture. Even to the reformers of the Qing dynasty trying to reform Chinese society with Western democratic thoughts, the quintessence of traditional culture was still intertwined with the theories of political reform. For instance, the 'perfect society' designed by Kang Youwei was in essence the enhancement of that described by Confucius.

Observations about modern society should reference ancient society. Without the ancient times, there would be no modern society. Without inheritance, there would be no large body of traditional culture; without inheritance, China's ancient civilisation would not have continued until now. Inheritance hinges on the universal value of traditional culture and mountains of positive energy in traditional culture for the social progress of today. Traditional culture is the most valuable material and spiritual wealth of the Chinese people which should be properly applied. We must not act as misers or black sheep. Instead, we should adhere to the principle of pursuing reform to remove or supplement elements of traditional culture for its proliferation, appreciation, better inheritance and accelerated advancement.

Volume 2

Develop fine traditional Chinese culture in accordance with the values of the times to uphold benevolence, 'people orientation', integrity, righteousness, harmony, concord and great unity so that fine traditional Chinese culture can become an important source of socialist core values.

— Xi Jinping

Chapter 1

Benevolence - Doctrine of Conducting Self-Perfection of the Chinese People

'Standing on earth, I consider how to become a good person.' It is quite easy to write the Chinese character '人 ren (person)' with one stroke to the left and the other to the right. Nevertheless, it is difficult to act as a 'person'. 'Without morality, personal cultivation is impossible; without attaining virtue, a person will not be fulfilled.' How to be a person? Traditional Chinese culture has given us a definite answer and edification. That is benevolence. Simply speaking, benevolence is to love, respect, be friendly to and help others. The manifestations of benevolence differ because of different subjects or objects. It is kindness of parents, filial piety of children, family affection of siblings, personal loyalty to friends, patriotism for the country, and love and support for the people. These different sorts of love converge to be benevolence. It is the core of Confucianism, and an indispensable part of Taoism and Buddhism. It counts for much in the entire traditional Chinese ideology and plays a positive role in building the present socialist core values.

1. Benevolence and boundless love

The Chinese character system abounds with words and expressions implying 'benevolence', for example, kindheartedness, mercy, benevolence, clemency, kindheartedness and justice, righteous person, and with both a benevolent mind and heart. These words and expressions mostly mean benevolence. The Chinese people take 'benevolence' as the core of moral principles to guide their own behaviour and extend it to be their great love to cultivate themselves and others, take others as brothers and share the life of all creatures. That great love bears the wisdom of their ancestors and silently nurtures the full invigoration and continuity of the Chinese nation.

(1) Benevolent people always care for and love others

Confucius was the initiator of 'benevolence'. He began to recruit students at the age of 30. It was like a private school today. In his teaching, 'benevolence', the core of his ideology, was extensively spread. As calculated, *The Analects of Confucius* totaled more than 15,900 characters and the character '仁 ren (benevolence)' appeared 109 times, 25 times mentioned by others and 84 times by Confucius himself.

Confucius said: "All the human virtues can be summed up as benevolence." (*The Doctrine of the Mean*) Confucius defined 'benevolence' as a human instinct and the fundamental essence of a human being. It was the source of a 'fulfilled person' and 'fulfilled benevolence'. The basic connotation of 'benevolence' can be shown in the anecdote that: "Fan Chi asked what 'benevolence' was. Confucius answered: 'To love others'." (*Yan Yuan* – a disciple of Confucius (521 to 481BC), also known as Yan Hui) Benevolence and love comprised 'kindheartedness' and became the core of Confucius's 'doctrine of benevolence' system.

Confucius's thought of 'kindheartedness' was primarily a specific moral rule, namely, love and kindness. Specifically speaking, Confucius's kindheartedness started from love, namely, the affection between father and son, the filial piety of a dutiful son for his father and fraternal love. Affection and filial piety show the love between father and son and fraternal love refers to devoted love between brothers. You Zi (You Ruo) said: "People who show filial piety to their parents and respect and love elder brothers rarely offend higher authorities. People who refuse to offend higher authorities never rise up in rebellion. Noble men concentrate their fundamental efforts on self-cultivation. If fundamental self-cultivation is attained, the doctrine develops from it. To show filial piety to parents, and love and respect to elder brothers are the fundamentals of benevolence. (*The Analects of Confucius - On Learning*) Therefore filial piety, and love and respect for elder brothers, are the fundamentals of Confucius's thought of 'benevolence'.

Although the thought of 'benevolence' originated from love for one's own family, it did not just stop there. Confucius considered others, and promoted 'kindheartedness' to the level of 'loving others' and 'universal love'. He required being close to kindhearted people. Confucius said: "People should be dutiful to their parents at home and respect their elder brothers outside. They should talk and behave discreetly, keep to their words, establish wide and new contacts and be on good terms with virtuous men. With additional capacity, they can learn all sorts of knowledge." (*The Analects of Confucius - On Learning*) That means the scope of kindheartedness can extend from kinship to others living in the same universe and even all men on earth. That is to say, 'moral integrity should be upheld in every corner of the world'. Confucius thought the friends around a person were quite important. The benevolent should make friends with brave, honest and upright gentlemen, learn from them and develop friendship to aid their righteous conduct. Confucius's advocacy for loving others and for getting on good terms with the benevolent were inherited by many thinkers. They further developed his advocacy in their own ideologies to enrich the content of 'benevolence'.

Based on Confucius's thought, Mencius connected benevolence with righteousness and took righteousness as the supreme principle of moral behaviour. He held the idea that compassion and the sense of good and evil permeated the natural instincts of people. He defined compassion as the starting point for benevolence and the sense of good and evil as the start of righteousness. It was described that 'people have compassion and the sense of good and evil' and that 'compassion is the starting point for benevolence and that the sense of good and evil is the start of righteousness'. (*Mencius - Gao Tzu Part I*) Besides, Mencius regarded benevolence as a fundamental element connecting man and nature, and the core of the political quality and morality of the rulers; and that, therefore, administrators should implement benevolent government and consider others out of kindheartedness. "If one implements benevolent government with understanding and compassion, the governance of the country falls into place easily." "Care for the elderly of our own and others; love the children of our own and others." (*Mencius - King Hui of Liang Vol.1*) That means benevolent government promises sound governance, otherwise, there is disorder. In practice, it was consistent with the 'universal love' advocated by Confucius.

Mo Zi proposed the ideas of universal love and non-aggression. He advocated great benevolence, great love and worldly ambition. He thought the greater self (the spiritual self) should benefit the world and that kindheartedness should not just be in mind but more importantly in practice. "The benevolent must do good for the world and remove the evils in the world. That should be a universal criterion. Anything that benefits mankind can be done, and one should refrain from doing anything that is not beneficial." (*Mo Zi - Non-Music Vol.1*)

The idea of kindheartedness was handed down by the Chinese nation for generations and specifically referred to the love for families, friends, others, the motherland and all living creatures. It plays a vital role in political rule and people's enlightenment in China.

(2) Benevolence depends on oneself rather than others

How can people become benevolent? Confucius thought: "Denying self and returning to propriety is benevolence. Once it is done, universal benevolence is achieved. Benevolence depends on oneself. Does it depend on others?" Benevolence depending on oneself rather than others is the main interpretation of Confucius for 'benevolence'. He deemed as long as people spoke and acted according to the moral principles and ethics of society, they could achieve kindheartedness.

How to become a virtuous sage or gentleman critically depends on whether one is willing to strive for 'benevolence'. "If I want to become benevolent, I will make it." (*The Analects of Confucius - Narrations*) As long as we bear in mind the goal of 'benevolence', it is achievable.

Similarly, Mencius discussed the possibility of 'becoming benevolent' from the perspective of humanity. He thought that people who were instinctively kind could become benevolent as long as they stuck to their conscience. Since human instinct is kind, why have many immoral events occurred in reality in society? Mencius believed that immoral people in real life were not born immoral but lost their conscience as they grew up. 'Benevolence', like 'righteousness', 'propriety' and 'wisdom', is an inherent human instinct. If they discard it, people become immoral. For this reason, if people with superior natural endowments cannot make self-examination, although they have 'four starting points'[1], they may tend to become evil. Mencius put forward that people should examine themselves to revive their own 'conscience and virtue'.

From the times of Mencius to the Song and Ming dynasties, the Confucian school always stressed planting 'benevolence' in the self-awareness of the subject and depending on oneself to attain benevolence. Zhu Xi said: "Benevolence rests in inherent morality rather than external

---

[1] The 'four starting points' refer to four virtues upheld by the Confucian school. That is to say, compassion is the starting point for kindheartedness; a sense of shame is the starting point for righteousness; yielding one's position to a more capable person is the starting point for propriety; and the sense of right and wrong is the starting point for wisdom. This is an important part of Mencius's thought and Mencius's major contribution to pre-Qin Confucianism.

appearance." (*Notes of Collected Works of Zhu Xi*) It means if a person wants to attain benevolence, benevolence is hidden in their heart. Conversely, if benevolence is not in their heart, it will be good for nothing.

In accordance with the inherent benevolence and the independence to attain benevolence, the Confucian school concluded that all the ethical norms came from innermost conscious selection and people should consciously obey and abide by social norms.

(3) Consider and do good to others

Confucius said: "The benevolent should help others accomplish something if they are accomplished and help others to prosper after they have prospered themselves." (*The Analects of Confucius - Ran Yong*) Benevolence also requires us to consider and help others. It is the basic moral cultivation of man. To consider others, one should primarily 'do unto others as you would have them do unto you'. That is a sort of empathy. If a person can experience the emotions and wishes of others and understand the positions and feelings of others, they will consider and handle problems from their own angle. People of all social strata in the West universally identify with this sentence, and it has become a golden moral rule observed by people all over the world.

In the story of Yu the Great controlling the flood, Yu the Great dredged nine great rivers finally flowing into the sea and swept away flood disasters in 13 years. In the Warring States period, a man named Bai Gui said to Mencius: "If I were Yu the Great, I would have done much better. As long as I had dredged the river, the flood would flow to the neighbouring countries." Mencius negated what he said unreservedly and said noble men would not do that at all. 'Noble men are always ready to do good to others.' (*Mencius*) In the case of water control, Bai Gui only considered his own country regardless of other countries. Although Yu the Great devoted a lot of time and energy, he did unto others as he would have them do unto him. He thoroughly eliminated flood disasters in his own country and those of other countries. It was indeed the benevolent mental realm worthy of others' reverence.

In addition to 'doing unto others as one would have them do unto you', it is further required to consider others and do good to others. Just as Mencius said: "Care for the elderly of our own and others; love the children of our own and others." (*Mencius*) That means treating the elderly and children of others as one's own. A political leader should even be more considerate about ordinary people. In the Spring and Autumn period, it snowed heavily in the State of Qi. Duke Jing of Qi stood at the window appreciating the snow-covered landscape in his warm robe made of fox fur. He expressed wonder at the beautiful scene and gladly told Yan Zi that it was surprisingly not cold but warm. Looking at the fur robe of Duke Jing of Qi and the warm stove in the room, Yan Zi said straightforwardly: "I hear that the ancient wise monarchs thought about the hungry while they were well fed, those who felt cold while they wore warm clothes and those who were tired while they enjoyed an easy and leisurely life. They often considered others and their countries prospered as a consequence. However, why don't you think about others?" Duke Jing of Qi was choked by Yan Zi. The supreme realm of doing good to others is to move beyond seeking individual gain to that of the entire country. 'Those who do good for their country deserve love; those who do harm to their country invite hatred." (*Collection of Words and Deeds of Yan Zi in the Spring and Autumn Period*) It is required 'to hear the sound of the wind, the sound of the rain and the sound of reading, and to care for the affairs of the family, the affairs of the state and the affairs of the universe'. (Gu Xiancheng of the Ming dynasty)

2. The spirit of great love handed down from generation to generation

In the Chinese history of more than 5,000 years, people with lofty ideals emerged endlessly and the spirit of great love was handed down from generation to generation. From Qu Yuan's lament for the harsh livelihood of people to Wen Tianxiang's patriotism to 'leave a loyal heart shining in the pages of history' and Zhang Zai's ideals of 'setting one's mind on heaven and earth, developing steadfastness to serve the people, carrying forward the lost knowledge of the past saints and bringing peace and tranquility for all ages', the seeds of benevolence were sown in every inch of land; the flame of benevolence warmed each heart; the notes of benevolence composed the song of China's triumph. All these elements converged into great love in the world, moved both heaven and earth, and were full of power and grandeur.

(1) Return parental love with filial piety

'Filial piety for parents and fraternal love are the essence of benevolence.'

Chapter 1

(*The Analects of Confucius - On Learning*) 'Benevolent people always care for others and regard family as the most important thing.' (*The Doctrine of the Mean*) Filial piety is the root of benevolence and care for others is the start of benevolence. At the New Year's greeting party in 2015, Xi Jinping proposed: "Whatever the changes of the era and life pattern, we should attach priority to family construction, especially, family members, family education and family tradition." Family is the basic cell of society and the first school of a person in life. The words and deeds of parents can teach their children to experience the impressive moral power and filial piety that enables children to bring their parents happiness from the inside.

The Chinese nation has highly valued family, family affection and family education since ancient times. In its long history, the Chinese nation has left the world many great and influential stories about family affection, including great parental love and dutiful children. 'The loving mother held threads in her hand, to sew clothes for the wanderer. Making the clothes with thick stitches, she feared he would return late. Who can understand parents' love? Gratitude should be shown to them for their love and care for their children since childhood.' (Meng Jiao's *Travelers' Song*); 'Being a stranger all alone in a strange land far away, I think of my dear ones on festive occasions more than ever.' (Wang Wei's *Thinking of My Brother on Mountain-Climbing Day*). These tuneful verses are true affirmations of how one misses one's parents and family affection. It can be said that family affection was the everlasting roots and veins of Chinese civilisation and the cornerstone of the continuity of the descendants of the Yan Emperor and the Yellow Emperor. They are all from a grateful heart fostered by benevolence.

After arduous replacement of successive dynasties, Chinese culture inevitably underwent some changes. Nevertheless, the culture of filial piety has always unswervingly commanded the direction of development of Chinese culture for thousands of years. Filial piety is the most important of all virtues and is the duty of each child. Chinese culture has endured so long and become a unique ancient civilisation worldwide until now thanks to the culture of filial piety. For instance, Shun's filial piety moved heaven; Zi Lu carried rice to his parents from far away although he himself had hardly enough to eat; Dong Yong sold himself to bury his father with the money; Ding Lan who had lost his parents in his childhood missed his parents so much that he carved wooden figurines and served them as if they were his parents; Yang Xiang clutched the throat of a fierce tiger with her weak small hands and saved her father and herself; Zhu Shouchang resigned from a high position to find his mother. Such affectionate stories have been handed down from ancient times to modern times. 'Huang Xiang warmed up the cold bed for his father in winter. His filial piety for his father should be continued.' (*The Three-Character Classics*) Huang Xiang showed filial piety to his father at the age of nine. He cooled his father's pillow and bed mat in summer and warmed his father's quilt in winter.

A happy family is surely based on some material conditions and social position. Nevertheless, 'the rise and fall of a family resides in rites and morality rather than wealth and high position.' There are numerous examples of affectionate families where children showed filial piety to their parents in *24 Stories of Filial Piety*. All the protagonists of filial piety cherish a grateful heart. It is just the grateful heart that always invigorates the family relationship within Chinese civilisation and becomes the valuable spiritual wealth of the Chinese nation.

(2) Love and sympathise with people to foster world peace

Benevolence requires cherishing people in one's heart. The roots, strength and bloodline of a country are its people. 'Wise monarchs should reward the kindhearted, eliminate people's troubles, love people as if they were their own children, protect people like heaven and tolerate them like the earth.' (Liu Xiang's *New Order - Miscellaneous I* in the Western Han dynasty) The ancients clearly put forward the view that officials should patronise their subjects like heaven and treat them leniently like the earth.

The Romance of the Three Kingdoms described a story: After Liu Bei defeated Cao Cao's troops in Xinye, Henan province, he moved to Fan city in Hubei province. To take revenge, Cao Cao personally led the eight-pronged attack upon Fan city. Cao Cao's troops were so mighty that Zhuge Liang anticipated that they would not be held off. So he persuaded Liu Bei to abandon Fan city, ford the Han river and retreat to Xiangyang. Liu Bei could not bear to abandon the people who had followed him for quite a long time and dispatched someone to announce in the city: "Cao Cao's troops are coming and Liu Bei cannot hold them off for long. Whoever wants to continue to follow Liu Bei can cross the river with him." The people in the city all braved death to follow him. Liu Bei asked Guan Yu to organise vessels at the river bank. People brought along all their family members, young and old, and they marched ahead and sobbed ceaselessly on both river banks. At this sight in his vessel, Liu Bei wept loudly from sorrow and said in sobs: "The people are suffering from such a disastrous calamity for my sake. Do I have the face to live on in the world?!" At that, he was about to throw himself into the river and drown himself. Others beside him hurried to grasp him. Everyone cried bitterly at the sight of it. Landing on the southern bank, Liu Bei looked back and saw innumerable ordinary people, unable to cross the river, wave and shout to the south. Liu Bei hurriedly ordered Guan Yu to expedite the process of taking people back in the vessels. After all the ordinary people were taken across the river, Liu Bei mounted his horse and left. Liu Bei's action of 'taking the ordinary people across the river' fueled the circulation of Liu Bei's reputation for loving people in the Central Plains area. Later, someone created a poem to praise him: 'Even in the face of danger Liu Bei considered the ordinary people, boarded the vessel in tears and deployed his troops. Paying a visit to the mouth of the Xiangjiang river now, the elders can still remember the king who loved, and was loved by, his people.' The benevolence of the rulers significantly strengthened the legal foundation for their rule.

The Tang dynasty, the peak of Chinese feudal society, was no doubt a world power in the modern global landscape in those years. The 'excellent governance' during the Zhenguan reign by Emperor Taizong of the Tang witnessed economic prosperity, people's wealthy life, social stability and even no robbery. The huge achievements were inseparable with the ruler's thinking that 'the people are more important than the ruler', 'the people are like water and the emperors are like a ship', and 'the people like water can both support and overturn the ship'. Then, the monarch and his subjects were of one mind. The emperor was fairly considerate to his subjects and his subjects were loyal to him and exerted their utmost efforts to support him. It was said that in May of the 19th year of the Zhenguan period in the Chinese lunar calendar, Emperor Taizong of the Tang personally led the army to attack Korea and showed his care for both generals and private soldiers without any distinction on the way. Once a soldier fell ill and could not set out with the rest of the troops. Taizong went to see him in person and entrusted him to the local government for his treatment. After the war, Taizong ordered the remains of the dead officers and men to be collected and buried properly, held memorial ceremonies for them in person and was choked with tears. The parents of the dead soldiers were deeply moved once they discovered that and said from their hearts: "We felt extremely grief-stricken to lose our son. But when the emperor cried and held memorial ceremonies for them personally, we knew they would rest in peace without any regret after death."

(3) Thousands of years of continuous patriotism

Patriotism is one of the cores of benevolence and more importantly the eternal theme of the Chinese people. As the song *My Chinese Heart* says: 'The Yangtze river, the Great Wall, Mount Tai and the Yellow river weigh quite heavily on my heart. They will be endeared in my bosom anytime and anywhere.' The song is a direct expression of patriotic feelings.

Legend has it that the Dragon Boat Festival held every year on 5 May in the Chinese lunar calendar was held in honour of Qu Yuan. After he threw himself into the Miluo river and drowned, the people of Chu felt anguish and sorrow. They swarmed to the Miluo river to mourn him. Some fishermen went to and fro to salvage his corpse and constantly threw traditional Chinese rice dumplings and eggs into the river because they thought the fish would not bite Qu Yuan's body after eating the food. Besides, a veteran physician poured a jar of realgar wine (*xionghuangjiu* or Chinese cereal wine) into the river because he wanted to prevent the flood dragon from hurting Qu Yuan. It was said that the day when Qu Yuan threw himself into the river was 5 May. After that, on this day each year, people would row dragon boats, eat traditional Chinese rice dumplings and drink realgar wine to commemorate Qu Yuan. That convention lasts until now and the Dragon Boat Festival has been established as a national statutory holiday.

Throughout Chinese history, patriotic figures like Qu Yuan have emerged endlessly. For instance, Su Wu 'kept the sceptre from disgrace, drank melted snow to quench his thirst, devoured fabric to satisfy his hunger and tended sheep along the North Sea coast'; Yue Fei served his country loyally and composed the eternal masterpiece by 'dedicating himself to his country's cause and risked everything to achieve it'; Wen Tianxiang's righteousness that 'death comes to all men and my loyalty may leave a page in the annals' moved heaven and earth; Zheng Chenggong braved his death to recover Taiwan and safeguarded Chinese sovereignty and territorial integrity; Lin Zexu burned opium stocks at Humen beach and safeguarded the dignity of the Chinese nation with unparalleled courage and determination…

'Even ordinary people are responsible for the fate of the nation.' It has been the source of the patriotic practice of the Chinese nation since ancient times to safeguard the homeland and territory, and to contest every inch of ground. As for invaders, the Chinese people have always been firmly determined to 'punish invaders of China however far away they were'. Japanese pirates invaded Taizhou in great force and were defeated by Qi Jiguang's troops in Linhai, Zhejiang province. They fought nine times and Qi's troops won nine times. Qi Jiguang hence created a poem 'Fighting north and south to respond to the war situation, I thought about my life smilingly in the frontier. All year round, I mostly marched ahead on horseback'.

Gong Zizhen, a Qing poet, once composed verses to eulogise the martyrs dying for the country: 'The remains of the loyal were buried everywhere in the green hills, and there is no need to carry the corpses back to the hometown; the fallen flowers are heartless, but will fall onto the earth and become great manure to nourish other flowers.' To safeguard national peace, even though Chinese die on the battlefield with their souls wandering in a foreign land, they will still turn into green manure and protect the flowers. That is the patriotism of the Chinese people.

3. Consolidate the moral foundation of the modern Chinese people with benevolence

The idea of benevolence has been handed down from generation to generation for thousands of years, prolonged and applied to educate, cultivate and guide generations of Chinese people to love their relatives, the people and the country. Today, as we build socialist core values, we should also carefully draw beneficial nutrition from it, absorb, transform and bring forth new ideas about it, and apply it in modern society in a bid to consolidate the moral foundation of the modern Chinese people.

(1) Practice benevolence entirely of one's own accord with caution and self-discipline

'Practicing benevolence entirely of one's own accord' means taking the initiative to be benevolent of one's own accord. It fully reflects autonomous benevolence. It means that people are actively required to turn moral requests for benevolence into moral standards of their own. It requires us to positively practice benevolence and strengthen our own moral cultivation, self-management and self-restraint. With wariness and self-discipline, a person can do good deeds completely on their own initiative. The loving heart is not exposed to the public but should nurture others and warm their hearts in a gentle way just like spring rain. Just like a quotation of Xi Jinping from *The Book of Rites*: 'Even the most covert and imperceptible words and deeds can reflect a person's character. Therefore, noble men should learn caution and self-discipline.' That is the highest state of moral self-discipline and benevolence.

Liu Shenglan was an elderly person of no family in Shandong who, in his 90s, persisted in eking out a meagre existence and helping students with their studies. Shandong province enjoyed 'five guarantees[1]'. In 1998 he accidentally read a newspaper report on supporting students in their study. From then on, 73-year-old Liu Shenglan donated his meagre salary. The students who received his donations gradually 'increased' from surrounding cities to the whole country. At his peak, he concurrently donated funds to more than 50 students. For 17 years, he had never tasted a piece of meat or bought himself new clothes. He even begrudged buying himself a steamed bun. However, in total he donated more than Rmb70,000 to more than 100 students. Liu Shenglan, having one foot in the grave, delivered his negligible contributions and composed a song of great love in the universe with his own old hands.

'Emulating those better than oneself' manifests people's pursuit of lofty moral values and moral self-discipline. More importantly, it is the conscious compliance and identification with the moral norm. In recent years, moral models have been appraised and chosen in various regions as marker posts and banners in society. They advocate a kind of orientation and pursuit to people. The model figures, with their lively and intuitive impressions, have deepened people's understanding of, and identification with, moral power. With their firm belief, lofty spirit and noble morality, they have interpreted the mainstream values of society and embody the standards of reference for individuals in moral practice. Models can generate infinite power and the typical images of the moral quintessence can bring people tremendous mental encouragement and innermost influence.

(2) Consider others and help others

The 'benevolent morality' in fine traditional Chinese culture is broad and profound. It is universal love considering others and the universe. The spirit of benevolent morality is not just a code of behaviour for people to

---

[1] The 'five guarantees' is a social insurance system in China for members of society that are incapable of working and without guarantees for living, namely, guarantees for their food, clothing, residence, medical treatment and burial.

get along with one another and with nature but is also an indispensable ethical practice for civilians. It is social morality. It is the simplest, lowest and most common code of behaviour in social life and the most fundamental condition to maintain normal, orderly and healthy public life. It requires the government to honour credibility, self-discipline and tolerance. It also requires us to cherish benevolence, kindheartedness and sympathy and to live on friendly terms with others and to co-exist with them harmoniously. In getting along with nature, we should respect the laws of nature and protect the environment. Only in that way can society develop harmoniously.

'Considering others' is also a benevolence that comes from empathy. It is often applied in handling interpersonal relationships. It is also a habitual method for people to consider some social public problems. 'Considering others' means judging others by oneself, deducing other people's intentions on one's own and putting oneself in someone else's position. 'Considering others' and 'empathy' are alike in a certain sense. Chinese people are kind, honest, gracious and helpful. Chinese family members respect, love and help each other. Chinese people make donations to charity and provide international aid to the international community. These are all collective manifestations of the compliance and identification of Chinese people with the ideology of benevolent morality which has been internalised in their hearts and externalised in their actions. In the face of right and wrong, Chinese people can clearly distinguish black from white. They can help others and make no distinction between 'you' and 'me', regions, nationalities, races and even national boundaries. China experienced the outbreak of 'SARS' in 2003, the Wenchuan earthquake in 2008 and the Yushu earthquake in 2010. Faced with these catastrophes, the Chinese people, with the spirit of boundless benevolence and great love, joined hands to overcome numerous difficulties associated with SARS, turned sorrow into strength and revived from the earthquakes. When the eruption of major epidemics and calamities occurred among the international community, the Chinese people considered others, showed their great love and offered humanitarian assistance to the international community for free. In March 2014, Ebola broke out in West Africa. China successively dispatched medical staff to offer aid there. Despite the possibility of being infected with the high-risk life-threatening disease, Chinese medical staff resolutely stood by the African people, shared weal and woe with them, and stood together regardless of the situation. Chinese people adopt the policy of empathy with others in both minor and major issues, and carry forward the spirit of boundless benevolence. It is a social morality and more importantly the moral foundation for social harmony and world peace.

Hold fast to benevolence and wait for golden opportunities as a return. 'Taking pleasure in helping others' is a traditional Chinese virtue, an important part of the thinking behind benevolence and the mark of personality sublimation. It warms the world like spring light and nurtures the earth like dew. In China's long history, there were typical cases of righteous, courageous and helpful figures, such as Lei Feng, Guo Mingyi and Fang Junming. In fact, in real society, no one exists in isolation but must have contact with others in life. Everyone may encounter some difficulties, conflicts and problems and need the care, protection, support and help of others. In social life, if everyone can care for and help others on their own initiative, start from themselves and minor matters, and develop helpfulness to be a common social practice, they can get others' help anytime and anywhere and sense the warmth of society.

All of us should carry forward the spirit of taking pleasure in helping others, and positively take the initiative to care for and help others. Public welfare is a new form of help. It reflects a new type of socialist interpersonal relationship and is closely linked with us. Each citizen should pay more attention to and support public welfare, be more charitable, spread love and live as a kindhearted person, especially in activities such as the following: relief, donation for study, voluntary blood donation, emergency aid, public welfare and charity. 'If someone presents roses to others, the fragrance of the roses will linger in their hands.' We should make donations to charity for the benefit of society and show sincere care for others so that society will become warmer and life will be filled with more fragrance.

(3) Be concerned about people all over the world and be determined to serve the country worthily

The 'spirit of dedication' is a sort of love and wholeheartedness for a person's career. It is a spirit of benevolent morality to love, dedicate and serve the motherland. It is also driven by a strong sense of social responsibility and historic mission.

The practice that 'even ordinary people are responsible for the rise and fall of their country' was the reflection of Gu Yanwu's patriotism in the Qing dynasty; the spirit of 'being concerned about the country and the people before anything else' interprets Fan Zhongyan's patriotism of 'being concerned about people all over the whole world'. It was just under the edification of the spirit of utter benevolence and devotion to 'being mindful of people throughout the universe' that when China was faced with the crisis of foreign invasion, innumerable people with lofty ideals cherished a strong sense of historic responsibility, risked their lives and those of their families to strive for national independence and people's emancipation, were ready to lose their heads, shed their blood, brave extreme danger and never refused to do so under any circumstances. In the burning of opium stocks at Humen beach, Lin Zexu was not afraid of foreign enemies but acted with dignity and honour; in the naval battle of 1894, Deng Shichang charged forward and forgot about his own life; reformers with ideals and integrity such as Kang Youwei, Liang Qichao and Tan Sitong advocated reform for national salvation; a large group of revolutionary heroes represented by Sun Yat-sen and Huang Xing struggled and dedicated themselves to democracy and republicanism. They were all outstanding representatives of patriotism.

From the smoke-smothered period of war and into the peaceful stage of socialist construction, men and women with lofty ideals mindful of the world and repaying the motherland boasted a strong sense of social responsibility and historic mission. Taking the rise and fall of the universe as their own duty, they made selfless contributions to the safety and peace of the country and the well-being of the people. Qian Xuesen reputed to be the 'father of the atomic and hydrogen bombs and man-made satellites', Yuan Longping noted as the 'father of Chinese rice' and Mao Yisheng celebrated as the 'father of Chinese bridges' had experience of studying, teaching or working overseas. Nonetheless, they vowed to serve their country and were driven by their patriotism to return to China. In their respective professional fields, they studied assiduously, bravely scaled new heights and delivered silent contributions. Huang Xuhua was renowned as the 'father of China's nuclear submarines' and one of the developers and founders of the first generation of nuclear-powered submarines. To develop nuclear-powered submarines, during more than 30 years, his father and eight brothers and sisters did not know what he was doing then. His mother longed to see him at 63 and finally succeeded in seeing him at 93. In 1964, Huang Xuhua finally led his team to develop China's first nuclear-powered submarine and made China the world's fifth country to possess nuclear-powered submarines. In 1988, deep diving tests of nuclear-powered submarines were launched in the South China sea to ascertain the design limits. Huang Xuhua dived 300m under the water in person and became the first chief designer to test the deep diving. He pledged to serve his country from the bottom of his heart and delivered his silent and diligent dedication. Nevertheless, he attained huge and infinitely powerful achievements.

The Qian diagram in *The Book of Changes* says: 'The law of nature is a combination of Yin and Yang, our living environment is the integration of rigidity and flexibility, and benevolence and righteousness are most important in interpersonal contact. Without benevolence and righteousness, a person will not keep a foothold in society. Benevolence is the virtue of the heart and the reason for love. A benevolent person must have lofty virtues and a loving heart.

Chapter 2

Focus on 'People-Oriented' Thought - The Foundation of the Chinese People's National Security

'People-oriented' means that 'the people are the foundation of the state and the state serves its people'. It stemmed from *The Book of History - Lament of Five Children*. As recorded, Tai Kang, grandson of Yu the Great, lacked any virtue, went on long hunting trips, put affairs of state aside, and finally incurred the repulsion of the common people. Afterwards, Hou Yi occupied his capital. His mother and five younger brothers were driven to the Luohe river. They recounted the admonition of Yu the Great and created *Lament of Five Children* to express their resentment and lament for 'losing the state'. 'People-oriented' in essence meant that people were the foundation and cornerstone of the state. After that, the connotation of 'people-oriented' was constantly enriched and became the core of China's traditional theories on managing state affairs. 'People-oriented' thought has been the essence of the culture of the Chinese nation for thousands of years. The connotation of being 'people-oriented' was incessantly diversified with the development of the times and presented a splendid view of China's national culture.

1. Trace back to the source of 'people-oriented'

'People-oriented' thought is likely to have come into being in ancient China. As early as 700BC, *Guan Zi - On Hegemony* recorded: 'Hegemony hinges on being 'people oriented'. The state will be secured if it is implemented or in danger otherwise.' The term 'people-oriented' here was different from that in the modern West. The term 'people-oriented' in the modern West refers to 'people' without any discrimination while the 'people' Guan Zhong described actually referred to 'nationals'. In those years, the 'people of Chu', 'people of Qi' and 'people of Lu' in the articles of the hundred schools of thought actually referred to 'nationals of Chu', 'nationals of

Qi' and 'nationals of Lu' and the term 'people-oriented' practically meant 'nationals-oriented'. Consequently, the descendants included the sentence of Guan Zhong in the 'people-oriented' thought as a sort of incisive interpretation of early 'people-oriented' thought.

(1) The rudiments of 'people-oriented' thought in the period of Three Emperors and Five Sovereigns

'The people are the foundation of the state' has two senses of meaning: First, that 'people-oriented' thought was a product of the state; second, that 'people-oriented' thought was the state ruler's philosophy of political governance. 'The people are the foundation of the state' was the political idea emerging with the appearance of the state.

It is generally held that 'people-oriented' thought originated in the Shang and Zhou dynasties. That is because, in the real record of the earliest oracle bone scripts, people found the first Chinese character '民 min (people)' in the history of Chinese characters. In the more distant ages before characters appeared, for instance, the Xia dynasty and even the earlier period of the Three Emperors and Five Sovereigns, 'people-oriented' thought had already made its debut.

An article notes: In ancient times, 'people drilled wood to make fire to eliminate the smell of urine'. Suiren Shi[1] made it possible for people to 'eat cooked food', which put 'people-oriented' thought into practice; by inventing 'building shelters with wood to avoid wild beasts and floods', Youchao Shi[2] practiced 'people-oriented' thought by teaching people to live in shelters; the Yellow Emperor worked hard for the people and won their hearts and support; Emperor Zhuan Xu (a legendary monarch in ancient China) 'cultivated materials to nurture the land… cultivated disposition for education'; Emperor Ku 'acted according to heaven's will, solved emerging problems for people, used local materials and economised on their use, instructed all the people and taught them what was beneficial'; Emperor Yao 'manifested the harmony of the nine clans (of a family) to the tribes'; Emperor Shun was able to 'pacify the domestic and overseas situation with the help of eight talented people'; Yu the Great 'toiled hard, felt deeply

---

[1] In ancient Chinese mythology, Suiren Shi was a matriarchal clan near Hetao in the early Neolithic period. They lived by hunting and found that sparks appeared when the stones they used to strike the wild animals collided with the mountain stones. Inspired by that, Suiren Shi invented drilling wood to make fire.

[2] In ancient Chinese mythology, Youchao Shi was the inventor of houses and buildings.

worried and refused to return home even when passing by' only to control the flood and benefit the people. In these ancient myths, the images of the Three Emperors and Five Sovereigns loving and benefiting the people passed before people's eyes. Among them, apart from the legend of Yu the Great that happened after the state had come into being, the other instances all happened among primitive tribes. Without character or state, the tribal leaders still showed their love and kindness for their clansmen.

It is said that the clan commune was actually the rudiments of a country and a country-like state. The relationship between the clan leader and clan members was practically similar to the relations between a ruler and the ruled. According to the *Records of the Grand Historian*, 'Chiyou was the most atrocious and could not be conquered. The Yan Emperor wanted to attack the feudal princes who finally surrendered to Xuanyuan. Xuanyuan mobilised the soldiers with his virtue, reorganised the army, researched changes in the solar system governing the seasons, planted five cereals (rice, two kinds of millet, wheat and beans), pacified the people, and measured the land.' The Yellow Emperor was the leader of the largest clan tribe in those years. 'Pacifying the people', the attitude of the ruling Yellow Emperor to the people, obviously displayed 'affection for the people'. Emperor Yao and Emperor Shun when in power also inherited the concept and undertaking of the Yellow Emperor of the rule of virtue. Although that period of history has descended into oblivion for lack of written records, the periods of Emperor Yao and Emperor Shun sketched by relevant myths handed down manifested an obscure era when the rulers were attached to their people. Otherwise, why did Du Fu, the poet sage of the Tang, write the lines 'To help the monarch surpass Emperor Yao and Emperor Shun, it is required to renew the glorious customs'? Why did great Chairman Mao Zedong compose the verse 'The 600 million Chinese are all sages like Shun and Yao'?

(2) Lessons from the fall of the Xia dynasty: loss of the foundation of the country

That 'the people are the foundation of a country' was the admonition of Yu the Great to his descendants. However, Emperor Jie, the 17th monarch of Xia, went against the teachings of the deceased. His dissolution and atrocities brought the utmost pain to the 'foundation' of the country. It is told that the subjects then pointed at the sun and cursed Emperor Jie of Xia: 'When you perish, I'd like to perish together with you.' Drawing lessons from the brutality of Jie, the Shang dynasty complied with the aspirations of the people and delivered the chivalrous deed of overturning the Xia dynasty. The Shang dynasty took the lead in seizing state power by force, overthrew the decadent Xia dynasty and broke the inexorable law that 'the emperors cannot be changed'.

After founding the Shang dynasty, Emperor Tang absorbed the lessons of the Xia, implemented the policy of 'rule of leniency' and attached importance to agricultural development and production. Hence, the Shang dynasty lasted up to 600 years in the hands of 31 emperors spanning 17 generations. Nonetheless, its fall was also caused by the brutality of its last monarch Emperor Zhou who brought calamity to the people. Emperor Wu of Zhou carried the torch that 'the decrees of heaven are not unchanging and the rulers can rule only with the assistance of morality' and violently attacked the decayed Shang dynasty. Zhou learned a good lesson from the fall of Zhou: Only by worshiping God and protecting the people can the crown be consolidated and secured, and can life be lengthened. The written imperial mandates in the first year of the Western Zhou dynasty saw the thought of 'protecting the people' of the nobles of that time. For instance, *The Book of History - Oath-Taking* records: 'God can see what we see and can hear what we hear.' 'If the Zhou dynasty wants to rule the country eternally, its descendants must protect the people forever. It can be said that the 'people-oriented' thought of China took initial shape then and became the guiding principle for the monarchs of Zhou to govern the country and administer political affairs.

(3) The chorus of many schools of thought and surge of 'people-oriented' thought

In the 'contention of a hundred schools of thought' in the Spring and Autumn and the Warring States period, 'people-oriented' thought presented a splendid sight. In the chorus of these schools of thought, 'people-oriented' was a resounding melody. It can be said that the ancient philosophers emerging in those years drastically differed in many viewpoints but astonishingly held an identical idea on the 'people-oriented' issue. A series of humanistic advocacies, for example, that 'the people are more important than the ruler' and 'people-oriented', were interpreted and amplified by the Confucian school, the Taoist school, the Mohist school, the Legalists and the Eclectics from different angles and converged into a torrential current of 'people-oriented' thought.

Chapter 2

In the Spring and Autumn period, in the face of the positive advocacies of the ancient philosophers, the rulers of all states, to maintain the interests of the ruling class, had to carefully consider the value of 'people-oriented' thought and took it as the basis to seek hegemony. 'People-oriented' thought gained momentum accordingly. That 'the people are the masters of god' and 'the monarchs are there to serve the people' evolved to be an important ethos. Among them, Confucius was the most influential. He reflected on the violence of the state, proposed the principle that 'the benevolent love the people', advocated priority for education and lenient punishment, and stressed 'using the resources of the people as discreetly as holding memorial ceremonies'. His thought of the association of sage and king being benevolent to people was actually, from a humanitarian perspective and carrying the banner of rising above ego and returning to propriety, the summarisation and sublimation of the concept of state management and ruling experience since the Zhou dynasty and the Spring and Autumn period featuring attaching great importance to the people, winning people's hearts, protecting the people, having a lot of people, loving the people, fulfilling the people, nourishing the people, benefiting the people, showing affection to the people, enriching the people and facilitating the people. The 'people-oriented' ideology was established on this basis.

Lao Tzu, called 'my teacher' by Confucius, quoted from the sage and proposed four requirements, namely the 'self-cultivation, self-rectification, self-prosperity and self-simplification' of people. In a word, it required people to make reforms with their own wisdom and strength, maintain a correct orientation, strive to develop the economy and keep simple and plain folk customs. It also required that the monarch adopt an attitude toward the people that 'nobility is based on humility'. Meanwhile, the rulers had to take the will of the people into full consideration. Just as it is said, 'the sages do not have their own will and they should take the people's will as their own.' He reminded the rulers that 'the people are hungry because their superiors have taxed them too much'. He warned the rulers not to exploit the people too much and not to push the people too far by saying that 'the people are not afraid of death, so why intimidate them with death?'

Some works researching the 'people-oriented' thought of the pre-Qin period highly praised Confucius and Mencius. As a matter of fact, the most vigorous advocate of being 'people-oriented' was Guan Zhong. For Guan

Zhong's method of state management, Confucius was full of praise: 'Duke Huan held meetings with sovereigns to form alliances not with chariots (military force) but with the efforts of Guan Zhong. What great virtue! What great virtue!' The two 'What great virtues!' here exhibited Confucius's full affirmation for the meritorious achievements and benevolence of Guan Zhong. The greatest point of Guan Zhong's 'benevolence' was love for people. The thought of love for people was shown in 'colonisation, prosperity, teaching and rectification of people'. The book *Guan Zi* is rich in 'people-oriented' thought, focusing on complying with the wishes of the people and adapting to the conditions of the people.

In the early stage of the Warring States period, 'people-oriented' thought was relatively completely expounded in the ideologies of the philosophers. The wording 'people-oriented' clearly summarised by the Legalists in the name of Guan Ying, the political fantasy of the agriculturalists to 'cook and eat together with the people', the profound thought of weakening the government power upheld by Lao Tzu and Chuang Tzu who bemoaned the state of the universe and pitied the fate of humankind and Mo Zi's thoughts of 'universal love and mutual benefit' and advocacy of 'thrifty use', 'thrifty burial', 'non-aggression' and 'reverence for the wise' all showed the multi-angle and multi-dimensional progress of 'people-oriented' thought. However, it was Mencius, a synthesiser of Confucianism, that directly promoted 'people-oriented' thought to new heights.

Taking virtue as the standard and teaching as his own duty, Mencius called loudly for the people to be saved from 'hanging upside down' and 'deep water and hot fire' (extreme suffering) and stressed the need to establish social harmony from the property rights system. Mencius measured the political importance of the monarch and the people, extended the relationship between the state and the people to that between the monarch and the people and came to the conclusion that went beyond politics that 'the people are the most important, followed by the country and the monarch'. Concurrently, Mencius further elucidated the thoughts of 'being concerned about the people's concerns' and 'sharing happiness with people'. He held that 'people will be happy with the happiness of the monarchs who are happy with the happiness of the people; people will feel worried about the worries of the monarchs who are worried about their worries. The monarchs who are happy with people's happiness and worried about people's worries will rule the state forever.' (*Mencius - King Hui of Liang Vol.2*) It made 'people-oriented' thought a real cultural faith, a spiritual realm and the era's pulse of the ideological trend of humanism.

Xuncius also particularly stressed 'people-oriented' thought. He advocated: "People are not born for the monarch; the monarch is born to serve the people." (*Xuncius - Grand Strategy*) It stressed that 'the people are more important than the monarch' from another perspective. According to Xuncius, people appeared not to surround and protect the monarch but the monarch was born only to serve the people. Social fairness, justice and national welfare were the ultimate aim while the establishment of the kingship was just a means. It theoretically distinguished the country from the son of heaven and the state from the monarch. Additionally, Xuncius compared the relationship between the monarch and the people to that between a ship and water: 'The monarch is like a ship; the people are like water. The water can carry the ship and also overturn it.' (*Xuncius - Politics of the Ruler*) It further affirmed the role of people in the political rule of the state.

The Spring and Autumn and the Warring States period were times when the feudal princes vied for power. The vassal states had the opportunity to seek hegemony only depending on their prosperity and military forces. Almost all men of insight became aware that the most fundamental way for the state to prosper and to strengthen their military forces hinged on 'people'. Human conditions are the key factor when weighing up favourable climatic, geographical and human conditions. Whoever won people's support would obtain state power, conversely, without it they would lose state power. In this way, like the theories of other schools, 'people-oriented' thought afforded a magnificent viewpoint in a changeable situation.

(4) The failure of 'people-oriented' thought: publicity and fall

From the period of the First Emperor of Qin, 'people-oriented' thought gradually approached the centralisation of state power. Monarchical power was strengthened but 'people-oriented' thought was weakened. It appeared when Xuncius and his disciple and Legalist Han Fei in the later Warring States period initially completed the theoretical transformation of 'people-oriented' thought. Especially, after the practice of Dong Zhongshu's idea of 'only worshiping Confucianism' in politics in the mid Western Han dynasty, 'people-oriented' thought and feudal politics were completely integrated. The advanced political concept of being 'people-oriented' was gradually reduced to being the power tactics and tool of the rulers and they lost the power to counterbalance the feudal centralisation of state power. Definitely, the evolution of 'people-oriented' thought was also highlighted then. For instance, 'people-oriented' thought was established as part of the ruling ideology of the state and partially legalised, which played a wondrous role in passing on 'people-oriented' thought in ancient times.

The tyranny of Qin, especially the burning of the books and the burying of the scholars, made the development of 'people-oriented' thought of that period almost negligible. When the passage of history reached the Han dynasty, 'people-oriented' thought revived and began to be re-integrated. As a result, only then were Confucian doctrines advocated. Since then, Confucianism has been the theme of the ideology and culture of all future dynasties. Some 'people-oriented' thoughts since the Qin and Han dynasties were not handed down as the advice of officials but as a sort of system. For instance, the notions that 'heaven was the advisor of the monarch' and 'the monarch was born to serve the people' became the main evidence of the implementation of the monarchy; that 'people paid allegiance to the state', 'the monarch showed benevolence, benefit and love to the people' and 'the monarch pacified the people and made policies for the people' became the main reasons for the monarchs to make regulations about honorific titles and posthumous titles; that 'heaven complied with the wishes of the people' and 'the mind of heaven and the aspirations of the people' became the vital reasons for the monarchical inheritance system; that 'the decrees complied with people's minds' and 'considering people's views' served as the primary reason for the system of airing views; that 'selecting officials for the people' and 'parenting the people' stood as the significant reason for the bureaucracy; that 'contributing to the people', 'influencing the people and forming moral customs' and 'serving all the people' became the predominant reasons for the state worship system….

The development of 'people-oriented' thought after Qin and the Han did not surpass the achievements in the Spring and Autumn and the Warring States period. However, the long history still shows the development path of 'people-oriented' thought coming down in one continuous line. Especially, the appearance of the imperial examination system, and honest and upright officials, seemed to be like a refreshing breeze for the practice of 'people-oriented' thought. The imperial examination system that arose in the Sui and Tang period blazed a new trail for the political development of civilians. 'Clean and honest officials' pledging for the people in the historical books of all dynasties were like a miracle upholding 'people-oriented' thought under despotism and high tension. A large number of biographies about clean and honest officials, part of historical books, novels and dramas in China, were written in praise of them. The *Record of the Grand Historian* called them 'merciless officials'. Many historical books including *History of the Han Dynasty* and *History of the Later Han Dynasty* were 'biographies of merciless officials'. There were innumerable legends about clean and honest officials in literature and folklore, for instance, Bao Zheng, Hai Rui and Yu Chengong. Bao Zheng was even revered as divine. It can be said that administration by clean and honest officials was jointly demanded by the upper-class governors and the lower-class people in feudal society. Besides, the thought of clean and honest officials had developed into a complex that permeated the innermost being of all members of society.

'People-oriented' thought after the Qin and Han period was also highlighted by the awakening of the underprivileged populace. Usually, when the monarchs lost 'people-oriented' thought, the appeal of the underprivileged populace for it became the strongest voice in society. The peasant uprisings of all dynasties shouted slogans with strong elements of 'people-oriented' thought. The peasants in the late Qin dynasty shouted: "Were powerful and noble people born into the upper class?" Similarly, in the Song dynasty, there prevailed a saying among the uprising heroes that: 'It takes turns to be the king and it's my turn next year.' Although rebellions burst out amid high tension, 'people-oriented' thought became people's pursuit. It was the historical progress of this thought.

Reviewing the failure of 'people-oriented' thought after the Qin and Han, we can find a rule: Almost all the founding fathers of the dynasties prioritised this thought; almost all the monarchs of conquered nations paid scant attention to this way of thinking. The more centralised the feudal group was, the more despotic the rulers were, and the more failure this thought would suffer. When the society was characterised by dark politics and mass impoverishment, 'people-oriented' thought turned out to be an ideological weapon for statesmen and intellectuals to denounce tyranny and advocate reform. The ups and downs of all the dynasties proved a saying in the Spring and Autumn and the Warring States period: Those who won people's hearts secured state power, those who did the opposite lost.

2. 'People-oriented' thought: A political doctrine amplifying benevolence

Traditional 'people-oriented' thought stressed the important position of people in social life and political affairs, revealed the basic law of public support and the vicissitudes of the dynasty, and advocated benevolence. In retrospect, attaching great importance to the people, loving people, benefiting people and complying with the people was a theme that always ran through China's traditional 'people-oriented' thought.

(1) Attaching great importance to the people: The people are more important than the monarch

Attaching great importance to the people is to place importance on their fundamental role in social life and political affairs. It was the theoretical basis of 'people-oriented' thought in ancient China. 'People-oriented' thought was extended and developed on this basis.

As the 'meta-theory of the ancient thought of attaching great importance to the people, the idea that 'the people are the foundation of the state' revealed that the people were the fundamental essence on which a state was founded and the pivotal cornerstone to safeguard national peace. In view of the lessons of the previous dynasty, the enlightened sovereigns of the Shang came to know people's power. Emperor Pangeng of the Shang said: "The sovereigns of previous dynasties all upheld 'people-oriented' thought." He believed that 'people-oriented' thought was a tradition handed down from the ancestors.

Evidently, the 'foundation of the country' in the mind of the ancients was not merely 'people' but also other factors including heaven (the Emperor of Heaven) and the monarchs. Nevertheless, the weight of these factors in 'people-oriented' thought changed. In the Shang dynasty, importance was laid on the people and more on the gods. In the early Zhou, the ruler reflecting on the lessons of the fall of the Shang recognised that the people were the critical strength deciding the fate of the dynasty. They combined the mandate of heaven with people's will and proposed 'worshiping heaven and protecting the people'. After moving the capital eastward to Luoyi, Emperor Ping of Zhou came to understand people's power more clearly and the position of the gods further dropped. National prosperity rested on the people rather than the so-called 'gods' because even the 'gods' stood by the people. In some good aspects, the 'gods' would act according to people's requirements. In the middle and late Spring and Autumn period, statesman Zichan of the State of Zheng further came up with the thought that 'the natural law is far away while humanity is near' (*The Commentary of Zu - The 18th Year of Duke Zhao*) and raised the curtain on the theories of pre-Qin philosophers about the relationship between humans and nature.

In the comparison between the people and the monarchs, Guan Zhong was the earliest to propose that 'the people of the State of Qi were also the foundation of the monarch', taking the people as the foundation of both the country and its monarch. He believed that 'politics prospers when it complies with people's hearts; politics fails when it goes against people's hearts'. The sentence of Lao Tzu that 'nobility is based on lowliness' interpreted the relationship between the nobility and lowliness from the philosophical dimension. 'Since ancient times, the enemies of the people have ultimately been, sooner or later, conquered by the people.' That raised the significance of attaching great importance to the people from the perspective of managing state affairs. Mencius's earthshaking utterances that 'the people are the most important, followed by the state and the monarch' directly placed more importance on the people than on the state or the monarch. Afterwards, Xuncius compared the relationship between the people and the monarch to that between water and a ship: 'The monarchs are ships; the ordinary people are water. The water can both carry the ships and overturn them.' After that, the thoughts attaching great importance to the people mostly originated from the numerous viewpoints in the pre-Qin period.

(2) Love the people: Take the common aspirations of the people as those of the monarch

If we say the rulers advocated 'attaching great importance to the people' out of affirmation and reverence for people's power which implied the 'monarch-based' political ideology and scheme, then Lao Tzu's theory of loving the people, namely, that 'the sages do not have their own will and they should take the people's will as theirs' implied 'people-oriented' thought. Loving the people was the best manifestation, or rather, a conscious thought attaching great importance to the people.

Starting from the thought that 'the benevolent love the people', Confucius required rulers to 'be thrifty, love the people, use the resources of the people in the farming season' and implement benevolent government. Mencius's idea of 'loving the people' stressed sharing happiness with the people.

Adopting the stance of ordinary people, Mo Zi hoped that the rulers could 'share the undertaking with the people' and 'toil with the people'. He further brought forward the advocacy of 'universal love'. Intellectual Tang Zhen in the early Qing dynasty worshiped the lofty ideals of Mo Zi and admonished the political rulers at that time: 'Monarchs should love the people, just like the heart loves the body.' To show their love for the people, the wise ancient monarchs did not just take the people as their own children - 'subjects like children' - but also asked all the officials to 'love the people as if they were their own children'.

Another point of loving the people was the advocacy for the monarchs to share sorrows and woes sentimentally with the people. Mencius was opposed to the rulers 'enjoying themselves alone' but advocated their 'sharing joy with the people'. Du Fu hoped that 'tens of thousands of mansions could shelter poor scholars so that they could smile with joy'. Fan Zhongyan's words about 'being worried about the concerns of the people and enjoying the joy of the people' became renowned for myriads of years. Tang Zhen in the early Qing thought highly of Emperor Yao and Emperor Shun's spirit of sharing pain together with the people and the spirit of utter devotion to the people: 'The monarchs should live in thatched cottages that are not trimmed, eat from earthenware rice bowls and drink from earthenware cups. Although they are as highly placed as emperors and rule the country, they are willing to have simple meals, wear warm but coarse clothes, promote good and do away with evil. It is no different from living in a field. They all show their sympathy for the people.'

Loving the people is a sort of feeling and the highest realm of 'people-oriented' thought. Only when the emperors love the people sincerely will they benefit the people selflessly, consciously comply with the people's will and give the people better opportunities for development. In this sense, 'people-oriented' thought is the amplification of the thought of benevolence in politics.

(3) Benefit the people: Bestow virtue on the people

So-called 'benefiting the people' is to bring benefits to the people. 'Benefiting the people' is the manifestation of 'people-oriented' thought in the economic concept. *The Book of History* reads: 'The people do not have permanent loyalty. Only benefit can win their support.' Benefiting the people is most likely to win people's hearts. It can be understood in two senses: to show affection to people and to update the people. To show affection to people, the monarchs should enable people to live a better-off life, help them settle down and acquire the fundamentals needed for living. To 'update people', efforts must be made to heighten their awareness and update their spirit and ideology. In the modern world, both the material and spiritual requirements should be satisfied.

In the Shang dynasty, 'people-oriented' thought was endowed with concrete contents, namely, 'bestowing virtue on people'. One of the reasons for Emperor Pangeng to move the capital to Yin (now Xiaotun village, Anyang city, Henan province) was to protect people from flood disasters. It progressed in the Zhou dynasty, stressing not merely 'bestowing virtue on people' but also 'admiring heaven and protecting people, namely, emphasising the protection of people's rights and interests. The rulers should perform the mandate of heaven, honour the teachings of the gods and the ancestors, protect the people of the country and become wise and virtuous monarchs. Duke Zhou further put forth the new political concept of 'protecting people'.

As to showing affection for people, *The Book of History* early on came up with such actions as 'nourishing people', 'keeping people healthy' and 'making people prosperous'. It was thought that it should be the most fundamental pursuit for the monarchs to rule the country by nourishing the people, bringing them tangible benefits and letting them live an affluent and healthy life. To 'help the people have a good harvest' and to 'protect the people' were Duke Zhou's admonition and requirements for Emperor Cheng as the new governor. 'The governor should always think about people's happiness and avoid neglecting government affairs for his private ends.' In commending the feats of Duke Wen of Jin, Emperor Ping of Zhou hoped that he could bring benefits to future generations and help them enjoy a peaceful and wealthy life. 'Rule of virtue is the best politics. Good politics makes people's lives better.'

The supreme goal of benefiting the people was to 'enrich the people' and help them live an affluent life. Confucius took 'enriching the people' as the premise of benevolent government. He thought 'even if the people live a rich life, can the monarch live an inadequate life? If the people live an inadequate life, can the monarch live an affluent life alone?" The moderately prosperous society he envisaged was a society in which people shared wealth. Mencius advocated 'giving wealth to people' so that the people could 'have enough food in bumper harvest years and survive in famine years'. Xuncius proposed that 'the upper class will become rich when the lower class becomes rich'. He was opposed to levying heavy taxes to draw people into poverty and thought 'since ancient times, poor people of lower class have all endangered the rule'. *Views of the Noblemen of All States - Views of the Noblemen of the State of Chu Vol.1* warned that 'if the people had not enough money for subsistence, would there be other ways out for the state except perishing?' Guan Zi said: "Only when the people have enough food and clothes can they consider etiquette and pay attention to honour and shame."

Afterwards, 'people-oriented' thought of all dynasties was reflected in their government policies of prospering and benefiting the people. After seizing state power, they all made compromise policies for the people, either announcing amnesty or reducing the burden of taxation and cost, returning grain plots to people and benefiting people so as to embrace social stability and enjoy an enlightened heyday.

(4) Favour people: Do not go against people's will

Those who win people's support will win state power. An important way to win people's support is to favour people. 'To favour people' was deemed by the enlightened ancient rulers as the one and only way to govern and make the state prosperous. To favour people advocated that one should not go against the will of the people, that the will of the people should be .seriously considered, and that favouring the will of the people was to comply with the mandate of heaven. Almost all the regime changes in history were launched under the banner of 'favouring the people'. The destruction of Xia by Shang was regarded as complying with the aspirations of heaven and the people; Emperor Wu of Zhou sent a punitive expedition to Emperor Zhou of Xia on the premise that 'heaven must follow the will of the people' and stressed that 'heaven can see what we see and hear what we hear'. Mencius pointed out that decision-makers should not make decisions arbitrarily but should listen to the views of the people. Huang Zongxi once uttered his famous views: "What the emperors think to be true may not be true and what the emperors think to be wrong may not necessarily be wrong. Even the emperors do not judge right or wrong by themselves. Right and wrong can be decided only in schools." Hence, the theory of 'favouring the people' was promoted to new heights.

Cherishing 'people-oriented' thought, the rulers must gain people's trust. Zigong, a disciple of Confucius, asked about politics. Confucius replied with 'enough food, enough soldiers and enough credibility'. Zigong went on to ask: "Which is to be removed if necessary?" Confucius replied: "Remove the 'soldiers'. If another one must be removed, it was 'food'." "Wouldn't people be starved if 'food' was removed?" Confucius explained: "Death has occurred to all men since ancient times but people cannot live without credibility." He took people's trust as being more important than life. Mencius further summarised the law of historical ups and downs as 'those who won people's support finally won state power'.

In the entire feudal period, the viewpoints in stark contrast with 'people-oriented' thought also included 'monarch-oriented' thought, 'official-oriented' thought and 'god-oriented' thought. An overview of history reveals such a law that the heyday of a dynasty was always the period when 'people-oriented' thought prevailed and the fall of a dynasty happened in the period when 'monarch-oriented' thought and 'official-oriented' thought dominated.

3. Integrating 'people-oriented' thought and democracy in China in the new century

The CPC absorbed a large amount of its essence from 'people-oriented' thought in ancient times and integrated it with the modern democratic spirit. The 'people' were taken as the basis of the party and the revolution, the foundation for building the country and the cornerstone for its governance. The new China was named the 'People's Republic of China'.

(1) A clear-cut stand of serving the people

In Yan'an, Mao Zedong wrote a memorial speech entitled *Serve the People* in honour of an ordinary soldier named Zhang Side. The classic article critically absorbed China's traditional 'people-oriented' thought and modern Chinese and Western democratic thought, applied the Marxist viewpoint on the masses (of people) in the specific practice of China's democratic revolution and carried forward and developed the Marxist mass viewpoint and China's traditional 'people-oriented' thought. Afterwards, 'to serve the people' became the tenet of the CPC.

The value and aim of 'people-oriented' thought in ancient China was to maintain the ruling status of the exploiting classes. In ancient society, 'the emperor represented state power', and political power, the state and the monarch were identical. Therefore, 'people-oriented' thought advocating that 'the people are the foundation of the country' and 'the monarchs will lose their throne without the people' was in essence a measure and tool of the monarchs to maintain their rule. Nevertheless, 'people-oriented' thought today aims to seek and stimulate development to realise people's fundamental rights and interests, to constantly satisfy their increasing material and cultural demands, to practically guarantee people's economic, political and cultural rights and interests, and to bring the achievements of development to all the people. That is to say, people are both the measures and the ultimate purpose of social development. People's overall development should be realised. To fulfill the goal is the ultimate purpose and ultimate mission of the power executors.

(2) Serve the people as public servants

Traditional 'people-oriented' thought stressed granting favours to people. It was tantamount to giving alms to people in the capacity of a saviour. Modern 'people-oriented' thought emphasises that all the power of the power executors is endowed by the people and they have been selected to serve the people. Therefore, they must serve the people unconditionally. There is a famous saying from Deng Xiaoping: "Leaders are public servants."

According to the positioning that 'leaders are public servants', the function of leaders should be to 'serve the people' as public servants. 'Public servants' are 'the servants of the public'. Such a positioning indicates that the leaders do not stand high above the people but on an equal footing with the people. The function of 'public servants' tells us that the power endowed by the people can be used only to serve and benefit the people. The power of the leaders is only the responsibility and obligation of public servants rather than the precondition to ask people for personal gain.

Xi Jinping read a couplet to district county party committee secretaries at a workshop in Heze, Shandong province. The second line of the couplet reads: 'The clothes were given by the people. The food was given by the people. Don't bully the people, because you are also ordinary people.' The couplet was written more than 330 years ago, namely, in the 19th year of the reign of Emperor Kangxi by Gao Yiyong, magistrate of Neixiang county, Henan, China. In modern society where 'people-oriented' thought is vigorously advocated, Xi Jinping read the couplet that 'you are also ordinary people' not to lecture and educate others but also to include oneself among them. If the magistrate of each village, county, city and province can consciously regard 'themselves as ordinary people', all the policies and administration will start from the practical interests and experiences of the people. There would not be any fear for a good cadre-people relationship and no problem amid reform and development would be left unsolved.

It is not just lip service to place leaders in the position of the 'public servants' of people. They must bear in mind the consciousness of public servants. If every leader could have had that consciousness, they would not have turned a deaf ear to people's appeals, neglected people's sufferings and damaged people's interests, for instance, by 'barbarous demolition' and 'land acquisition by force'.

Since leaders are public servants, CPC members, especially the leaders of every rank, must practice the mission and tenet of service, strive to enhance service quality and consciously implement 'four prevents' in 'service': The first is to prevent 'flippancy', that is to say, to prevent a flippant work style that does not go deep into the realities of life or among the people; the second is to prevent 'oversimplification and crudeness', that is to say, to prevent an oversimplified and crude working style, acting arbitrarily or acting as a tyrant, or bullying and oppressing people; the third is to prevent 'arrogance', that is to say, to prevent conceit and complacency, putting on airs and graces and looking down on people; the fourth is to prevent 'shirking', that is to say, to prevent hankering for a life of ease and comfort, and unwillingness to work in harsh environments, to address complicated conflicts or to struggle arduously together with the people.

(3) Manage affairs for the people and let them be their own masters

'Officials who fail to manage people's affairs would be better off resigning and selling sweet potatoes.' The words of the ballad vividly interpret 'people oriented' thought in ancient times. Amid the promotion of modern democracy, many people think that interpretation is out of date. They believe that true democracy is to let people be their own masters. As a matter of fact, the people share many rights which cannot be exercised independently as individual subjects. For instance, the maintenance of state sovereignty, social peace and the natural environment; none of these things can be undertaken by one or two individuals or groups. 'Representatives' have to be selected by people to safeguard these rights.

A characteristic of the marriage of modern democracy and traditional 'people-oriented' thought is that it does not negate the advocacy for 'managing people's affairs' in traditional 'people-oriented' thought and stresses 'letting people be their own masters'. To achieve this end, 'managing people's affairs' and 'letting people be their own masters' should be strictly demarcated. The party and the government should manage the affairs that are beyond the ability of the people to manage, and should give people a free hand to handle the affairs within their power. For instance, the promotion of democracy at the grassroots level since the reform and opening up was an example of management of grassroots affairs by the people themselves.

The reform and opening up promoted since the third plenary session of the 11th central committee of the CPC was in a sense to return power to the people. That is to say, it returned the initiative for social reform and development to the people through the reform and opening up so that the people could become self-reliant and independent masters of society. From the earliest rural land joint contract to the present land transfer, the peasants have become the real land owners. The establishment of the socialist market economic mechanism was to tap the fullest potential of everyone and offer everyone the greatest room for free activities. It helped people independently strive for their social benefit.

It should be pointed out that there is a misunderstanding about the judgment of democracy in modern times: Some believe that the reason for the high degree of democracy in Western countries is due to their mass elections'. As a matter of fact, the general elections in some Western countries are often realised through 'a race of money', that is to say, the campaign funds raised by cliques (party groupings) represented by the campaigners. And the providers of campaign funds are the wealthy. Moreover, the leaders who win the general election may not necessarily do good deeds or achieve what the voters wish. Wasn't Hitler elected by general election? In real life, there are many cases where presidents were ousted from power soon after being elected. Can such democracy be said to be advanced and modern democracy? Actually, the judgment of the degree of a modern country's democracy should not be made on how the leaders in charge of public affairs are elected but, more importantly, on who the elected leaders speak for, handle affairs for and stand for.

(4) Whether rulers love the people or not can be measured by the level of popular support

'The ordinary people serve as the steelyard measuring the right and wrong between heaven and earth.' People can most clearly see and most sensibly judge whether the practice of the party and the government complies with people's will or represents people's interests or not. That is because people's evaluation most conforms to objective standards. For this reason, what the party and government is doing or is going to do should be checked and evaluated by the people. What the people embrace, favour and are happy with should be done with indomitable will and without hesitation. Conversely, anything the people are against should not be done at all.

To have the people act as the judges is not to have them judge the actions of the party and the government on a certain issue in a certain period of time. It is aimed at mastering people's microscopic evaluation on a certain issue or a certain governing behaviour and pays special attention to their macroscopic evaluation on the party and the government. The issues embraced and approved by the people should be done perfectly well by the party and the government. Otherwise, the people will ultimately not be happy about it. Our advocacy to build the party for the interests of the vast majority of people and to hold power for the people does not represent people's interests just in word. Only when the party and the government do good for, and bring benefit to, the people in a down-to-earth manner can they become the advanced representatives approved by the people, can they attract people's trust around the leading group of the CPC central committee, and can the ruling status of the party in the new century be further cemented.

Chapter 3

Honesty - The Foundation of the Chinese People

Confucius said: "A man cannot succeed without honesty." He ranked honesty in the first place of governance, which indicated its greatest importance in ancient times. In fact, honesty has always been the unfading topic of Chinese culture. It is also deeply rooted in Chinese culture and the innermost being of every Chinese. It is the foundation for our survival and development, the basis of accomplishments and the moral standard maintaining social harmony.

1. Honesty is the bond that unites people and holds them together

The word 'honesty' was first proposed by Guan Zhong. *Guan Zi - Shu Yan* records: How to consider 'honesty' as a strategy for state governance has been widely discussed. Definitely, as to who first invented the word 'honesty', some regard that it was the *Record of the Events of the Zhou Dynasty* rather than *Guan Zi* that used 'sincerity' and 'faithfulness' (jointly meaning 'honesty') together. It is because of the *Record of the Events of the Zhou Dynasty*, that 'sincerity' and 'faithfulness' were used together several times. For instance, 'the people do not have to repay even in bumper harvest years; help the people with sincerity and honesty to get rich' and 'there should be filial piety of children for their parents, friendship between brothers, loyalty of ministers and officials to the monarch and faithfulness between townspeople.' Here, 'faithfulness' and 'sincerity' actually mean 'honesty'.

(1) Consistence of sincerity and faithfulness

Before 'sincerity' and 'faithfulness' were used together, the two words of similar meaning were two independent concepts. The word 'sincerity' first appeared in *The Book of History*: 'Ghosts and gods cannot enjoy sacrificial offerings but the worship of devout disciples.' Here, 'sincerity' shows the devout attitude to ghosts and gods - earnest belief. However, 'sincerity' as a 'virtuous' concept first appeared in *The Book of Changes*: 'To be irreconcilable with evil, to keep sincere and to refine language to establish truth.' Here, sincerity refers to the virtue of being true rather than presumptuous and being antagonistic to evil. In *The Book of Changes*, 'faithfulness' also appears several times. For instance, *The Book of Changes - The System of Hexagrams Vol.1* records: 'What can help people? Faithfulness.' It means that it is faithfulness that offers people help.

The Book of Rites - The Doctrine of the Mean reads: 'Sincerity is self-improvement.' It means 'real'. Zhu Xi, one of the representatives of neo-Confucianism, in footnoting the chapter on 'sincerity (sincere intention)' in *Great Learning*, pointed out that: 'Sincerity is earnest; intention comes from the bottom of the heart.' It means that only with sincerity can a person match their words to their deeds, start from kindness and end up with kindness. He explained 'sincerity is a great universal truth and pursuing sincerity is a fundamental principle of conduct' in *The Doctrine of the Mean* and *Mencius*, and that 'sincerity' means keeping it real without being presumptuous or false, and it is the naturalness of heaven and the motive power of natural movements and changes in heaven; 'consciousness of sincerity' or 'being sincere' are certainly humane. That is to say, people, through their moral cultivation of self-discipline, achieve 'sincerity' from heaven and upgrade to the moral realm featuring fairness, selflessness and keeping it real without being presumptuous, false or a cheat. It is the principle and obligation of being a person. In short, 'consciousness of sincerity' and 'being sincere' constitute the practical acts of people pursuing 'sincerity'.

As to faithfulness, the ancients also had many explanations. Confucius and Mencius took 'faithfulness' as the foundation of conduct and one of the five cardinal relationships.[1] *Mencius* reads: 'Those who are kind are faithful.' *The Doctrine of Mo Zi* says: 'Faithfulness means the words accord with the intention.' *The Study of Confucian Classics at White Tiger Temple - Nature* proclaims: 'Faithfulness is sincerity and single-mindedness.' *Views of the Noblemen of All States - Views of the Noblemen of Jin* says: 'To act

---

[1] The five relationships in feudal China refer to the ethical relationships between the monarch and the ministers, between father and son, between brothers, between couples and between friends.

according to one's character is faithfulness.' *Collection of Jia Yi's Works on Taoism* reads: 'To honour one's word is faithfulness.' *The Book of Rites - Interpretation of the Classics* says: 'If people attain their wishes within reason, it is faithfulness.' Faithfulness is shown in trustworthiness, in character and morals, adherence to moral etiquette and honouring commitment.

Since both sincerity and faithfulness mean 'honesty' and share literal implications, they are often used to explain each other. In *Word and Expression*, Xu Shen said: 'Sincerity is faithfulness.' 'Faithfulness is sincerity.' Their basic connotation is honesty, no cheating, honouring commitment, conformity of words with deeds and truthfulness both within and without. However, strictly speaking, the difference between the two words is just like two sides of a gold coin: the one side is internally genuine and the other is overtly genuine. However, the ancients' explanation of sincerity and faithfulness shows that, although they share a similar meaning, they are 'differentiated'. In the general sense, 'sincerity' means honesty, mainly referring to the inherent moral quality of the subject; 'faithfulness' means credit and trustworthiness, primarily implying the externalisation of the inherent 'sincerity' and the trust of others. 'Sincerity' is the intrinsic and inherent truth and 'faithfulness' is the externally manifested truth. 'To be sincere' as Mencius said, is to apply the intrinsic truth in practice - shown externally. It is the principle and law for people to emulate the laws of nature and to pursue sincerity. In a word, 'sincerity' is 'sincere at heart' and 'faithfulness' is 'to be externally faithful to others'. Sincerity comes from the inside and faithfulness refers to something outside. The combination of 'sincerity' and 'faithfulness' comprises a phrase with an internally and externally rich connotation. 'Sincerity' and 'faithfulness' used together contain both their respective meanings and their extended connotation, which fully reflect the ancient philosophical theory that 'man is an integral part of nature'.

(2) Cultivation of oneself and others rests in honesty

In traditional Confucianism, honesty was regarded as an important prerequisite and the ethical focus to abide by in order to seek self-cultivation, handle family and state affairs well, and unite the world. It is the essence of morality and the source of behaviour. Nevertheless, the origin of 'sincerity' is man himself. Wanting to be sincere, people should uphold sincerity and earnestness, further develop their sincerity and achieve internal and external consistency through 'consciousness of sincerity'. To develop inherent 'sincerity' in terms of their conduct, people should 'indulge in self-reflection three times a day - whether they give their advice and suggestions loyally, whether they get along or cooperate with their friends faithfully and whether they often review what their teacher has taught them'. With respect to what they say and do, 'gentlemen will lose dignity without seriousness; learning can relieve people of ignorance; loyalty and faithfulness should be cherished'; as to managing state affairs, it is required to 'be devoted to work, be thrifty, love the people, and use the resources of the people in the farming season'...Therefore, *The Doctrine of the Mean* stresses: 'Sincerity is the beginning and end of everything. Without sincerity, a man can accomplish nothing.' It means that everything depends on 'sincerity' and loses its value without 'sincerity'.

Many chapters of Lao Tzu's *Tao De Jing (Book of Changes)* talk about honesty. For instance, 'I believe both sincere and insincere people; it is my virtue', 'sincere words may not sound pleasant to the ears and good words pleasant to the ears may not necessarily be sincere' and 'is making accommodation for the sake of overall interests as described by the ancients empty talk without any reason? We should sincerely and completely follow and accept the teachings of these forthright admonitions on the philosophy of life'... Deeming sincerity and faithfulness as the moral state that should be pursued in life is the basis for displaying indispensable morality. Honesty is also an important concept in the works of Chuang Tzu, another prestigious figure of Taoism. In his *Chuang Tzu - The Secular World*, he stressed 'men of lofty morality are worthy of trust'. In his *Chuang Tzu - Fisherman*, he emphasised: 'Truth results from absolute sincerity. Without truth or sincerity, men cannot arouse others' feelings.' In his *Chuang Tzu - Xu Wugui*, he said people should 'foster sincerity to comply with nature rather than disturb its law.' In Chuang *Tzu - Gengsang Chu*, he stressed that 'sincerity can smash gold'. Chuang Tzu took 'the real look' as the utmost sincerity and held the view that without sincerity people would not be touched. The view elevated honesty to a new realm.

Guan Zhong also 'cherished honesty'. The role of 'honesty' is frequently talked about in *Guan Zi*. He emphasised that 'those who are not real businessmen should not do business; those who are not real craftsmen should not work in that capacity; those who are not real peasants should not do farm work; scholars unworthy of their names or titles should not work as officials in the court'. (*Guan Zi - Economic Plan*) 'Insincere administrators should not be appointed as high-ranking officials.' (*Guan Zi - On Rights*)

'People of sincerity and faithfulness can obtain good reputations.' (*Guan Zi - Explanation of the Situation*) 'The sages are all sincere and faithful and should be treated with benevolence.' (*Guan Zi - On The Situation*) 'To be sincere, faithful and benevolent'. He translated the concept of honesty into policy measures and official management strategies as well as economic measures. He thought that scholars, peasants, workers and businessmen in society would not be equal to their social roles without honesty. He even stressed that the honest in society should become rich first. Afterwards, such cultural sages as Yan Ying, Sun Wu, Sun Bin, Mencius and Xuncius followed this principle and developed honesty as a tradition in the State of Qi. The people of Qi had many statements and much practice on honesty. Especially, Han Feizi absorbed the concept of honesty of the Legalists in the early stage and advocated honesty. He believed that 'honest monarchs and states do not cheat their people' and that the image of monarchs as sincere and faithful should be established on the basis of 'rewarding esteem and faithfulness'.

In the Spring and Autumn and the Warring States period, the Mohist school stood alongside the Confucian school as an equally 'famous school'. Two statements of Mo Zi were quite famous, namely, 'people without strong ambitions will not be smart and those without honesty will accomplish nothing.' The first sentence stressed that people without strong ambitions would not give full play to their wisdom and the second emphasised that aspirations would not be realised without honesty - they attached more importance to the practice of honesty.

In brief, the ancient sages extolled honesty as a lofty virtue, which fully demonstrated the value and position of honesty in the mind of the Chinese people.

(3) Loyalty, courage and utmost honesty

The elucidation of the concept of honesty by neo-Confucianism in the Song and Ming dynasties was originally because it bracketed 'faithfulness' together with loyalty, sincerity and righteousness, and was deemed to be the philosophy of life. 'Loyalty and sincerity', 'fidelity' and 'faithfulness' began to be frequently applied in practice. Zhu Xi said: "The principle of conducting oneself is to be loyal and faithful… Without loyalty or faithfulness, life is like a tree without roots and water without a source. Even worse, nothing is left." Actually, the original meaning of faithfulness is to honour promises, show the inner truth to others and stress sincerity and trustworthiness between people. Nevertheless, loyalty, sincerity and faithfulness, linked together, have become a lofty, great spirit and the supreme realm of honesty pursued by the Chinese people. The *Record of the Grand Historian* comments on Qu Yuan 'dedicating his loyalty and wisdom'. Future generations eulogised Yue Fei for his 'dedication and loyalty to pay back his homeland'. There are also many proverbs and maxims relating to 'loyalty', for instance, 'be loyal and faithful', 'exceedingly faithful', 'unswervingly loyal', 'a person of supreme sincerity and nobility', 'die the cruelest death', 'absolute loyalty and deep patriotism' and 'loyal through the sun and the moon (utmost loyalty)'. They constitute the grand and magnificent culture of honesty of the Chinese nation.

Loyalty refers to the sincerity in contacts between particular people and issues. Trying one's best to help others is called 'loyalty'. Confucius took loyalty as the condition for implementing 'benevolence', namely, the highest moral principle. Mencius also deemed 'loyalty' as an important moral norm. Similarly, 'loyalty' is 'sincerity' to the external elements. But the objects of 'honesty' are all materials and people. However, the object of 'loyalty' is the wholehearted trust, particularly in materials and people, and the great spirit a person is willing to safeguard even at the cost of their life. Therefore, loyalty is also called 'lofty ambition', 'utmost mission' and 'strongest political integrity'. A Peking Opera called *Chinese Orphan* relates that: In the Spring and Autumn and Warring States period, General Tu Anjia of Duke Ling of Jin, due to conflicts with loyal official Zhao Dun and the jealousy of Zhao Shuo, the son of Zhao Dun and the emperor's son-in-law, astonishingly killed 300 family members of Zhao Dun, leaving only an orphan to be rescued by Cheng Ying. Tu Anjia ordered all infants from one to six months old all over the state to be killed to eradicate hidden dangers. Cheng Ying and senior official Gongsun Chujiu 'substituted the fake for the genuine' and successfully retained the last bloodline of the Zhao family at the cost of the sons of Gongsun Chujiu and Cheng Ying. Twenty years later, the orphan named Zhao Wu grew up. Cheng Ying drew a picture to tell him about the hatred of his family and the state. Zhao Wu finally got his revenge. As early as the Warring States period, Mencius once said: "Life is what I want; righteousness is also what I want. But they cannot be obtained simultaneously. Then I will choose righteousness at the expense of life." Loyalty is a responsibility that drives every loyalist to make selfless contributions.

Loyalty is a kind of power. The Chinese people not merely treat loyalty as a character trait but also as a moral competence and as the chief and core of all competences. Loyalty is the critical joint closely linking the state and the people. The state is the core and the people are the foundation. The state is responsible for the people, specifically shown in keeping honest and safeguarding people's interests. In that way the state can obtain cohesion and centripetal force. The people are loyal to the state, concretely reflected in their patriotic and collective spirit and their conscious protection of the national and social interests. No organisation is willing to employ a disloyal person. However talented they are, they will be discarded by society, for instance, traitors to China. A loyal person has belief and great virtue. Their deeds can live up to the expectations of both the state and the ordinary people.

2. Honesty: The timeless practice of the Chinese people

As a Western intellectual once commented, traditional Chinese culture is distinctively characterised by stress on 'pragmatism' from whatever theoretical perspective. In the words of the Chinese people, it is 'humanistic pragmatism'. That is to say, it is like 'writing articles for the need of the times'. As to honesty, the ancient Chinese did not merely rest on its theory, but more on its practical application.

(1) Conduct oneself in society based on honesty and honouring commitments

The ancient Chinese cherished honesty. The first point of emphasis was to practice what one preached and take resolute action. *Chuang Tzu - A Robber Called Zhi* tells a story: A man named Wei Sheng and a girl agreed to meet under a bridge. But the girl did not come. The surging river inundated the bridge. But Wei Sheng still held onto the bridge girder, continued waiting and drowned. The story was widely read by later generations. In his poem *The Trader's Wife*, Li Bai of the Tang wrote: 'If you are as faithful as Wei Sheng holding the bridge girder, I will not climb to the Frowning Cliff to mourn you.'

The ancients firmly knew the dialectics of honesty. Sometimes, honesty seemed to be fulfilled at the cost of one's own interests. However, the honest ones would gain more. Ji Bu in the Han dynasty overcame death thanks to his honesty. The *Record of the Grand Historian* comments: 'The acquisition of 100 *jin* (catties) of gold is not as good as acquiring Ji Bu's promise.' When the Chu and Han fought against each other, Ji Bu offered advice to Xiang Yu who defeated Liu Bang thanks to the advice. Liu Bang, after becoming the emperor, still bore a grudge about it and ordered Ji Bu's arrest. Many people clandestinely helped him. Soon afterwards, Ji Bu disguised himself and worked as a hired labourer with the Zhu family in Shandong. The Zhu family took him on knowingly and went to Ruyin Duke Xiahou Ying to plead for mercy for Ji Bu. As persuaded by Xiahou Ying, Liu Bang repealed the order for Ji Bu's arrest, appointed him to be *langzhong*, a high-ranking official position of the Han, and soon reappointed him as chief of Hedong prefecture.

Governance by *Civilisation* records a story of death due to dishonesty. In the story, the boat of a businessman in Jiyang sank and he cried for help. A fisherman rushed to save him after hearing his cry for help. The businessman promised to give him 5kg of gold. After he was rescued, he only gave the fisherman 0.5kg of gold. The fisherman had no alternative but to leave disconsolately. Unexpectedly, the wealthy man was shipwrecked again at the same site. Another man wanted to save him. But the fisherman once cheated by the businessman told him that: "He is the one who breaks his promises!" At last, the businessman drowned. If a person goes back on his word, he will not be trusted by increasingly more people. When he loses everyone's trust, he cannot move a single step.

It was accidental that the businessman encountered the same fisherman when his boat sank twice. But his tragic end was no surprise. Ancient China was an acquaintance society. The influence of honesty was quite obvious. If a person was dishonest, they would lose others' trust. Once they were in trouble, no one was willing to save them and they had no alternative but to await their doom. Conversely, if a person kept to their promises, more and more people would respect, trust, help and follow them of their own accord.

(2) Honest management of family affairs and the paramount value of family harmony

In a family, honesty is the basic guarantee of harmony. Wei Zheng, a minister of the Tang, said: "A husband and wife must be sincerely affectionate to each other. Otherwise, they will be separated." As long as the couple, father and son, and brothers treat each other with sincerity, loyalty and faithfulness, they can get along harmoniously. If family members lack loyalty and sincerity to each other, the family will fall apart one day. Therefore, Sima Guang of the Song dynasty said: "Good governors do not bully their subjects; good managers of family affairs do not bully their kin."

As to family education, people take delight in talking about the story of Zeng Zi killing his pig. Zeng Zi was a disciple of Confucius. Once, Zeng Zi's wife wanted to go shopping. Their son cried to follow her. His wife coaxed him: "Wait at home for me and I'll kill the pig and cook it for you." Their son believed her and stopped crying. When his wife returned from the market, she saw Zeng Zi ready to kill the pig. She hurried to stop him and said she had simply coaxed their son. Zeng Zi responded seriously: "How can we cheat a child?" He really killed the pig. Zeng Zi taught his son by his own example and was praised by future generations.

The best manifestations of honesty in managing family affairs are filial piety and fraternal duty. Confucius attached high importance to filial piety and fraternal duty. He deemed them to be the foundation of self-conduct and learning in the world. He taught his own disciples: 'People should be dutiful to their parents at home and respect their elder brothers outside. They should talk and behave discreetly, keep to their word, establish wide and new contacts, and be on good terms with virtuous people. With additional capacity, they can learn all sorts of knowledge.' His disciples understood it: 'People can do their utmost to serve their parents; they can devote themselves to serving the emperor; they can get along faithfully with their friends and honour their words. Although such sages modestly say they have not read many books, I still believe they are knowledgeable.' In truth, filial piety and fraternal duty reflect 'faithfulness' and 'sincerity'.

(3) Start business with honesty and take it as the source of abundant wealth

In ancient China, the commodity economy was not advanced. However, the highest-ranked occupation 'went to business' in ancient China. It was Fan Li of the State of Yue in the Spring and Autumn period. After helping King Gou Jian of Yue win overlord status, he retired and did business in the alias of Tao Zhugong together with Xi Shi. Thanks to his proficiency in business operation, he soon became a tycoon. The *Record of the Grand Historian - Social Economy Commentary Section* records: 'To buy and sell there are good opportunities to make a profit of 10%. Soon afterwards, his properties amounted to a huge number.' One secret of Fan Li's success was his persistence in fair transactions.

'Honesty' is a traditional virtue of Chinese businessmen. People stress honesty in commodity transactions. Sima Guang of the Northern Song lived a less affluent life in his later years. He asked his steward to sell a tall horse at the market. The horse was good-looking but had lung disease. Sima Guang told his steward: "The horse's lung disease will recur in summer. You must tell the buyer about it." The steward smiled and told the buyer about it when the buyer examined the horse. But the buyer knew it was the horse Sima Guang once rode, did not counter offer and agreed to pay the asking price for the horse. After returning to the mansion, the steward reported the transaction excitedly to Sima Guang. Sima Guang felt that 50 strings of copper coins was too expensive for a sick horse. He asked the steward to tell the buyer clearly and changed the negotiated price to 30 strings of cash the next day. He told the steward: "It is not important how much money a horse is sold for. But it is a big deal if a person tells lies and gets defamed. We must conduct ourselves sincerely. Otherwise, we will lose more." On that, the steward felt ashamed and truthfully told the buyer that the horse had a disease. He also told him Sima Guang specially warned him not to fool the buyer and get into trouble. Everyone who knew about it at the market eulogised Sima Guang's honesty.

In the Ming and Qing dynasties, China's commodity economy developed step by step. The stronger businessmen flourished mostly because of their honesty with old and young customers alike. Some have discussed why the businessmen of the ancient Jin were able to prosper. Their secret was honesty and attaching more priority to 'reputation' than to 'profit'. Qiao Zhiyong was most noted among the businessmen of Jin. His time-honoured 'Da Shun Chang' Shanxi mature vinegar workshop in Baotou was trusted by customers. He heard someone say: "The quality of the mature vinegar produced by the Qiao family is far worse than in the past." He found out the reason, punished the swindlers, exchanged the poor quality product and doubled the indemnity for customers. His actions won the customers' trust, warned his peers of their misdemeanours, taught his clerks in his stores how to conduct themselves and do business, and restored the reputation of the time-honoured brand of 'Da Shun Chang'. He fulfilled his 'multiple purposes' at one stroke.

(4) Honest governance and happy people living in a peaceful country

Honesty is the foundation of a country. The people are the subjects of the country and the sovereignty of a country belongs to all its people. Since ancient times, China has been taught that 'the people are the foundation of a state and the state serves the people' and 'the monarchs who win people's support will have state power and those who lose people's support will lose state power'. These statements are still famous and applicable today. What is the basis for state leaders to unite the people? They depend on their wise policy and spiritual beliefs. 'Honesty' is the cultural spirit and moral conviction to win people's trust and unite people. Among enough food, enough military forces and people's trust, Confucius would rather have lost military forces and food to maintain people's trust. Just as Wang Anshi said: "Since the ancient times, faithfulness and sincerity have been the driving forces for the people and one sincere statement is heavier than gold."

In the Warring States period, Shang Yang of the State of Qin was keenly aware of the essential truth that rulers should win people's trust. In promoting the State of Qin to unite the seven states in those years, Shang Yang implemented a series of reforms. To have the people believe the reform was real, Shang Yang took an unexpected action beforehand. He ordered the erection of a piece of 10-metre-long wood outside the southern gate of Qin and promised in public: Whoever can move the wood to the northern gate will be rewarded with 10 pieces of gold. People did not believe in pennies from heaven. None of the numerous bystanders tried to move it. Afterwards, Shang Yang raised the money reward to 50 pieces of gold. The generous reward roused one person to heroism. A man had a go at carrying the wood to the northern gate. Shang Yang immediately paid him the reward. Shang Yang's action let others know that he was a man of his word. After that, the new law promulgated by Shang Yang won people's trust and was rapidly promoted in the State of Qin. It fueled Qin's growing prosperity day by day until it finally reunified China.

In the place where Shang Yang 'erected the wood to show his trustworthiness', an ironically famous farce of 'crying wolf' occurred 400 years ago. It is historically recorded that, in the reign of Emperor You of Zhou, Bao Si became the favorite princess consort. She was a cool beauty. Emperor You wanted to make her laugh and followed the bad idea of a courtier to light the beacon fires on more than 20 beacon towers near the capital for Bao Si to appreciate. Beacon fires were used to give border alarms in ancient China and could only be lit to summon the feudal princes to the rescue when enemies invaded. As a consequence, the feudal princes saw the beacon fires, led their soldiers there in a hurry and left in indignation after realising that the fires had been lit by the king only for the amusement of the queen. When Bao Si saw the awe-inspiring feudal princes beside themselves with anger at that time she finally smiled. Five years later, the Xirong people launched massive attacks on Zhou. Emperor You lit the beacon fires again. But no feudal princes came to help - no one was willing to be cheated again. As a result, Emperor You was forced to cut his throat and Bao Si was captured.

The first story was about 'erecting wood for trustworthiness' and that a promise must be kept; the second related the game of 'crying wolf'. Consequently, the reform of the former succeeded and the national strength was heightened; the latter resulted in disgrace, suicide and the collapse of the state. It thus can be seen that 'honesty' plays a decisive role in the rise and fall of a country.

3. Modern trends of thought on honesty

As the quintessence of traditional Chinese culture, honesty is more valued in modern China. The call for honesty can be heard everywhere.

(1) Lack of honesty is the concern of the times

Honesty is a fine character trait of the Chinese nation. However, in modern society, honesty has become a scarce resource. An honesty crisis hangs over the head of the whole society like the sword of Damocles. Despite fast-track economic growth, people's worries about lack of honesty increase every day. Even whether to support the fallen aged or not has aroused hot social debate. The exclamations about an 'honesty crisis' and 'lack of honesty' are pervasive throughout society.

It is a common occurrence that forged and fake commodities and swindling pervade the market. On the one hand, deceptive advertising is dazzling; on the other hand, the making and selling of fakes has emerged endlessly. 'Problematic food' infringes on the legitimate rights and interests of consumers and even threatens their lives. In commodity circulation, swindling has become the 'magic key' for some people to get rich. Dishonesty and fraud in the stock market has made stocks the carrier and focus point of funding risks. And swindling by means of contracts has become the poison of the market economy. What's more, there are also debt chains between enterprises, default and repudiation of debt between operators, tax evasion, smuggling and foreign exchange fraud in the market. In the securities market, all sorts of counterfeit situations often arise. Financial fraud through cooking the books, inflating profits, concealment of major events and forging bank statements are shocking sights to behold. Morevoer, some intermediaries whose job it is to safeguard market fairness and justice, such as those in the domains of accounting, auditing, assessment, supervision and service consultancies, in addition to their low service quality, often violate their professional ethics of being independent, fair and honest. These phenomena have seriously disturbed the normal development of the market economy.

When a crisis of market confidence occurs, that also leads to a decline in government credibility. Some cadres neglect ideological and moral cultivation and practice. Many problems are waiting to be settled in terms of ideological style, work style, leadership style, lifestyle and learning style. For example, some people overtly agree with but covertly oppose the ideals and convictions, and the lines, guidance and policies of the party; their words do not conform to their deeds; they act differently in public and in private, to one's face and behind one's back, with superiors and inferiors, and with others and themselves; they practice fraud in their ages, credentials, diplomas, professional titles, experience, models, auditing, assessment and commitment, deceiving their superiors, deluding their subordinates and pursuing fame and profit; they massage their 'work performance' regardless of the interests of the people, at the cost of resources and through freeloading; they work for appearance's sake and formalism neglecting the actual results, follow the trend and even 'go through the motions carefully'.

Moreover, in cultural and academic circles where lack of honesty is bitterly despised, some men of letters who praise themselves 'for their honesty amid dishonesty' have also been plagued by academic corruption. A professor of law once said that academic corruption has spread to most academic fields and that scholars of almost all Chinese universities and colleges have been involved in academic cheating or corruption including thesis corruption and fabrication of academic credentials, patents for invention and overseas entrepreneurial experience… However, people do not despise such cheating behaviour but most of the time condone it instead, which has indirectly fueled academic cheating.

(2) Return of honesty a call of the times

Compared with the ancients, modern people have more of a need to be honest. After entering modern society, everyone becomes a genuine 'social being'. In the past, a peasant tilling land could settle most of the materials needed for production and living without participating in market exchange. But now, a peasant going in for farming cannot till the land without a supply of production materials from the outside world. Seeds, pesticides and fertilisers… are all purchased externally. Even peasant households planting rice and corn themselves buy processed grain from stores. Amid increasingly frequent interpersonal contact, the issue of honesty involves all the aspects of people's production, living and even survival and has become the most important factor influencing the quality of people's production and life.

Modern society is in the era of the market economy. Honesty is the lifeline of the market economy. A market economy is subject to good reputation, honesty is its brand, money and capital. It is the magic weapon to win in competition. In the market, 'centuries-old stores' and big and powerful modern enterprises attach much importance to their corporate image and prestige. They are keenly aware of the fact that image and prestige come from honesty, as do their corporate profits and development. With a good reputation, their products can be sold at higher prices and achieve a bigger market share. Modern people are willing to spend more on buying genuine products; with a good reputation, enterprises can borrow or lend money for their operation. Banks will not be afraid that their loan will turn bad or turn into dead loans; with a good reputation, even small enterprises can compete with large ones and even compete against international financial groups. Without honesty, however strong an enterprise is, it will be finally weeded out from the market. It can be said that the market can best experience the pain of a crisis of honesty and is most eager for honesty.

Since ancient times, China has been taught that 'the people are the foundation of a state and the state serves the people' and 'the monarchs who gain people's support will have state power and those who lose people's support will lose state power'. These statements are still famous and applicable today. If a state is dishonest to its people, it will inevitably lose the people's support; only when it is honest with people can it establish its own prestige. Xuncius also held the view that the state would grow stronger if its government decree won the trust of people and weaker if not. For this reason, when governing a country or running for a position as a government official, one should establish faithfulness and morality as the objective and roots. To a state and a government, 'honesty and trustworthiness' reflect the 'national character and morals'; domestically, it is a focal prop for the people to support and be in favour of the government; internationally, it is a symbol of statehood and national dignity. It is a vital strength for a country to stand among the nations of the world with self-reliance. It is also a mark of good 'international image' and 'international reputation'.

(3) Build an honest society with joint efforts

Despite the present worrisome situation of lack of credibility and a crisis of honesty, it should be noticed that social honesty is not going from bad to worse. Some shining points of honesty always appear everywhere and illuminate the path toward building honesty. The 'politics' section of *xinhuanet.com* once published a series of 'stories on the honesty of grassroots people', including 'an honest porter' who took pains to find the owner of goods worth Rmb10,000 and returned the goods to the owner; 'an honest father in his 80s' who repaid debts for his sons; 'an honest salesman' who refused to take away other people's possessions, even if they amounted to Rmb5 million'… These stories tell us that China's honesty construction is moving in a good direction. Definitely, to really restore honesty, efforts should be made in the following four aspects:

First, efforts should be made to promote positive energy and foster honest citizens. The CPC central committee issued a *Civic Virtues Construction Programme* and clearly proposed 'honesty' as the basic norm of civic virtue. This proposal carried forward traditional Chinese virtue and complied with the trend of development of the times. The report of the 18th National Congress of the CPC included 'honesty' in the socialist core values and advocated it as one of the important values and principles identified by modern Chinese. It is necessary to complete an honesty education promotion system, enhance everyone's consciousness of honesty, establish a social and cultural environment of honesty and trustworthiness, carry out effective honesty and morality cultivation and education, ingrain honesty in the mind of each citizen and finally internalise it as part of their basic character.

Second, endeavours must be made to build market integrity. Based on learning from and absorbing the scientific and successful experiences of mature market economies, explorations should be launched into building a credit system that conforms to China's realities. Primarily, before a major credit system for the whole society is established, a market economy credit system should be built. The key point is to build a unified market social creditworthiness reporting system. Secondly, 'honest enterprises', 'honest companies' and 'honest areas' selection activities should be held frequently to motivate the main market players to consciously pursue honest operations and to optimise the market environment. Thirdly, dishonest market behaviour should be more severely punished. Many countries have stipulated that companies and individuals with poor credit records will be restricted in applying for loans and employment. Fourthly, based on improving the corresponding market management system, construction of honesty and faithfulness should be brought into the legal orbit. Fifthly, it is necessary to take supervision over honesty as the foothold and establish a credit regulator. On the one hand, the aim of this is to inspect and supervise the credit information of individuals and companies and, on the other, to accept reporting on and investigation into credit violations in a bid to inspect and punish whoever and whatever violates honesty, offer the victims channels to lodge their complaints and recover their losses, and protect the interests of the victims.

Third, work should be done to build an honest government and a team of honest public servants. Modern governments manage the affairs of the society not by their authority but with their services. The honesty of modern government officials is chiefly shown in serving the people. Honest government is based on a team of loyal and honest public servants. How honest the public servants are plays a decisive role in the degree of government credit. They should be 'honest and trustworthy' to their superiors, inferiors and the ordinary people, tell the truth and seek truth from facts. The building of an honest government requires the public servants to treat ordinary people sincerely, enhance their sense of identity of the public with their honest practice, win people' s support and trust, and appeal to the public to consciously follow their example so as to develop fine social customs based on sincerity and focused on integrity.

Fourth, a social credit system should be established so that the dishonest ones cannot move a single step. Based on the support of science and technology, especially internet popularisation in modern society, it is completely feasible to establish a complete social credit system. We find that the words and deeds of some publicly scrutinised figures, including the delinquents, can be traced to each period of time after birth via a 'man hunt'. Even the embarrassing anecdotes in their infancy and childhood cannot escape scrutiny. Through 'Internet+', a social credit system of powerful functions and a basic platform can be established to record and enquire about the credit information of public citizens and the main market players. Delinquent behaviour can be meticulously recorded with the aim of providing an accurate basis for the credit system executors to punish delinquents. Definitely, the internet is just a tool. It is more important to establish a mechanism featuring division of labour, fair competition and fair allocation among and within social organisations (strata) in a move to form a complete credit system and credit reference system. Such a system will fully expose delinquency to public scrutiny. The punishment mechanism for dishonesty is not just a rigid regulation but is supported by strict laws and regulations. It can provide a legal basis to sanction seriously dishonest behaviour so that the honest and trustworthy behaviour of everyone in society is underpinned by laws and regulations.

Chapter 4

Uphold Righteousness - The Selfless Kindness of the Chinese People

In traditional Chinese, 'righteousness' is a complicated concept with abundant connotations. In the mind of the Chinese people, it is shown in all the rightful, reasonable issues, views and actions, all the pursuits for the truth, the good and the beautiful, the castigation of the false, the evil and the ugly, the adherence to social fairness and justice and the opposition to social unfairness and inequality. The criterion of 'righteousness' refers to benevolence toward, and help for, relatives, friends and even ordinary people in the narrow sense and the responsibility for the country and the whole society in a broader sense. In a word, all materials, words and deeds complying with natural and humane laws are 'righteous'. 'Righteousness' in Chinese tradition includes all the components of this concept in modern society.

1. The long history of the theory of 'righteousness'

The Chinese writing system boasts a unique worldwide feature: ideographical expression. That is to say, readers can read the writing and understand its meaning. The writing systems of other countries are phonetic. That is to say, the meanings of the characters need to be expressed additionally. The new words and expressions are formed with the combination of syllabic alphabets.

(1) Explanation of the meanings of 'righteousness' and 'justice' in *Analytical Dictionary of Characters*

The explanations of the two words 'righteousness' and 'justice' in the *Analytical Dictionary of Characters* are: 'The character '正 *zheng* (righteousness)' means rectification and making something appropriate. The word form takes '止 *zhi* (stop)' as the word root and the designated symbol '一 yi' is used to indicate 'preventing errors'. All the characters relating to righteousness can use '正 (righteousness)' as a radical on one side of a Chinese character.' It was interpreted by later generations as: '正' is composed of '一' and '止'. '一' represents the unification of heaven and '止' indicates that wars cease and the world is unified. So its meaning extends to be 'unification of heaven' and 'the standard of the unification of heaven'. The complex traditional Chinese character '义 yi (justice)', namely, '義', is an ideographical character composed of '我 wo (I)' underneath and '羊 yang (sheep)' on top. It has a vertical structure, with '羊' on top and '我' below it. '羊' represents sacrifice while '我' implies weapon and guard of honour which is an upheld flag. The combined meaning is to sacrifice for the flag of faith. That is 'justice'. These two characters created by the Chinese people's ancestors are quite meaningful.

The origin of '正' can be dated back to the earliest oracle bone scripts. In the oracle bone scripts, a small box above represents the ancient city wall and the '止' below indicates 'foot'. It symbolises that the feet of many people move toward the city wall, meaning the troops going on an expedition. The original meaning of '正' is 'expedition'. As time went by, '正' gradually lost its original meaning and evolved to be 'uprightness' and 'righteousness'. The later coined character '征 zheng (expedition)' completely replaced '正' in the original meaning. Hereafter, people mainly used the extended meaning of '正'. For instance: 'If the name is not correct, the words will not ring true.' (*The Analects of Confucius - Zi Lu*) 'The genuine ancient books' (*Collected Works Written by Han Yu and Revised by Zhu Xi*, Han Yu of the Tang dynasty); 'fair attitude and integrity' (*History of the Han Dynasty - Biographies of Li Guang and Su Jian*); 'Those who indulge in shooting will not miss the mark.' (*The Book of Songs - The Glamour of the State of Qi - Exclamation*) Additionally, the character '正' is used as a verb, it means 'making it up to the standard'. For instance, 'to rectify oneself from virtuous men' (*The Analects of Confucius - On Learning*) Based on the numerous items, the character '正' appears in the articles and speeches of some people meaning 'correct, pure, rightful, upright, normal treatment, rectification and adjustment'. After the ancient Chinese combined '正 (righteousness)' and '义 (justice)', various extended meanings of '正' were added to the phrase '正义 (righteousness)' and further stressed the rightfulness and rationality of '义 (justice)'.

Now let's say something about '义 (righteousness)'. '义' is an associative compound, namely, combining two characters and encompassing their meanings so as to enrich the connotation of the new words. The '羊 (sheep)' above was written as '義', meaning 'auspicious', the good omens shown in sacrifices to ancestors and the practice of divination; the lower part is '我' which was a weapon with sharp teeth and represented a 'war expedition'. The original meaning of the phrase was coined for the grand ceremony before a war expedition and the prediction of good or bad luck through sacrifices to ancestors and the practice of divination. If it was a good omen, it showed that the war was benevolent and fair. A benevolent war sanctioned by the gods was a war of kindness and a war of good omen. Concurrently, sincere the upper part of '义' was the sacrifice for grand fetes - '羊 (sheep)' and the lower part was '我 (I)', the character was endowed with divine majesty and was extended to mean universal appropriateness and the ordinance of poetic justice. Hereafter, it was further extended to mean universally accepted morality, truth and word connotation. As a matter of fact, in ancient China, '义' was an amiable, good character. Almost all the good deeds indicating fairness, justice and responsibility in society were crowned with the appraisal of '义'. It was tantamount to the highest evaluation, for instance, kindheartedness and justice, ritual philosophy, good faith, ties of friendship, loyalty, a sense of justice, code of brotherhood, obligation, chivalrous deeds, philanthropic relief, charitable contributions and gratuitous treatment. Even the dogs that would rather die than leave their owners and protect their owners at any time were called 'righteous dogs'.

In brief, the above quotations show that when the ancient Chinese coined the characters '正' and '义', they endowed them with abundant connotations and masses of positive energy. It left more room to incorporate the two and expand and enrich their connotations.

(2) 'Of the four dimensions', one's 'righteous spirit' reaches up to the clouds

Guan Zi - The Herdsmen records: 'The country has four dimensions… namely, a sense of propriety, righteousness, honesty and honour.' 'If the four dimensions were not advocated, the state would perish from the earth.' Here '义 (righteousness)' was upgraded to be the critical line and essential for the survival and governance of a country.

As the Chinese saying goes, one's high morality reaches up to the clouds.

It is sourced from *The Book of Song - Biography of Xie Lingyun*, where it is written: 'Qu Yuan and Song Yu initiated a fresh poetic style; afterwards, it was carried forward by Jia Yi and Sima Xiangru whose beautiful verses were inscribed on ancient bronze objects, with the high morality in the argumentation reaching up to the clouds.' Here, it eulogised the righteousness of Qu Yuan and others that reached up to the clouds. From then on, people applied it to describe the lofty spirit of a person struggling for righteousness. It is quite suitable for the idiom to be used to depict the connotation of 'righteousness' in traditional Chinese culture and the status of 'righteousness' in social life.

'Righteousness' stands quite high in Confucianism. It appears frequently in *The Analects of Confucius* and is taken as the criterion to distinguish men of noble character from villains. It is said that 'men of noble character highly value righteousness while villains attach more importance to benefits'. It is believed that only being righteous is the behavioral pattern of men of noble character. In the moral system of 'benevolence, righteousness and etiquette' determined by Confucius, 'righteousness' coordinates the other two - righteousness is the external manifestation of benevolence and etiquette is the mode of external manifestation. 'Righteousness can be shown through etiquette' and benevolence can be seen through righteousness.

Dong Zhongshu said: "The rule of righteousness is to rectify oneself rather than others." (*Luxuriant Dew of the Spring and Autumn Annals - The Rule of Righteousness*) In his view, the benevolence of the Confucian school was to pacify the people. Therefore, it required being benevolent to others; however, righteousness was to rectify oneself through morality and justice. Liu Jiuyuan thought: 'People of morality and talent take righteousness as the root of their conduct in society. The righteous ones are respected and the unrighteous are slighted; it is quite glorious to act with righteousness and disgraceful to act in bad faith." (*With Guo Bangyi*) It required that all people's behaviour should be based on morality and justice.

In traditional Chinese culture, righteousness was not merely a very important moral cultivation and personality state but a sort of code of behaviour for the ancients. The literal research of 'the five relationships' reveals a secret. Among the five indispensable qualities of 'benevolence, righteousness, propriety, wisdom and trust', only 'wisdom' is at the level of knowledge and the basis of morality while the other four items are at the level of moral principles. In this sense, 'benevolence, propriety and trust' are comparatively independent moral elements - the ancient Chinese seldom used them together. Only 'righteousness' was often used together with other moral elements, for instance, kindheartedness, ritual philosophy and good faith. This demonstrates that all the ethical categories can be included within the connotation of 'righteousness', or that righteousness is a standard of conduct running through all the ethical categories.

(3) Difficulty of handling people who talk frivolously

Not many classical articles of the ancient Chinese can be retrieved as the source of 'justice'. '正' and '义' were used together firstly in *Xuncius - The Functions of the Confucians* which appeared slightly later. It was written there: 'People without knowledge and morality and who do anything for the sake of their own private gain are all losers.' *The Record of the Grand Historian - Biographies of Famous Knights* by Sima Qian notes: 'Although the knights' behaviour does not conform to moral laws, they must stand by their words and must not stop their actions until success is achieved.' The 'righteousness' here seems to be extended to unified social regulations. *The Statement of a Hermit - Lament of the Hermit* by Wang Fu of the Eastern Han dynasty reads: 'Fan Wu, an important official of the State of Jin, and Hua Yuan, a major official of the State of Song in the Spring and Autumn period, were exiled and returned to Jin. Nevertheless, when they returned, the crafty and evil officials all escaped from their homeland. Therefore, the righteous people cannot be reconciled with the wicked.' Here the meaning of 'righteousness' is basically close to how modern people would understand it.

Since 'righteousness' is rarely seen in ancient classical books, some people have the idea that the concept of righteousness was a modern concept imported from the West. How ridiculous!

From the previous discussion about 'righteousness' in traditional Chinese culture, it is basically clear that there is much overlap between 'righteousness' and 'justice'. Apart from the fact that the 'righteousness' occasionally mentioned in some ancient works had the meaning of 'fairness and uprightness', the original and extended meanings of 'righteousness' not only encompass all the contents of the modern viewpoint of justice, but the range of their content was much broader. 'Righteousness' as the norm of behaviour in ancient China was applicable to almost all people and objects, and everything that one could wish for. The single character 'righteousness' in ancient Chinese was generally tantamount to 'justice' in modern Chinese. In fact, the ancient words combined together with 'justice' implied 'righteousness' and even more, for example, righteous army, righteous men and righteous deeds.

Moreover, according to the lexical structure of Chinese, 'righteousness and justice' are attributive structures. 'Righteousness' is the attributive modifier of 'justice'. For thousands of years, 'justice' did not frequently appear in all sorts of classical books. However, 'righteousness' can be seen everywhere because 'righteousness' conveys all the connotations of 'justice'. Therefore, Confucius sighed with emotion: 'Some people cannot articulate their ideas clearly… It is exceedingly difficult to teach such people." (*The Analects of Confucius*)

To further differentiate the relationship between righteousness and justice, we may as well compare 'justice' in the modern sense with 'righteousness' in the ancient sense.

In the broad sense, the connotation of justice is compliance, fairness, impartiality, lawfulness, reasonableness and rationality. The so-called compliance means what complies with nature, the law and god's will. It is the justice that complies with god; the so-called fairness, impartiality and lawfulness refer to the relatively fair and impartial distribution mechanism for power, wealth and reputation among people of all social strata which can be promoted and implemented under legal conditions; the so-called reasonableness and rationality indicate that the words and deeds of country, social classes and individuals conform to the ethical and emotional principles of society and its members. Any of the three major categories can be referred to as 'justice'.

The approach to realising fairness and justice in the West is the implementation of law. That is to say, the law requires people to conduct themselves according to the norm. In ancient China, fairness could be realised in various ways. In addition to laws, there were also restrictions in etiquette and customs, education and public opinion. There was a saying among the people that 'law is no more than human relationships'. It meant that the ties of friendship could bend the rules at times. Definitely, to the ancient Chinese, it was most important for righteousness to conform with social norms, including the law. Confucius said: "Gentlemen took righteousness as the most fundamental, promoted it with etiquette, expressed it with humble words and completed it with loyalty. That was the essential element of gentlemen." (*The Analects of Confucius - Duke Weiling*) The value of etiquette was shown in the principle of righteousness. Without righteousness, etiquette performed practically no function and meant nothing. *The Book of Rites - Continual Etiquette* quoted from Confucius: 'It is most important to know the meaning of 'etiquette'. The complicated etiquette can be followed. But it is fairly difficult to understand the connotation of 'etiquette'. If the meaning of etiquette can be known and the etiquette can be followed, the world can be ruled in an orderly fashion and in great unity'. Etiquette is a social norm and a form of righteousness. Righteousness is the soul of etiquette. Etiquette is fostered under the principle of righteousness and is accordingly the best way to uphold justice.

Modern justice stresses social equality. In traditional culture, fairness and justice are very closely related. In traditional society, chivalrous and righteous men robbing the rich to feed the poor and taking delight in gratitude and revenge were often deemed as envoys of justice. Peasant uprisings in history always carried the torch of 'equivalent humility, wealth and rank' and it was even thought that 'one should take turns to be the emperor'. Definitely, the pursuit of lower-class people for justice caused two diametrically different responses. The authorities would judge chivalrous men as 'being against the law or discipline'; with regard to ordinary people, they upheld justice.

In the modern viewpoint, justice is shown in the fair pursuit of profit. The market economy is the economic system maximising the interests under the premises of fairness and justice. In the modern view of justice, although wars are deemed as inhuman actions, they cannot be avoided but should be judged in the sense of being just or unjust.

Surely, we must admit the differences between the righteousness in ancient China and the justice in modern China and the West. The greatest difference hinges on the fact that the justice in modern society has a clear direction but the viewpoint of righteousness in traditional Chinese culture was extensive in meaning and covered anything good within the scope of justice. For instance, in traditional Chinese society, having a strong sense of justice and being ready to help the weak seemed to be the way to conduct oneself in society and such life goals were revered by the public. In modern society, behaviour that takes delight in gratitude and revenge is most of the time against the law. Nonetheless, laws are the best way to uphold justice in modern society. We must bear this in mind in the transition from a traditional value standard of justice towards a modern value standard.

2. Righteousness, the common value historically pursued by Chinese nationals

The righteous actions taken by Chinese throughout their history are too numerous to mention one by one. There were too many righteous men with their sparkling righteous spirit and they jointly comprised the grand, glittering and soul-stirring chapters of the righteous actions of the Chinese nation.

(1) Ancient legends eulogised righteousness

The era of great antiquity saw the flourishing and emergence of the traditional Chinese viewpoint of righteousness. Although the ancient myths and legends were not recorded in official history, they disclosed the information that the ancient Chinese cherished righteousness.

Although there are diverse versions of the characters and stories of the 'Three Emperors and Five Sovereigns', they were largely identical but with minor differences and remained essentially the same despite various superficial changes. The major characters, incidents and timing basically remain the same and the righteousness and selfless spirit hinted at in the characters and incidents are still unchanged. Suiren Shi drilled wood to make fire and taught people how to make, use and keep fire. Thanks to the use of fire, mankind evolved from the stage of eating uncooked food to eating cooked food, which markedly enhanced people's physiques and lengthened people's lifespans. It was a righteous action for human beings. Fu Hsi invented the fishing net, the hunting trap, original cuisine and especially the wise trigram so that the descendants could deduce the relationships and changes of everything in the space and time of the world. To save human beings, Shen Nung not only personally climbed mountains to collect herbal medicine but also tried it in person to identify the medical performance regardless of the possible harmful side-effects. Legend has it that he experienced '70 kinds of poison every day'. The Yellow Emperor upholding justice led his tribe to bravely fight and triumph over the intrepid and uncouth Chiyou tribe. He showed his bravery, resourcefulness and lofty spirit in battle; he did not ruthlessly kill his defeated opponents but tolerated them and encouraged intermarriage with them. All this manifested his all-embracing and inclusive mentality.

The story of abdication from Emperor Yao to Emperor Shun, two of the 'Five Sovereigns', more clearly reflects massive righteousness. Legend has it that after the Yellow Emperor, three outstanding tribal leaders emerged in succession, namely, Emperor Yao, Emperor Shun and Emperor Yu. The aged Yao wanted to find a successor. Once, he called together the tribal leaders from all around for consultation. His son Dan Zhu and Gong Gong, the God of Water in ancient Chinese mythology, in charge of water conservancy, were recommended to succeed to the throne. However, the recommendation was rejected by Yao. Finally, he decided to pass on the throne to Shun. After Emperor Shun passed away, he did not hand over power to his son but to Yu the Great who delivered meritorious contributions to water control. After Yu succeeded to the throne, he established the Xia dynasty. Since he rose from among the people, he embodied profound 'people-oriented' thought.

Studies of the tribes in primitive society show that the viewpoint of justice flourished in ancient times. The elements of justice, including equal division, fairness, equality and openness began to take shape in the primitive clan communes. Among the primitive peasants, equal division was the unique mode of property distribution. It was the so-called absolute form of justice. The principle of fairness was applied in material wealth distribution. Nobody had the right to occupy, eat, gain or have more material wealth of the clan or tribe. Similarly, all the primitive tribesmen were essentially equal in discussing, determining and handling official business. There was no distinction between lowliness and nobleness or closeness and distance between tribal leaders and ordinary tribespeople or between the core habitation of the tribe and other tribespeople living in other habitations. In the early period, 'equality' was not distinguished by gender. Gender inequality did not appear until the matriarchal and patriarchal societies came into being.

(2) Twenty-five histories manifesting justice

In ancient China, it was the imperial historiographer who most faithfully recorded history. It was the best convention of the Chinese historiographers to defy brute force and persist in writing down the truth.

As *The Commentary of Zuo - The 25th Year of Duke Xiang of Qi* records, Cui Zhu, a minister of State of Qi, killed Duke Zhuang who committed adultery with his wife. The imperial historiographer then wrote down on the bamboo slips truthfully: 'Cui Zhu killed the monarch.' Cui Zhu flew into a rage and killed the imperial historiographer. Two younger brothers of the latter portrayed things as they really were and were also killed by Cui Zhu. Cui Zhu said to the last younger brother of the imperial historiographer who persisted in writing down the facts: "Your three brothers have been killed by me. Don't you fear death? You'd better record the death of Duke Zhuang as a result of a sudden attack of a serious illness." The younger brother of the imperial historiographer responded with a severe countenance: "It is the obligation of a historiographer to record history strictly according to the facts. I'd rather die than commit dereliction of duty for survival. What you did will surely be known sooner or later. Even if I don't write it down, you cannot cover up your criminal liability. On the contrary, you will be reduced to a laughing stock." Cui Zhu had nothing to say and released him.

The traceable history of China, from the establishment of the Xia dynasty in 2070BC, underwent a total of more than 10 dynasties. The 25 historical books recorded the glorious deeds of the Chinese in practicing justice in different historical periods.

The *Record of the Grand Historian* was the first general history presented in a series of biographies. Suffering the greatest humiliation in life, Sima Qian still stuck to his objective stance as a historiographer and evaluated historic figures. For instance, although Xiang Yu was an unsuccessful hero, the *Record of the Grand Historian* still recorded him as an emperor and included him in the series of 'biographic sketches of emperors' (in the *Record of the Grand Historian*, biographic sketches record stories about emperors). For example, Chen Sheng and Wu Guang, leaders of a peasant uprising in the late Qin dynasty, in the traditional view, were bandits defying their superiors and started a rebellion. They could not be recorded in official history. Nonetheless, the *Record of the Grand Historian* included it in the 'aristocratic family' series (In the *Record of the Grand Historian*, the 'aristocratic family' series were the biographies recording the stories of the feudal princes) and voiced the slogan 'social equality' through the mouth of Chen Sheng - 'Are powerful and noble people born into power and nobility?' Sima Qian initiated the genre of 'historical biography' to

Chapter 4

record important figures. He proposed in the index of the *Record of the Grand Historian* that: 'Historical biographies record the stories of officials and can be handed down to future generations.' Among them, *Biographies of Famous Knights* gives an account of the historical facts about eminent chivalrous people such as Zhu Jia, Ju Meng and Guo Jie of the Han dynasty. Although Sima Qian thought the behaviour of the knights 'went against the law and discipline', namely, conflicted with the traditional viewpoint of justice. He made a realistic analysis of different sorts of knights, fully affirmed the 'civilian knights', 'country knights' and 'village knights' and eulogised their righteous behaviour as 'being trustworthy, purposeful and determined to realise their promises; helping others out of difficulties at the cost of their own lives... and not showing off their abilities, merits and virtues'.

Almost all the historical books in each dynasty after the *Record of the Grand Historian* inherited the tradition of the book and truthfully recorded the righteous actions of righteous personages. Some officials of ordinary rank and moderate contributions were recorded in the annals of history. For instance, the Twenty-Five Histories recorded the two 'most righteous officials' in history. One was Bao Zheng of the Song and the other was 'Hai Rui' of the Ming. They were called incarnations of righteousness.

In addition to the Twenty-Five Histories, *History As A Mirror*, a chronicle, was reputed to be a complete collection of the righteous people in ancient China. Its author Sima Qian wrote: 'People's specialties (moral quality) have a bearing on their rise and fall. Good moral qualities should serve as the quintessence while bad ones should function as the criteria to punish others.' He sampled and related some major historical events so as to 'reflect the vicissitudes of the previous dynasties and measure the success and failure now, reward kindness and punish evildoings, accept the right and reject the wrong'. Since the completion of *History As A Mirror*, emperors, generals, ministers, men of letters, poets and very important people from all walks of life have competed to read it. Numerous emperors, virtuous feudal officials, learned scholars and modern statesmen, intellectuals and scholars have commented on the book. Mao Zedong said that he had commented on it 17 times in total and his appraisal was that "I benefit from every reading of the god-given good book... with its pervasive dialectics."

History is like a long river of great waves sweeping away sand. Many emperors, generals and ministers were temporarily powerful but forgotten forever. However, the names of righteous personages still glitter in the annals today.

(3) *Song of the Guerrilla* resounds through the ages

Prime Minister Wen Tianxiang of the Ming dynasty lost a battle and was captured in Haifeng, Guangdong. For three years in prison, he suffered all kinds of coercion and bribery. Faithful and unyielding, he created the *Song of the Guerrilla* which was as eternally famous as *Passing by Lingdingyang*. In the introductory part, it reads: 'Righteousness pervades heaven and earth; it exists in different forms. On earth, it forms rivers and mountains; in the sky, it forms the sun, the moon and the stars. In people, it is called awe-inspiring and is a great spirit which is forceful and majestic and permeates the entire universe.' The awe-inspiring spirit was the righteousness pursued by ancient Chinese people. In the critically harsh times, it was manifested to be the paramount moral integrity of the celebrities for their touching deeds and remained in the long history of China. 'The imperial historiographer truthfully recorded the history of the State of Qi written on bamboo slips without regard for his own life; imperial historiographer Dong Hu made faithful records of the State of Jin with his writing brush; Zhang Liang dispatched a man of unusual strength to kill the atrocious First Emperor of Qin with his iron hammer; Su Wu was exceedingly faithful to the Han dynasty and always held the sceptre given by the emperor in his hand; General Yan Yan would rather be executed than surrender; Privy Counselor Ji shed blood and fought desperately; Zhang Juyang took a mass pledge and crunched his teeth; Yan Changshan scolded the culprits and his tongue was cut off as a consequence; Guan Ning running away from social upheaval in eastern and southern parts of Liaoning province liked wearing a white hat symbolising that his lofty character surpassed the whiteness of ice and snow; Zhuge Liang, author of the *Northern Expedition Memorial*, moved the spirits and gods with his loyalty until his death; Zu Ti crossed the river for the northern expedition with his oars and vowed in an impassioned tone to conquer and annex the northern barbarian tribes in ancient China and people of the Jie nationality; Duan Xiushi dealt a heavy blow to and broke the heads of treacherous men.' They were all righteous men in different circumstances.

'The bamboo slips of the imperial historiographer' and 'the ink of Dong Hu's writing brush' respectively represent the upright imperial historiographers of the State of Qi and the State of Jin in the Spring and Autumn period; 'the iron hammer refers to Prime Minister Zhang Liang of the State of Han in the period of the Five Dynasties who arranged for a man of unusual strength to attack the First Emperor of Qin in a royal procession with an iron hammer; 'Su Wu's sceptre' indicates that Su Wu was sent on a diplomatic mission to Xiongnu in the reign of Emperor Wu, refused to surrender and was exiled to Beihai (now Baikal in Siberia). He was a shepherd for 19 years and flatly refused to surrender; 'The execution of General Yan' tells a story that General Yan Yan would rather have been executed than surrender in the Three Kingdoms period; 'Privy Counselor Ji shed blood' refers to his bravery in safeguarding the monarch with his own body and blood in the royal family of Emperor Hui of Jin; 'Zhang Juyang crunching his teeth' and 'Yan Changshan scolding the treacherous men only to have his tongue cut by his enemies' relate the stories of two ministers captured by rebels that would rather die than surrender and sent armed forces to suppress the rebellious elements in An Lushan's rebellion; 'the hat of Guan Ning in the eastern and southern parts of Liaoning province' narrates the story of Guan Ning who made light of power, lived in seclusion and out of office, and became well known for his lofty qualities of honesty, uprightness and satisfaction with poverty and teaching in the late Eastern Han dynasty; 'the Northern Expedition Memorial' indicates that Zhuge Liang in the Three Kingdoms period submitted a memorial to the last ruler of the Shu Kingdom of the Han before dispatching armed forces to attack Wei, one of the Three Kingdoms that showed their determination to fight until the end for the undertaking of unification; 'to cross the river with oars' is a story about the patriot Zu Ti of the Eastern Jin dynasty who led his troops on a northern expedition, struck the oars and pledged to crush the rebellion in the Central Plains in the north when he crossed the river; 'to strike the treacherous man with a sceptre' relates that Zhu Ci plotted treason and summoned Duan Xiushi to discuss it in the reign of Emperor Dezong of the Tang. Duan Xiushi refused to comply with the request and smashed Zhu Ci's head with a sceptre…

In the on-again and off-again dynasties, whenever China was invaded, some patriots put themselves forward, safeguarded their homeland and had no scruples about fighting in battle until their last drop of blood and perishing together. The most famous faithful patriots included Huo Qubing and Wei Qing who drove out the Xiongnu in the Western Han dynasty, the generals who repelled the Tujue, a nationality in ancient China; Yue Fei who served the emperor and the country loyally and bravely; Deng Shichang, the chief escort of the 'Zhi Yuan' vessel who died for his country in the Sino-Japanese Naval War (September 1894 to April 1895). They were shining paragons of zeal, uprightness and the practice of upholding just values with their life and blood in the course of Chinese history.

3. Revitalise modern society with the spirit of fearlessness and positive energy

At different stages of historical development, China's just values were not merely stable and continuous in general but also distinctively characteristic of their times. In different times and societies, their contents and forms were different. But they all moved ahead and reached their peak.

(1) Socialist core values refresh traditional just values

Socialist societies should have different values from those of other societies, namely, socialist core values. Rather than a type of value system without foundation, they have been extracted on the basis of inheriting and carrying forward traditional Chinese values and absorbing the values of other civilisations and modern civilisation. They are the development, promotion, innovation and improvement of traditional Chinese values. They are the 'greatest common denominators' jointly identified and followed by people of all ethnic groups in modern China, featuring advancement, epochal character, creativity and comprehensiveness.

Socialist core values can be divided into three levels: 'prosperity, democracy, civility and harmony' are the value goals in the country dimension; 'freedom, equality, justice and rule of law' are the values in the social dimension; 'patriotism, dedication, integrity and friendship' are the value criteria at the individual level.

'Prosperity, democracy, civility and harmony' are both the objectives of building China into a socialist modernised country and the chief value objectives at the highest level of socialist core values. 'Prosperity' means national prosperity, which is the material basis for the Chinese nation to realise national prosperity and for people's happiness and good health to flourish. 'Democracy' is the decent demand of human society. The democracy we pursue is that of the people, whose essence and core is that people are the masters of their own country. 'Civility' is an important sign of social progress, the summary of the national, scientific and popular culture and the vital support of the great rejuvenation of the Chinese nation. 'Harmony' collectively reflects the lively situation, namely, to teach people's learning, get paid for work, enjoy medical treatment for illness, be looked after properly in old age and have houses to live in. It is also the pivotal guarantee for economic and social harmony and stability, and for lasting and sound development.

'Freedom, equality, justice and rule of law' are the vivid expression of a good society and reflect the basic attributes of a socialist society with Chinese characteristics. 'Freedom' refers to free human will, existence and development. It is also the social value objective pursued by Marxism. 'Equality' means that citizens are equal before the law; that human rights should be respected and guaranteed; and that everyone has the right to equal participation and development according to law. 'Fairness' means social equality and justice. 'Rule of law' is the basic mode of governing the country, and the basic requirement of democratic politics, and rule of law is the institutional guarantee to safeguard and protect citizens' fundamental interests and to realise freedom, equality, fairness and justice.

'Patriotism, dedication, integrity and friendship' are the basic moral regulations for citizens and the value standards for evaluating their moral behaviour. 'Patriotism' is the deep emotion of individuals for their motherland and the code of conduct for regulating the relationship between individuals and the motherland. 'Dedication' is a reflection of the vocational ethics and civic spirit including devotion to duty, diligence, practicality and willingness to work hard. 'Integrity' refers to honesty and trustworthiness. It is a vital component in building socialist ethics and stresses faithful labour, keeping promises and sincere treatment of others. 'Friendship' emphasises mutual respect, care and help among citizens for their harmony and amity so as to make a great effort to form a new type of socialist interpersonal relationship.

In a word, the spiritual essence of the specific expressions and meanings of the 24-character socialist core values at three levels is directly or indirectly linked, connected and integrated with China's traditional just values. With more clear levels, richer connotations and better systems, they are the inheritance, development, innovation and improvement of traditional just values.

(2) The light of justice shines on the Chinese Dream

The Chinese Dream is also a dream of revival to reinvigorate the past brilliance of the Chinese nation. The progress of national development largely depends on the guidance of socialist core values. To realise the Chinese Dream, efforts should be made to energetically foster and practice socialist core values in a bid to strengthen the spirit of Chinese nationals, bring together their minds and wisdom, motivate their positive energy and give full play to the functions and effects of socialist core values to realise the Chinese Dream for the great rejuvenation of the Chinese nation.

While pursuing the Chinese Dream, it is necessary to create a fair and just development space and a stage where everyone is willing to strive for the dream and everyone has the chance to fulfill their dream. On that stage, everyone is entitled to equal rights, equal opportunities and equal regulations. Equal rights offer everyone the chance of development and progress, equal treatment, a brilliant life and the fulfilment of their dreams. These changes do not differ due to family background or social status. Equal regulations require everyone to conduct themselves in accordance with the same regulations - everyone is equal before regulations. Fairness and justness are the prerequisites for realising the Chinese Dream of everyone in practice. Only with equal rights can the dream take off; only with equal opportunities will people have the impetus to strive for their dreams; only with equal regulations can people get closer to their dreams.

The Chinese Dream is superimposed over everyone's Chinese Dream and maximises the value of every Chinese person. However, the Chinese Dream of individuals cannot be realised without justice. Everyone's happiness and prosperity cannot be gained through unjust measures or by swindling, but through entrepreneurship, dedication and hard work. Just as Confucius pointed out, 'gentlemen make money without doing evil.' Through decades of practice of reform and opening up, the material wealth of the Chinese people has rapidly increased. People's spirit has also undergone gigantic changes and their mindset has become more diversified. For this reason, it is urgently required to advocate and foster new socialist core values at the level of the entire society, to gradually establish sound social customs, to develop a good social consciousness in citizens' minds and to lay a solid foundation for the Chinese Dream.

(3) Develop awe-inspiring righteousness and energise modern society

China has always upheld justice and selflessness. The ancients laid down their lives for justice because of their awe-inspiring righteousness and sense of justice. In stark contrast with the righteous spirit of the ancients, it is commonly seen in modern society that people ignore justice or dare not uphold it. For this reason, carrying forward the fine tradition of the Chinese nation to uphold justice is based on fostering Chinese people's sense of justice.

To foster the modern Chinese people's sense of justice, it is necessary to distinguish justice from injustice. As mentioned above, the viewpoint of justice assumes the distinctive characteristics of a particular era and differs among different social strata in different historical periods. Defending someone against injustice and satisfying oneself with dramatic vengeance was often deemed to be upholding justice in ancient society. But today, it might be regarded as unjust, radical behaviour or even as a crime. In modern society, the actions of abiding by laws and discipline, loving the aged and the young, having good manners, healing the wounded and rescuing the dying, helping the poor and doing rescue and relief work, are all manifestations of a sense of justice. Fostering a sense of justice adapted to the requirements of the times is based on distinguishing right from wrong in reality, knowing the laws and moral standards of modern society, developing the good habits of observing social systems and regulations, and making just moves within the scope of the law rather than going against laws and moral principles.

Fostering the sense of justice of modern Chinese people should follow on from creating a social atmosphere which can stimulate a sense of justice. This sort of social atmosphere should be based on systems, norms, public opinion and examples. Among them, institutional guarantee is the critical point for ultimately giving play to people's sense of justice and the achievement of social justice. American scholar John Bordley Rawls expressed the thought that: the moral evaluation and selection of systems should be superior to those of individuals; the sense of justice of the members of a society plays a fundamental role in all sorts of strength in the institutional scope; only a society regulated by a sense of justice will be a harmonious and stable society. In system construction, importance should be placed not only on punishment for injustice but more importantly on incentives for just behaviour. An incentive mechanism can encourage people to practice justice, protect the righteous from suffering losses and greatly propagate just behaviour. Moreover, the positive guidance of opinion and examples plays a great role.

Leaders and cadres should take the lead in fostering the sense of justice of modern Chinese people. Ji Kangzi asked Confucius about political affairs. Confucius responded: "Government officials should be righteous themselves. If the commander is righteous, who dare not be?" That is to say, the leaders' behaviour merits close public attention and is a reference point for 'those below to follow the behaviour of those above'. The justice practiced by leaders and cadres embodies the cardinal principles of righteousness in the highest level of state. They should have 'four properties': the ambition of unwavering pursuit of ideals and faith; the heroic spirit of honesty, trustworthiness and inspiring awe by upholding justice; the courage to launch innovative practice; the uprightness of being devoted to duty and holding power for the people.

Chapter 5

Concord - The Beautiful Harmony of the Chinese People

The Chinese people have always upheld 'concord' since ancient times. 'Concord' is primarily a concept and a philosophical viewpoint. It has two meanings: one is harmony and being of one mind, extended to mean the union of men and women. The other is the harmony and unity of all sorts of factors and relations of things. In social life, 'concord' is a harmonious, balanced and beautiful status and the objective and ideal pursued by human society. Today, we apply the concept and way of thinking of 'concord' to handle numerous problems in socioeconomic development and international disputes in a move to create a harmonious society and a world that cherishes 'peace as being most precious' and 'mutual learning of fine culture' and that shows the beautiful harmony of the Chinese people to the world.

1. A historical interpretation of harmonious interaction and sincere cooperation

'Concord' first appeared in *Views of the Noblemen of All States - The State of Zheng*: 'Through the education of five sorts of moral obligation and standards, the people can settle down and get on with their pursuits.' The 'education of five sorts of moral obligation and standards' refers to five dimensions of ethics: 'Righteousness of the father, loving kindness of the mother, fraternal love of the older brother for the younger brother, respect of the younger brother for the older brother and filial piety.' For this reason, the initial meaning of 'concord' referred to the mode of coordinating different sorts of relations, norms and administration of the country. 'Concord' is abundantly elucidated in traditional Chinese culture. Both *Views of the Noblemen of All States* and *The Commentary of Zuo* mentioned the concept of 'concord'; *The Book of Changes* talks about concord between

Yin and Yang; *The Book of Songs* relates a story about 'adding seasoning to a soup'; Confucius advocated 'taking a mean course' and 'harmony and peacefulness are prized'; Lao Tzu said: "Knowing the principle of harmony and balance is called 'the objective convention'"; The *Scripture of the Great Peace* proposes the 'concord of Yin and Yang'; Buddhism advocates 'the concord of principal and subsidiary causes'; people in the Han and Tang dynasties developed the theory that 'man is an integral part of nature'; people of the Ming dynasty proposed 'the oneness of body and utility' and 'the unity of knowing and doing'.

(1) Concord of Yin and Yang, endless growth and multiplication

Upholding harmony is a major characteristic of Chinese culture. Mention and discussion about the idea of concord can be found in many ancient books and records.

As *Views of the Noblemen of All States* records, in the late Western Zhou dynasty, Shi Bo proposed that: 'Concord is the combination of different elements. Disparity and difference are the prerequisites of 'concord'. Only in that way can 'concord' last long. What's in concord can grow luxuriantly. If 'concord is eliminated and only difference is left', then it is close to perishing. It can thus be seen that 'concord' and 'sameness' are two different concepts'. 'To treat others as equals' is based on dissimilarity and correlation. Dissimilar objects can be coordinated, advance and develop together; 'To overlap the same objects' will only stifle vitality. 'Concord' and 'sameness' are different. 'Concord' is the mutual vibration and integration of different elements of different objects manifested in the unity of otherness. 'Sameness' is the overlapping of completely identical objects and the uniformity eliminating differences. Therefore, 'concord' seems vibrant and 'sameness' is lifeless. 'Concord' is a mode of thinking that can create a colourful world.

In the Spring and Autumn period, *The Commentary of Zuo* records a dialogue between Yan Ying and Duke Jing of Qi on 'concord and difference'. Yan Ying said: "The deceased emperors mixed the seasoning and made the five tones harmonious and pleasant to hear so as to pacify the mind and register political achievements. The principle of music, like flavour, is composed of well coordinated items including one airflow, two sorts of dance forms (Yin and Yang), three sections of *The Book of Songs* (songs about social customs, songs for the imperial court and songs for temples), products produced from four corners of the world, five tones, six rhymes, seven pitches, wind from eight directions and nine songs that complement each other. Pure and turbid, small and big, short and long, fast and slow, sad and happy, rigid and soft, late and fast, high and low, in and out, thoughtful and negligent, two extremes help each other. Noble men accept it to pacify their mind." Yan Ying thought the emperors should know how to bring everything into 'concord'; just like the blending of five flavours and the harmony of five tones, everything in nature reflects the truth that opposites attract and differences complement each other. Only when monarchs came to know this truth could they secure peaceful and tranquil politics and social harmony.

The concept of concord is fully developed in *The Book of Changes*. The book stresses supreme harmony, which is the ideal state to pursue supreme harmony. It emphasises that 'the sages move the will of the people and the world is at peace' and 'the foothold of practice is the highest realm of harmony'. In pursuing it, the practice is always in a harmonious status. They stress the value and significance of 'concord' to all things in the world and to world order. *The Book of Changes* holds the view that 'Yin and Yang constitute the way'; the binary concord system of a structure of trigrams is enough to simulate the changes of the universe. For instance, heaven and earth comprise the universe; men and women, different social classes and different nations constitute society; day and night become a day. All these can be regarded as the way of Yin and Yang. Yin and Yang are mutually connected, interpenetrating and entwined with each other in harmonious development. In a word, because of the fusion of Yin and Yang, all living things on earth can co-exist together.

In philosophy, the Confucian school advocated the distinction between and the concord of the two extremes of objects. It thought 'attaining a state of harmony' could demonstrate the view that 'heaven and earth had their own position and everything developed'. This awareness gradually evolved into the theory that 'man is an integral part of nature'. In *The Analects of Confucius*, it stresses 'fully knowing and understanding problems' and 'applying them'; Mencius upholds the theory that 'man is an integral part of nature' and advocates 'complying with the function of destiny because of the awareness of it'. From the epistemological perspective, *Xuncius* proposed the theory of 'integration of two objects'. It held the view that 'the mind' plays the role of knowing both sides and the exclusive side of issues; therefore, it is required not to hinder the experience and observation of 'the one side' because of the cognition of 'the other one'; only when that is achieved can 'unity' be realised, namely the binary concord of the 'integration of two objects'. In the specific environment of the early Han dynasty, Dong Zhongshu established a set of systems regarding the universe featuring 'concord of materials' and 'heaven-human interaction', politics and ethical thoughts. Through the theory of Yin and Yang and five elements, Dong Zhongshu developed the idea of 'heaven-human interaction' in *The Spring and Autumn Annals*. He thought that the universe is composed of the five elements wood, fire, earth, metal and water with different attributes. These five different attributes intergenerate and conquer each other and comprise a reasonable universal relationship. For instance, wood generates fire, fire generates earth, earth generates metal, metal generates water and water generates wood. Conversely, water conquers fire, fire conquers metal, metal conquers wood, wood conquers earth and earth conquers water. The intergeneration of the five elements is an intergenerating relationship. Although Dong Zhongshu's viewpoints had obvious divine touches, the integral thinking fueled the formation and deepening of the idea of harmony.

It was Zhang Zai, a neo-Confucianist of the Song dynasty that explicitly brought forward the theory that 'man is an integral part of nature' to explain the idea of the harmony of the Chinese people. In *Western Inscription* he declared that theory: heaven and earth are like the parents; human beings and other living things are mothered by heaven and earth and nurtured by air; the essence of air is the essence of human beings and other living things; the people are all my brothers and living things are all my friends. The ideas of 'peace and tranquility' and 'great unity' (an ideal or perfect society) have been the social and political ideals since the Duke of Zhou and Confucius. In the Northern Song dynasty, the statesmen and intellectuals represented by Fan Zhongyan and Li Gou advocated 'peace making'. Zhang Zai's thought was more penetrating, not limited to the 'peaceful' order prevailing at that time but looking to the foundation of 'peace' for 'all ages' with a deeper vision. That thought was distinctive in this sense.

The idea of 'harmony' is one of the general characteristics of Buddhism, Taoism and even the thoughts and theories of ancient philosophers. It can even be said to be a general feature of the whole Chinese culture. The Taoist view of harmony realises the harmony and common prosperity between man and the world in the realm of free growth. The Taoist school held the view that objects in the world were two opposite extremes originating from 'oneness'. They placed priority on distinguishing harmony and concord and the involution of two extreme objects to the origin. They required people to master the binary concord of negative objects. Nevertheless, the 'harmony' in Buddhist scripture means 'perfect penetration without obstruction' which is intact, full and 'integrated'.

In brief, Confucianism, Buddhism and Taoism are all rich in the spirit of 'harmony' featuring all-inclusiveness, intergrowth, co-existence, succession and inheritance, that is to say, mutual supplementation, balance and harmony.

(2) Etiquette and harmony secures peace for family and country

Confucius developed the 'supreme harmony' in *The Book of Changes* to become the viewpoints that 'gentlemen seek harmony but not uniformity' and 'harmony and peacefulness are prized' which reflected the Chinese people's view of harmony. *The Analects of Confucius - On Learning* reads: 'Etiquette should be applied and peacefulness is prized. That is the way of former kings and is regarded as beautiful.'

That 'etiquette should be applied and peacefulness is prized' means that standards of etiquette and the system of personal status should be applied to manage state affairs and harmony should be taken as the highest principle for dealing with interpersonal relations. It dialectically indicates that it won't do to handle everything only with etiquette and without 'harmony'. Conversely, if everything is handled in accordance with the principle of 'harmony' without any control by etiquette, it will get nowhere either. Etiquette and harmony are two opposite and interdependent sides in coping with administrative affairs and interpersonal relationships. They are opposite, complementary and mutually helpful. Neither can be neglected. Only in that way can one maximise safety in society and maintain it in a harmonious and orderly state.

In *The Book of Rites - The Doctrine of the Mean*, 'harmony' is explained as follows: 'If pleasure, anger, sorrow and joy are not expressed, it is called the 'mean'; if these emotions are expressed and moderate, it is called 'harmony'.' The so-called 'mean' means moderation and appropriateness. *The Analects of Confucius* reads: 'The benevolent should fulfill others if they want to fulfill themselves and make others prosperous if they want to prosper themselves' and 'do unto others as you would have them do unto you'. It is actually the principle of 'harmony', namely, the criterion to handle the relationship between people, between families and countries, and between man and nature. Mo Zi proposed: 'If universal love pervaded society, countries would not attack each other, families would not be in disorder and there would be no thieves or bandits... the country would be in good governance.' It can be seen that the Chinese strategic culture upholding harmony has taken pride in farming-learning and drawn lessons from wanton engagement in military aggression.

(3) Harmony of body and mind and concord of knowledge and action

Wang Yangming, a neo-Confucianist master in the Ming dynasty, was the first to come up with the theory of concord of knowledge and action. That is not the general relationship between knowledge and practice. 'Knowledge' primarily refers to people's moral consciousness, thoughts and ideas; 'action' chiefly represents people's practical acts of ethics. 'The concord of knowledge and action' reflects neo-Confucianism's mastery of the heavenly principles, the exploration of the universe and human society, the cognition of body and function, and the understanding of the thing-in-itself (the concept of noumenon) and effort. It evidently possesses the characteristic of holistic thinking.

As a matter of fact, both 'the oneness of body and utility' and 'the unique truth of everything' put forth by Cheng Yi and Zhu Xi or 'the mind is principle', 'no principle outside the mind', 'no object outside the mind' and 'concord of knowledge and action' advocated by Lu Jiuyuan and Wang Shouren were all imbued with the Confucian theory of 'concord'. If the theory that 'man is an integral part of nature' principally discusses the harmony between humanity and the law of nature, the idea of 'concord of knowledge and action' places more emphasis on thinking about the harmony between thoughts for life and actions. Wang Yangming held the view that knowledge is the thing-in-itself of action and action is the effort of knowledge. Knowledge is the start of action and action is the accomplishment of knowledge. Starting from the theory of concord of knowledge and action, Wang Yangming particularly criticised the two sorts of separation of knowledge and action, namely, 'action without knowledge' and 'knowledge without action'. He thought that sort of separation would lead nowhere. On 25 March 2014, Xi Jinping published a signed article entitled *Special Friends and Win-Win Partners* in France's *Le Figaro* newspaper. He said: "The Chinese people uphold the 'concord of knowledge and action' and the French people advocate 'forging iron to be a blacksmith'. Both ideologies stress translating thoughts into actions."

2. Benign interaction between the Chinese people and the universe

'Concord' is the externalisation of the theory that 'man is an integral part of nature' and closely related with world peace, national stability and individual harmony. If the spirit of harmony reflects the benign interaction between the Chinese people and the universe, the 'beauty of harmony' is the highest realm of Chinese ideology and culture, and traditional Chinese aesthetics. It is collectively reflected in natural harmony, artistic harmony, social harmony, and physical and mental harmony.

(1) Man and nature stand aloof from worldly success

It is often said that the Confucian school highly values ritual and music, and that the Taoist school cherishes nature. In other words, the former stresses social harmony and the latter emphasises natural harmony. Lao Tzu advocated 'learning from nature'. 'Doctrine' and 'nature' are the same and harmonious. 'Nature' is characterised by 'doctrine' and the origin of 'doctrine' is nature. Lao Tzu pointed out: 'Disasters are invited by greed and the greatest fault is desire.' He proposed to reach the 'mysterious', 'harmonious' realm by keeping a low profile and staying away from complacency and greed. Only with an innovative and open state of mind can the harmonious realm be achieved. The development of things is not aimed at reaching a status, nor can it stay in a certain status. It is impossible to go against the law of nature only to stay in a certain status. Once successful, the environment and conditions are changed. The best way out is to quit while one is ahead. This is the requirement and reflection whereby Lao Tzu included the doctrine of heaven in the doctrine of mankind. By standing aloof from worldly success and integrating with nature, people should take good care of themselves to govern the world and become integrated with others to realise the harmony between themselves and others.

In discussing the way to realise harmony between man and nature, Chuang Tzu proposed 'purifying the heart' and 'sitting in oblivion' (or 'sitting in a state of forgetfulness', a form of meditation to empty the mind of superfluous thoughts) to achieve harmony. The so-called 'purifying the heart' was to remove distractions from the mind, maintain concentration and then treat everything in a void. The so-called 'sitting in oblivion' meant sitting quietly and attentively to forget about something. It required people to be generous and open-minded, lenient and not to seek fame and wealth. Understanding the 'doctrine' in this way, people would see a new, harmonious world. Chuang Tzu strove to return to harmony in a generous mentality and admonished people to examine the position of man in nature and the private interests of individuals with broad vision and leniency in their daily lives. Furthermore, they should be content and eliminate anxiety.

(2) Artistic harmony like nature itself

Harmony is distinctively shown in all artistic forms. Chinese paintings, architecture and literature all display the integral harmony in the two dimensions of space and time. Before painting, the ancients would first check the size of the picture and make overall arrangements to harmonise the whole with the various parts. The emperors in Yan Liben's *Painting of A Line of Kings* stand in the centre. For instance, in *Emperor Wu of the Jin Dynasty*, the emperor is depicted to be tall. Two shorter servants stand on both sides, with their heels drawn to be in a higher position. With both hands unfolded forward, the emperor is supported by two servants. From the theory of perspective, the servants are unable to support him at all. However, Chinese paintings should be appreciated as a whole. That painting is an immortal masterpiece highlighting the stateliness of the emperor and the whole composition is exceedingly harmonious. The harmony of Chinese culture primarily stresses overall harmony.

Similarly, Chinese architecture shows a sense of the group. It is not aimed at the height of individual perfection but at the spectacular bearing of the group. For instance, the Temple of Heaven in Beijing used to be the sacrificial altar where the emperors of the Ming and Qing dynasties worshiped heaven. It was not merely an altar to offer sacrifice to heaven but also developed a unique artistic conception. It is like a philosophical poem or a freehand brush work. Its artistic conception does not rest only on the amusement of ordinary people. It is also reflected in the loftiness, auspiciousness and brightness between heaven and earth and the consideration, imagination and experience of the ancient Chinese people for the universe and their enjoyment of artistic beauty. The buildings at the Temple of Heaven display the techniques of artistic expression exclusive to ancient China, for instance, allegory and symbolism - the size of the circular mound altars and the amount of components concentrated and repeatedly featuring the number '9' to symbolize 'heaven' and the relations with 'heaven'. The Hall of Prayer for Good Harvests in the Temple of Heaven was built in a circular shape with its blueness symbolising heaven, and the large columns in the hall and the standard widths in between respectively symbolising the four seasons, 24 solar terms and twelve months of the year, 12 two-hour periods of the day (in ancient times, a day was divided into 12 two-hour periods) and the constellations, namely, the fixed stars in heaven.

In literature, Lin Yutang once said: 'Tao Yuanming was the greatest Chinese poet and the most harmonious cultural product of China.' Tao Yuanming's poems were most characterised by 'harmony'. The poet was like the poems and the poems were like the poet. More than 130 extant poems of his truthfully reflect his complicated, harsh and tortuous experiences of 'self-realisation'. The countryside in his writings was no longer a self-existent objective entity but rather, the subjectivised, emotionalised and personalised nature and habitat of the mind and natural instincts of the poet. Liang Qichao said: "He (Tao Yuanming) could appreciate the natural beauty and experience the subtlety of life." His poems reached the high realm of 'truth' and great harmony between man and poetry.

Chuang Tzu also put forward such important aesthetic categories as 'great beauty' and 'truth-orientation' and upheld the aesthetic view of 'letting things take their own course'. In the opinion of Chuang Tzu, naturalness and innocence are the highest standard and dimension of beauty. The calligraphy theories of all dynasties take 'naturalness' as the highest artistic grade in evaluating calligraphic works. Calligraphy cherishes naturalness and true disposition as the most important. The cursive-script calligraphers in the flourishing Tang dynasty, Su Shi, Huang Tingjian and Mi Fu in the Song dynasty, and Xu Wei in the late Ming dynasty, all expressed their true emotions in their work. These calligraphers avoided external disturbance, surpassed the subjects, reflected the origin of the artistic images with an empty, calm and clear mind, and realised integration and coordination of man and 'doctrine'. This realm is the 'purification of the heart' and 'sitting in oblivion' advocated by Chuang Tzu. It can be said that the unique calligraphy of China reflects the natural and harmonious beauty of traditional Chinese culture.

(3) Social harmony and each in their proper position

Traditional Chinese culture cherishes 'harmony'. 'Harmony is the most precious'. Not merely does everything in nature 'cherish peace' but society highly values 'harmony'. That 'etiquette should be applied and peacefulness is prized' means that 'harmony' is the value orientation of 'etiquette' and the functions and roles of 'etiquette' rest in that people of different social classes can be in their due positions and satisfied with their positions. Only in that way can 'harmony be realised in it' and the society be orderly and harmonious. In Chinese history, 49 reign titles for the emperors of all dynasties implied the meaning of 'harmony'. It shows that 'harmony' was the value goal pursued by the rulers on one hand and reflects the important status of 'harmony' in the core values of traditional society on the other. 'Harmony' is not just institutional ethics and political ethics but the fundamental principle for handling interpersonal relationships - 'gentlemen seek harmony but not uniformity'. The idea of 'harmony in diversity' includes lenience and inclusiveness toward different cultures, for example, how to handle the relationship between Confucianism, Buddhism and Taoism and achieve acculturation. In the modern sense, 'harmony in diversity' also includes absorbing the fine cultural achievements created by mankind. On 27 March 2014, Xi Jinping pointed out in his speech at the UNESCO headquarters: "We need to embrace different civilisations with a mind broader than the sky." "We should seek wisdom and absorb nutrients from different civilisations, provide spiritual backup and mental consolation for the people and jointly address all sorts of challenges confronting the human race." It needs to be pointed out that the 'harmony' or 'harmony in diversity' in traditional culture refers to the sum of people of all social strata. That is to say, 'each should be in their proper position' and 'each is satisfied with their proper position'. 'Satisfaction' with their 'position' in essence protects the privileges of people with special social status. Throughout history, only when privilege was eradicated and equal rights and social justice were realised were interpersonal and social harmony really accomplished. To inherit and carry forward the values and idea of 'harmony' in traditional Chinese culture, it is necessary to spare no efforts to achieve social fairness and justice including equal distribution and judicial fairness, to firmly oppose special privilege and the culture of 'official standards' and build 'harmony' on the basis of the equal rights and human dignity of different people.

(4) Physical and mental harmony aim at supreme goodness

Various internal and external pressures, especially people's endless pursuit of sensory enjoyment in modern society, often lead to physical and psychological imbalance and split personalities in people. Psychiatric disorders, excessive drinking, murder and suicide emanate from psychological imbalance and result in physical and psychological distortion. It has become a social disease because the victims have lost the harmony inside and outside their bodies and minds. Traditional Chinese culture shows that the ancient Chinese had similar anxieties. Confucius stated: "I feel worried that people will not cultivate their morality, practice the truth and correct their wrongdoings." This tells us about the principle of conducting ourselves in life from the other side: we should 'cultivate our morality', 'focus on learning', 'make rectification' and 'turn towards good'. Confucius was profoundly aware that it was not easy to 'cultivate morality'; it required lofty ideals and the mentality of caring for the social welfare of mankind; it not merely necessitated greater wisdom but also assumed social responsibility for cultural education. It requires great courage to take such responsibility. Nevertheless, it was more difficult to make corrections and turn towards good 'day by day'. Therefore, the ancient Chinese regarded 'cultivation of moral character' as the first lesson in life.

The *Great Learning* interprets 'self-cultivation, management of family and state affairs, and world peace' in this way: whether it be the heads of state or plain citizens, people should take self-cultivation of moral character as the basis. Efforts should be made primarily to cultivate moral character and then handle family affairs; only when family affairs are well handled can the country be well governed; only when the country is well governed, all is at peace. That order cannot be reversed. Especially, the roots cannot be dropped. Otherwise, it would be impossible to manage family and state affairs well.

A person of social responsibility chiefly requires self-cultivation so as to bring physical and psychological harmony, internal and external accommodation and optimal status. Only when physical and psychological harmony is achieved can the 'supreme good' realm be accomplished step by step in a bid to realise the general objective of life.

3. Modern practice of the idea that 'harmony and peacefulness are prized'

The historical mission of the CPC is to rejuvenate the Chinese nation. That includes both the national rejuvenation of the socialist PRC and the cultural revival of the Chinese nation. During the cultural revival of the Chinese nation, many valuable innovations have been made. Among them, the modern practice of the idea that 'harmony and peacefulness are prized' is an important innovative move.

The major problems of present-day human society can be concluded in three aspects: first, the relationship between man and nature; second, the questions among human beings; third, the questions inside and outside the mind and body. The greatest problem of modern human society is the conflict between man and nature, among human beings and between the inside and outside of the mind and body. How to solve these conflicts? The traditional Chinese theory that 'man is an integral part of nature', 'unity of self and others' and 'harmony of body and mind' can serve as meaningful ideological references.

(1) Harmony and common prosperity of man and nature

Over the past 200-300 years, people utilised and conquered nature during the industrialisation and modernisation processes. Although it played a gigantic role in improving people's living conditions, it was extremely destructive to the natural environment. That was related with the traditional Western philosophical viewpoint of 'the duopoly of nature and man'. Traditional Western culture regarded the relationship between the spirit and materials as respectively independent and irrelevant external relations. That thought process took the 'mind' and 'materials' as independent binary elements regardless of 'nature' to satisfy 'people's needs'; the conquering of 'nature' does not have to consider the living conditions of 'people'. However, the way of thinking of China's Confucian school is fundamentally different from this. The Confucian school thought the research of 'nature' (the laws of nature) necessarily involves 'man' (humanity); similarly, the research on 'man' will surely involve 'nature'. At present, in the face of 'global dilemmas' and modern crises such as population expansion, resources tension, ecological crisis, environmental pollution and climate warming, adhering to and developing Marxist natural dialectics will help to correctly recognise the nature of, and the relationship between, man and nature, to dissolve the acute conflicts between man and nature and to strive to pursue and realise harmonious development between man and nature.

Since the birth of human beings, people have drastically rebuilt and destroyed nature. It strikes people that they must review people's activities in nature and the relationship between man and nature; and must deeply reflect on the causes of the worsening relationship between man and nature from the perspective of nature. In 1992, 1,700 scientists from 69 countries, including 99 Nobel Prize winners, jointly signed their names to the warning: 'Man and nature are in conflict.'

People have begun trying to rebuild ecological ethics to improve the relationship between man and nature, changed their view from being the masters of nature to being the friends of nature, established a large ecosphere including man, society and nature, and have strived to realise a positive cycle for the large ecosphere. Chinese people are positively seeking the correct direction and reasonable path for the harmonious development of man and nature, and have included ecological civilisation into moving forward the diversity of social civilisation. The 18th National Congress of the CPC creatively proposed the 'five-pronged' general plan including economic construction, political construction, cultural construction, social construction and ecological construction. It enhanced ecological civilisation, stressed creating a good production and living environment for people, focused on promoting the harmonious co-existence of man and nature amid the modernisation process and endeavoured to bring China's modernisation drive onto a sustainable development path. That is the innovative transformation of traditional Chinese culture during socialist modernisation.

(2) The harmonious interaction of humans and society

Social harmony includes three aspects, namely, the harmony between man and nature, the harmony between man and society and the harmony among humans. Among them, the harmony between man and society is the core of social harmony. That is because man has not merely natural attributes but also social attributes. The harmony between man and nature and the harmony among humans must be based on the harmony between humans and society. Social morality requires individual interests to be subordinated to overall interests, which play a leading role in the relationship between man and society; however, in some cases, the overall interests must compromise with individual interests. That is because there are two sides to a harmonious relationship and things must be considered from both sides to establish harmony. Man and society are consistent in pursuing their interests. In a society where all sorts of interest relationships can be effectively coordinated, man and society must get along harmoniously. For this reason, the correct handling of all sorts of social relationship must properly learn from the idea of concord in traditional Chinese culture.

Only when the relationship between man and society, namely, between individual interests and overall interests, is properly dealt with can all social undertakings develop in a coordinated way.

At present, with diverse relations of social interests and forms of organization, and amid overall social harmony and stability, different individuals, groups and social strata are bound to have differences and conflicts. People's values unavoidably tend to be diverse and conflicts resulting from different values challenge social harmony and stability. These differences and conflicts should be rationally and dialectically treated in line with the idea of concord without avoiding, concealing, exaggerating or intensifying them. They should be solved through communication and negotiation. An inclusive attitude must be adopted to treat diverse values, accept the diversity of values and to balance and coordinate different values so as to ease and even eliminate the alienation and conflicts between different individuals and social groups. It is also necessary to respect and tolerate diverse values, seek common ground in the case of differences, champion diversity, foster and carry forward socialist core values, and lead the harmonious development of diverse values through socialist core values so that each citizen has the equal human dignity, rights and opportunities to enjoy the accomplishments of social development.

The harmony between man and society must be guaranteed by corresponding systems. Systems are the only fundamental guarantee of social fairness and justice, and effectively bring the idea of concord into all human relationships. There are two ways to maintain orderly and normal social development: one is the legal system and the other is moral strength. Democracy and law are the hallmarks of modern political civilisation and the primary feature of a harmonious society. Therefore, based on determining the moral code for citizens, China further proposed overall promotion of the rule of law, gradually established a fair and reasonable mechanism for the distribution of social interests and really benefited all the people with the abundant achievements of reform and development in an effort to realise the social development goals of shared common prosperity.

(3) A strong country without hegemony for harmony and win-win

The spirit of 'harmony' is something long nourished and internalised by traditional Chinese culture. In ancient China, the Great Wall was built for defence. Zheng He and his fleet went to the West seven times without occupying an inch of other countries' land. The humiliation of the Chinese nation in the last 100 years indeed aroused its resistance against foreign aggression and its strong aspirations for national independence and emancipation, on the one hand. On the other hand, it motivated the Chinese people to have a deep appreciation for the value of peace and prompted an urgent need for development after miserable experiences of wars and poverty in modern times, and to firmly believe that only peace can enable people to live in peace and contentment, and that only development can provide people with enough food and clothing. Xi Jinping stressed: "The Chinese nation is a peace-loving nation pursuing and carrying forward the firm ideas of peace, concord and harmony. The blood of the Chinese nation does not contain the genes of aggression and world hegemony. The Chinese people will not accept the logic that 'a powerful state must be a tyrant'. We are willing to get along and seek harmonious development with people around the world and strive for, protect and share peace with them."

In fact, different nations and countries should reach certain 'common ground' through cultural exchanges, dialogue (negotiation) and discussion. This is a process from 'difference' to mutual 'identification' in a certain sense. This mutual 'identification' is neither annihilation nor 'assimilation' of one by the other. It seeks the intersection of two different cultures and the stimulation of the cultural development of both sides on this basis. This is precisely the function of 'harmony'. For geological, historical or accidental reasons, different nations and countries developed different traditional cultures, had abundant and colourful human culture, and formed complementary and interactive patterns. Cultural differences may give rise to conflicts and even wars. But it cannot be deemed that 'differences' are bound to cause conflicts and wars. As a consequence, we must endeavour to have dialogue between different cultures, narrow the differences with the idea of 'concord' and get along harmoniously. Amid economic globalisation in the 21st century, all countries have reached such a consensus in terms of enhancing and improving international cultural exchanges and cooperation: to boost the understanding and expectations of people of all countries for a harmonious world and enhance the sense of responsibility and role of all countries in establishing a new international economic order so as to give full play to the economic effects of international cultural cooperation. Through establishing a harmonious world, international economic cooperation will last longer and be more stable; through international economic cooperation, all countries can get along harmoniously and the new international economic order will be built more quickly. International cultural exchanges and cooperation are an important channel to form this consensus, create the new power of international economic cooperation and build bridges to resolve conflicts.

In September and October 2013, Xi Jinping respectively proposed the concept of building the 'Silk Road Economic Belt' and the '21st Century Maritime Silk Road'. The proposal of this concept reflected the idea of concord in traditional Chinese culture. Both the Economic Belt and the Silk Road will involve many countries and nations. Hence, the critical point of promoting the 'One Belt, One Road' initiative is joint development and win-win. Since ancient times, the Silk Road has been not just a road of commerce and trade but a carrier of the cultural connotation of intercourse between different nations in Eurasia. With the sound of camel bells and clops, the road saw the gathering of numerous people along the route, bore the cultural exchanges between the Chinese people and the people along the route, and developed the unique Silk Road spirit. The Silk Road spirit advocates inclusiveness and mutual learning, respects the diversity of civilisations, encourages mutual exchanges between different civilisations, advocates mutual inclusiveness of all civilisations and realises the harmonious co-existence of diverse Eurasian civilisations. It has become the common value pursuit of the Shanghai Cooperative Organisation and Eurasian peoples.

China's 'One Belt, One Road' Initiative is the specific practice of a new security concept, a new cooperation concept and a new development concept focusing on mutual respect, cooperation and win-win. It will provide new carriers and links to inherit and carry forward the Silk Road spirit so as to inject new vigour and vitality into the ancient Silk Road. The joint development of the 'One Belt, One Road' should start from 'five points' (policy communication, road linking, smooth trade, currency circulation and communication of popular sentiments) so as to foster closer ties among the Eurasian countries, deepen their cooperation and broaden their development. As long as efforts are made to seek wider cooperation in trade and investment based on fully considering the interests of all parties, to give more scope to the potential of all countries for cooperation and to complement each other's advantages, common development and prosperity will surely be achieved. On 28 June 2014, Xi Jinping attended a meeting to mark the 60th anniversary of the initiation of the Five Principles of Peaceful Coexistence and delivered a speech: "The sky, the earth and the world are large enough for the common development and prosperity of all countries. The more prosperous some countries grow, the poorer and more backward other countries will become in the long term. That is unsustainable. A person's social elevation benefits those related to them and everyone's development will bring common prosperity." In pursuing their own development, endeavours should be made to positively stimulate the common development of other countries and to bring more and better benefits from development to people around the world.

Chapter 6

Quest for Great Unity - The Ideal Situation for the Chinese People

Since birth, human beings, from chipping stone tools to casting bronze, from hunter-gatherers in fields and forests to cloning creatures, from setting sail on the seas to pursuing dreams in outer space and from the ideal city-state of Plato to the communism of Marx... have all incessantly cherished their dreams, incessantly yearned for the future and incessantly carried out arduous explorations for the fulfilment of their dreams. Dreams are both the fulfilment of a person's life pursuit and a vision of social development. The society of 'great unity' delineated by the ancient Chinese people thousands of years ago is the simplest imagination of an ideal society. The Chinese nation has never ceased to pursue such an ideal society. The society of 'great unity' reflects the dream shared by myriads of Chinese people in the past dynasties and has become their inexorable impetus to work hard for national rejuvenation and prosperity.

1. The dream of the sages for great unity

Two sorts of social conditions were depicted in *The Book of Rites - Continual Etiquette*. The first was 'great unity': 'When the great way prevails, the world is equally shared by all. Worthy and able men are selected to be office holders. This breeds mutual confidence and the development of good neighbourliness. Hence, people do not take only their own parents as parents, nor do they treat only their own children as children. Provisions are made for the aged until their death, adults are given employment, and the young can grow up. Widows and widowers, orphans, the old and childless, as well as the sick and the disabled, are all well taken care of. Men have their proper roles, women their homes. While they hate to see wealth lying about on the ground, they do not necessarily keep it for their own use. While they hate the behaviour of not devoting effort to public work, they do not necessarily develop hatred for private gain. Thus evil scheming is repressed, and robbers, thieves and other lawless elements fail to arise. So that outer doors do not have to be shut. This is called 'the Age of Great Harmony". The second was 'affluence': 'Now the great way has vanished and the world has become private. People only respect and love their own parents, love their own children and make financial and physical endeavours only for their own sake. The emperors and feudal princes took demising the throne to their sons and brothers as a rite. The moat functioned as the defending facility. As the criterion, rites and morality were applied to set right the relationship between the monarch and the ministers, purify the parent-child relationship, harmonise fraternal relations and marriage bonds, and establish systems, especially the household registration system. According to rites and morality, the brave and astute ones were deemed to be sages (because of the thieves and brigands) and people regarded themselves as meritorious.' It thus can be seen that the 'great unity' was the upgrading of 'affluence' and a more ideal social form of a higher hierarchy. In the viewpoint of Confucius, the eras spanning the reigns of Emperor Yu, Emperor Tang, Emperor Wen, Emperor Wu, Emperor Cheng and Duke Zhou could be considered as 'well-off'. Nevertheless, the society of 'great unity' did exist in the ancient times of Yao, Shun and Yu but had been long gone. For this reason, the society of great unity was both a view of an ideal realm far away in the imagination of the philosophers, and the blueprint of the future ideal society that they longed for. The analysis of the standard of the all-round well-off society that we presently pursue shows that the all-round well-off society presently being realised is not the one described by Confucius but encompasses the features of the society of great unity. Or rather, when the nation state was unified in ancient times, our ancestors pursued great unity of the great way amid the pursuit for a comfortable level of living. So do people in modern times.

(1) The whole world is one community and selection should be done on merit

That 'the whole world is one community' is widely known in modern society. It is closely related with the strenuous efforts of Sun Yat-sen, a great forerunner of China's democratic revolution. However, the understanding and aspiration of Sun Yat-sen that 'the whole world is one community' differs from that of the ancients.

The notion that 'the whole world is one community' was explained thus by Zheng Xuan of the Eastern Han dynasty: 'The community is for the public: state power should be demised to wise successors rather than family members.' Kong Yingda of the Tang made it clear that: 'The world belongs to all the people. The throne of the emperor should be demised to those who are virtuous and able for the public good rather than to their descendants for private ends.' In this thought, the so-called 'whole world is one community' means that the monarchy symbolising state power is owned by all the people across the world and the country should be ruled by the virtuous and able ones. For instance, Yao demised the throne to Shun and Shun demised it to Yu rather than to their own descendants. This was fundamentally different from the practice of the well-off society in which, for instance, Yu privately demised the state power to Qi, and Emperor Wen to Emperor Wu.

What was the era of Emperor Yao and Emperor Shun like on earth? It was unknown in the times of Confucius and even modern times. The 'great unity' in the era of Yao and Shun was probably an ideal depiction of the hypothetical 'utopia' of the pre-Qin thinkers; nevertheless, their imagination of a society of 'great unity' was not merely retrospective but a hope for the future. The *Book of Songs* envisages the wonderful world of 'paradise', 'happy state' and 'joyful suburbs'. In the 'happy state', there is no exploitation or 'big rat (exploiter)' that profits from other people's toil.

In the times when the ancients aspired for 'the whole world to be one community', state power was owned by all the people and the throne was demised to the ablest and most virtuous successors. Concurrently, the virtuous and able ones were elected and appointed to administer the state, which was critical to rule and administer the world, in the viewpoint of Confucius. In discussing administration of state by the monarch, he emphasised moralising and handling political affairs was just like the north star being in a fixed position surrounded by a group of stars. Possibly through the example of state affairs management by the monarchs of the Zhou dynasty, the 'well-off' society could be said to be 'the whole world as one family'. Nonetheless, 'exercising government by means of virtue', like 'electing the virtuous and able ones' was the idea behind administering 'the whole world as one community' featuring 'great unity'. It is indicative that 'well-off' was closely tied with 'great unity' and was the inevitable path to 'great unity'.

At its founding, the CPC made it clear that the party has no special interests of its own but only the interests of the workers and the great majority of people. Its tenet to serve the people actually pursues the policy that 'the whole world is one community' rather than 'the whole world is one family'.

(2) Treat others like relatives and love indiscriminately

'Great unity' means 'the whole world is one community' and 'electing the virtuous and able' in terms of the political ideal of state governance and refers to benevolence and equality in terms of the pursuit of morality. In a 'well-off' society or in times characterised by 'ritual collapse', people might not be benevolent to others apart from their own relatives and children. Nevertheless, in the ideal society of 'great unity', it is full of 'benevolence': People treat the parents and children of others as theirs. It is precisely with the benevolence among people that the aged can die a good death, that the young can find favourable positions for the use of their skills, that children can grow up smoothly, and that widows, orphans, the disabled and patients can be well supported.

Since benevolence is the essential attribute of human beings, why do people 'only take good care of their own parents, relatives and children', 'do everything for their own interests' and 'attribute merit to themselves'? The 'four ends' theory of Mencius gave a reasonable explanation for this. Mencius said: 'The sense of compassion is humanity; the sense of shame and hate is justice; the sense of reverence is propriety; the sense of right and wrong is wisdom.' These four senses were respectively the germination of benevolence, righteousness, etiquette and wisdom. These four sorts of emotion were carefully conserved and grew to become benevolence, righteousness, etiquette and wisdom. Hence they were called the 'four ends'. It can thus be seen that 'benevolence' also originated from this source. Without 'benevolence' in their hearts, people are likely to be hoodwinked because they do not take sufficient care to foster its growth. In a society of 'great unity' and a 'well-off' society, the differences between 'people treating the parents and children of others as their own' and 'people only taking care of and loving their own parents, relatives and children' result from being hoodwinked by 'benevolence' and unconsciously discarding the germination of 'benevolence'. Just because of this, the transformation from a 'well-off' society to a society of 'great unity' led to the universal regression of 'benevolence'. On the one hand, it required people to find the 'benevolence' discarded by mankind. For example, just like moral cultivation, people needed to improve morality in the realm of the mind; on the other hand, the transfer from 'for one's own' was not only 'for oneself' but also required treating the relatives and children of others as one's own.

Benevolence and equality are interwoven. It is precisely because of benevolence that we can treat the relatives and children of others as our own. And in that way, 'the aged can die a good death, the young can find favourable positions for the use of their skills, children can grow up smoothly, and widows, orphans, the disabled and patients can be well supported.' Since people are all equal, selflessness perishes from society: Although people hate articles to be discarded on the ground, they do not take them as their own; they are willing to do their utmost and devote all their strength, but they do not do it for their private gains.

Definitely, the equality here is not absolute. As a matter of fact, there is no absolute equality at all. It is like the fact that 'great unity' is not complete 'identification'. Benevolence is not absolute love 'without difference'. People may 'treat the relatives and children of others as their own'. But affinities do exist. So there is no absolute consistency or equality. There are differences between men and women, the aged, the young, children, widowers, widows, orphans, the childless and the disabled. People of 'virtue and ability' should be selected for state governance. That is to say, there are differences between the virtuous and the immoral, and between the able and the incapable. They are also unequal.

However, in the final analysis, the society of 'great unity' in the imagination of the ancient philosophers stressed benevolence and moral equality, love for others, self-esteem and equality. Because of this, the ideal society in which 'the aged can die a good death, the young can find favourable positions for the use of their skills, children can grow up smoothly, and widows, orphans, the disabled and patients can be well supported' was worthy of people's permanent aspiration. The proposal made in the report of the 18th National Congress of the CPC to solve the most direct and most practical issues of interests of most concern to people made continuous headway in that knowledge was taught, labour was paid for, disease was cured, the aged were well supported and the homeless had homes to live in. To strive to make people's lives better is not just an ideal but an objective that is being realised! There is possibly a gap between the reality and the ideals. But we can already see the light at the end of the tunnel.

(3) Universal harmony with good neighbourly relations

The society of 'great unity', conceived by the ancient Chinese and stressing 'good neighbourly relations', was an ideal society of honesty and harmony. Here, honesty and harmony were in the dialectical relationship of cause and effect: the honesty between men stimulated social harmony which further consolidated honesty and trustworthiness.

The so-called 'honesty' is 'internally honest and externally trustworthy'. Only when a man is internally honest can he trust others and win the trust of others. Being 'internally honest' can be said to be the most fundamental moral deposit and the basis of trust between people and between countries. Just because of this, in Chinese Confucianism, there is a special emphasis on 'self-cultivation, proper management of family and state affairs, and ruling of the world'. 'Innermost integrity' and 'honesty' are the key points of it.

The harmony of state and society originates from harmony of the heart, including benevolence, equality and honesty. The harmony deeply rooted in people's minds can encourage social harmony. It seemed to be harmonious, stable and orderly under the rule of Emperor Wu and Emperor Wen of Zhou. However, it was no 'great unity' but a method of smoothing the relations between the monarch and the officials, and of developing a harmonious fraternity bound by ritual and morality. In the society of great unity, thanks to the harmony in the mind, there is no need to regulate society, attain innermost tranquility and foster social harmony through ritual philosophy.

The longing for 'good neighbourly relations' in the society of 'great unity' reflected the corrupt minds and fickleness of people and the discord and mutual bullying among states in the pre-Qin period. In those times, some would be currying favour for high positions and great wealth; some weak states even changed their loyalty frequently and dealt with other states in a fickle attempt to gain temporary advantage. Without honesty and trust, different peoples and different states could not enjoy a harmonious neighbourhood. The good neighbourly relations featuring honesty and harmony of the society of 'great unity' were similar to 'utopia', a small country with a small population depicted by Lao Tzu: 'Neighbouring states face each other. The cocks that crow and dogs that bark in one state can be heard in other states. People never engage in wars.' Here, it can be understood that there should be no war or conflict, cocks crowing and dogs barking can be heard in two adjacent states (or villages) and people do not engage in wars or conflicts with each other from their birth until their death.

In brief, the society of 'great unity' depicts the ideal, grand spectacle of political flourishing, high morality, harmonious public feeling and social stability. The picture of the ideal society can be said to be the beautified memory of the ancient Chinese thinkers for the primitive communist society of the distant past and the vision and conception of the ideal society featuring equality, benevolence, honesty and harmony without any war.

2. Tracing the history of the Chinese people's pursuit of great unity

The society of 'great unity' was merely a vision of an ideal society proposed by the ancient Chinese and could not be realised in a feudal society implementing a patriarchal clan system. The ideal of 'great unity' was merely a visionary blueprint. Nevertheless, arduous efforts have still been made by people for thousands of years: they reinterpreted and supplemented the dream for the society of 'great unity' according to their understanding; fought unyieldingly against the real society and moved ahead towards the ideal vision; carried the torch of 'great unity' and took it as a tool of regime change… Looking back over the course of history, among them were thinkers, revolutionists, statesmen, poets, artists and even illiterate ordinary people. They were all inspired by, built a consensus and drew vigour from 'great unity'. Even now, it can still enlighten us and lead the way toward our dream.

(1) Uphold virtue and harmony, and the pursuit of equality

Although the concept of 'great unity' was proposed in *The Book of Rites*, a classic Confucian work, it is not just the thinking of the Confucian school but integrates the thinking of 'a small country with a small population' of Lao Tzu of the Taoist school, the ideas of 'upholding virtue' and 'upholding harmony' of Mo Zi of the Mohist school, and the view that 'rulers should labour together with the peasants' of the agriculturalist school. Especially, Mo Zi's idea of 'upholding harmony' proposed 'selecting the virtuous and competent to be the emperor, administrators of the three main areas of public expenditure and senior officers'. Since the virtuous and able ones were elected from top to bottom, 'the people of the world were the same as the emperor', people from bottom to top could reach consensus and the states and the world could be unified and harmoniously managed. Mo Zi presupposed an absolutely right 'god'. If the emperor and god were inconsistent, disasters would befall as punishment.

Since its birth, the dream for a society of 'great unity' has aroused people's attention and has been deemed as the blueprint for an ideal society. That is because class inequality, oppression from influential officials and undistributed wealth forced people to aspire for a harmonious and unified society without oppression or class differentiation. Tao Yuanming of the Eastern Jin dynasty described a remote land of idyllic beauty. In it, there are fields crisscrossed with paths and two places are very close to each other; people live and work in peace, contentment and pleasure. Nevertheless, since it was fairly difficult to find an ideal world completely isolated from the realities of the outside world, the 'peach garden' depicted by Tao Yuanming was only a utopian daydream.

In the late Qing dynasty, Hong Xiuquan led a peasant uprising, integrated Western Christian thought with the traditional Chinese thought of 'great unity', promulgated *The Land System of the Heavenly Kingdom* and proposed to build the ideal Taiping Heavenly Kingdom (1851-1864) where 'people have land to plough, food to eat, clothes to wear and money to spend together, everything is evenly distributed and everyone is warmly dressed'. The vision of a shared ideal society pooling together the strength of the peasants enabled the revolt to accomplish periodic success with an irresistible force. However, due to the limitations of class consciousness, the leaders of the revolt did not correctly know the real impetus for historical progress; concurrently, the peasant uprising encountered a frenzied counterattack by the feudal class and the foreign bourgeoisie in those years. The uprising failed and the ideal blueprint that 'everything is evenly distributed and everyone is warmly dressed' was nothing but a mere scrap of paper and the society of 'great unity' fell through.

(2) Great unity, reform and 'continual etiquette'

'Great unity' has aroused people's extensive attention right up until modern times, which was closely related to the dissemination by Kang Youwei, a reformer in the late Qing dynasty. He witnessed the decay and incompetence of the Qing government and the backwardness of Chinese society at that time. He advocated following the example of Western bourgeois democracy, promoting reform, implementing constitutional monarchy, reforming the political and educational systems and developing industry, agriculture and business. Although the Hundred Days' Reform led by him ended up with the deaths of the 'six gentlemen' and the failure of the Constitutional Reform and Modernisation, the political reform objectively stimulated ideological enlightenment and emancipation, and drove the ideological and cultural progress of modern Chinese society.

The core idea of Kang Youwei's *Great Harmony Book* is consistent with that of *Continual Etiquette*. They all took the dream of a world of great unity featuring benevolence and equality as the core of their discussion. Nevertheless, Kang Youwei's explanation was more meticulous and concrete. He said: "Benevolence is humanity." His statement was extremely similar to that of Confucius and Mencius on 'benevolence'. Kang Youwei also stressed the importance of equality and held the views that 'everything started from gender equality' and ended up with the fact that 'all men are born equal' and that 'the whole world is one community with interpersonal amity and equality, and is one of great unity'. After all, Kang Youwei lived in a period when feudal society was beginning to collapse and Western democratic ideas and concepts of equality and universal love were beginning to be introduced to China. His profound Confucian thoughts and traditions explicitly underwent the baptism of Western civilisation in modern times.

The so-called world of 'great unity' defined by Kang Youwei was the ideal society breaking down the 'nine boundaries'. The 'nine boundaries' included: first, the national boundary divided into tribal territories; second, class boundaries divided into nobleness, lowliness, clarity and obscurity; third, racial boundaries divided into the yellow race, the white race, the brown race and the black race; fourth, gender boundaries divided into male and female; fifth, family boundaries between father and son, husband and wife and brothers; sixth, industrial boundaries, including agriculture, industry and business; seventh, chaotic boundaries of unjust, illogical, different and unfair laws; eighth, boundaries between species, the distinction between people and birds, beasts, worms and fish; ninth, boundaries of bitterness, where bitterness breeds endless inconceivable bitterness. Kang Youwei further proposed: "The way to relieve bitterness is to eliminate the nine boundaries." That means seeking equality among human beings of different races and different genders, showing universal love with benevolence and equality, eliminating the differences between countries, eradicating poverty and striving for peace. The removal of the 'nine boundaries' is in essence an ideal state surpassing reality.

(3) The whole world as one community settled by the Three People's Principles

It is reckoned that Sun Yat-sen liked writing works on the 'political ideal for a beautiful society'. Throughout his life he wrote 32 works on that theme and gave them to his friends, subordinates and revolutionaries for mutual encouragement. Driven by the thought that the world belongs to all the people, he created the Three People's Principles (nationalism, democracy and people's livelihood) and the Five-Power Constitution (providing for five branches of central government - legislative, executive, judicial, examination and censorate) and launched armed struggles. Although the 10 revolts led by him all failed, he still dashed forward without flagging to overcome difficulties.

Sun Yat-sen was deeply in love with the concept of an ideal society that 'belongs to all the people'. He thought that 'the whole world as one community' and the world of great unity were endowed with 'infinite hope and the greatest ideals'. That 'the whole world belongs to all people' had richer connotations to Sun Yat-sen. He said in his speech entitled the *Three People's Principles*: 'The Three People's Principles refers to 'civilian-owned, government by the people and government for the people'. This means that the country is owned by all the people, political affairs should be handled by all the people and the interests should be enjoyed by all the people. In that sense, the people should share everything in the country, not merely for communism,. This is the real principle of people's livelihood and the world of great unity hoped for by Confucius.' He added: "The principle of people's livelihood is socialism, or communism, namely, cosmopolitanism." It thus can be seen that the 'cosmopolitanism' put forward by Sun Yat-sen was different from the Taiping Heavenly Kingdom established by Hong Xiuquan and the world of 'great unity' in the view of Kang Youwei. Although it was slightly utopian, it absorbed Western theories on democracy, human rights and socialism based on the Three People's Principles and the ideal of 'great unity' of the ancient Chinese. In the viewpoint of Sun Yat-sen, the 'Three People's Principles' was the route to 'the whole world as one community'. For this reason, he called on 400 million Chinese people to 'make a dash with one mind, meet the trend of the world as a nation with a fine 5,000-year-old civilisation and build the politically most enlightened and peaceful country housing the happiest people.' To realise the ideal of 'the whole world as one community', Sun Yat-sen struggled throughout his life.

3. Contemporary interpretation of great unity

The social vision depicted by great unity has motivated the Chinese nation to unremittingly struggle in pursuit of it for thousands of years. Nonetheless, in the modern era, China was reduced to being a semi-colonial and semi-feudal society and the idea of 'great unity' seemed to recede into the distance. National salvation and revitalisation of the Chinese nation has become the most direct and urgent topic of the times and the historic mission of the whole nation. Innumerable people with lofty ideals came and went through thick and thin for the rise of China. Especially, under the leadership of the CPC, the Chinese people fought dauntlessly and exerted all their efforts to make the country prosperous. They have not merely established a socialist society where the people 'jointly have state power, jointly manage state affairs and jointly share the national interest' but they have also built China into a country with unprecedented conditions for realising the goal of rejuvenating a great nation.

At this historic new point of departure, Xi Jinping proposed the Chinese Dream to bring about a great rejuvenation of the Chinese nation. The Chinese Dream is aimed at the revival of national prosperity and people's happiness. It should be realised through China's peaceful rise, namely, through peaceful development, cooperation and win-win, the further promotion of socialism with Chinese characteristics, building a generally affluent society and realisation of the great rejuvenation of the Chinese nation. The Chinese Dream inherits the legacy at the core of the Chinese nation for thousands of years to pursue the ideal society and provides a scientific path and inexhaustible impetus to realise this ideal. It is more realistic, more practical and richer than a utopian vision and hence makes 'the ideal of great unity' increasingly more realistic.

(1) 'Two centenaries' and the Chinese Dream

To a modern country, the important standard of its development and progress includes political democracy, economic prosperity and progressive civilisation. More than three decades after the reform and opening up, China's development achievements are apparent in both economic construction and the overall development of politics, society and culture. Especially, the 18th National Congress of the CPC proposed the 'two centenaries' struggle objective: to establish a generally affluent society by the 100th anniversary of the CPC; and to build China into a modern socialist country featuring prosperity, democracy, civilisation and harmony by the 100th anniversary of the founding of the PRC. The objective of the 'two centenaries' is regarded as the specific content to realise the Chinese Dream and the idea of 'great unity' of the ancient Chinese has changed to become the specific practice of the joint endeavours of the Chinese nation.

Based on the fundamental establishment of an affluent society, the CPC proposes to 'build a comprehensively affluent society' for the first time for all the people to enjoy the fruits of prosperity. 'Comprehensive establishment' means not merely building economic, political, cultural, social and eco-friendly development of an affluent and flourishing country but benefiting billions of Chinese people with the achievements of economic and social development and reform, and building a paradise for the affluence of all the people. It is an affluent society laying a solid foundation for realising the grand objective of the socialist modernisation drive and the great rejuvenation of the Chinese nation. 'Building a prosperous, democratic, civilised and harmonious socialist modern country' will lay a more solid foundation for the realisation of the Chinese Dream for the great rejuvenation of the Chinese nation.

The Chinese Dream is not just the dream of the Chinese people to seek development and great rejuvenation of the Chinese nation but also the strategic thought to realise the revival. Xi Jinping emphasised that: the Chinese Dream is, in the final analysis, the dream of the Chinese people. It must be realised by the people and benefit the people. In this sense, the Chinese Dream is the dream shared by all the Chinese people and the dream for the Chinese people to bring about national prosperity and revival. The people are the fundamental driving force for the endless progress of history. The realisation of the Chinese Dream also needs the joint efforts of the Chinese nation. State power is shared by all the people. The people jointly govern their own country, pool their strengths and struggle together to realise their shared dream.

(2) People's splendid lives and fulfilling the dream

On many occasions, Xi Jinping has quoted a sentence from the *Tao Te Ching*: "Governing a large country is like cooking a small fish." It compares governing a country to cooking a small fish. The 'large' and 'small' vividly reveals the universality between governing a country and cooking a dish. Philosopher Wang Bi of the State of Wei thought that governing a country was like cooking a small fish; the fish should not be stirred frequently and governing a large country should not disturb the people; only that way can one win the wide support of the people and can the country be well managed.

There is evidently a profound reason for Xi Jinping quoting this sentence several times. When he met Chancellor Merkel of Germany in April 2014, he mentioned 'governing a large country is like cooking a small fish'. Xi continued: "The achievement, however large it is, divided by 1.3 billion Chinese is small; a problem, however small it is, multiplied by 1.3 billion Chinese will be amplified. With a big ship like China, one cannot afford to make the mistake of capsizing it." This clearly shows that it is a great challenge to govern such a large country as China with a population of 1.3 billion and to take good care of each individual in each area. Special care should be taken in making policies and avoiding complications. Besides, to make the Chinese people as affluent as those in developed countries and to tackle everyone's problems, it is much more difficult to govern a large country than a small one. He believes that the good governance of China does not rest only on avoiding disturbing people but in making people enjoy a better and more wonderful life. To that end, he has further pointed out: "The Chinese people living in our great motherland in this great era share the opportunities of enjoying a wonderful life, fulfilling their dreams and growing and progressing together with the motherland and the times."

People share the opportunity of enjoying a wonderful life, fulfilling their dreams and growing and progressing together with the motherland and the times. As a matter of fact, the people are the builders of socialism and are enjoying the fruits of their labour. One of the important symbols of the ideal society of 'great unity' is that the labourers share the fruits of their labour. To give all the people the opportunity to enjoy a wonderful life and fulfill their dreams, especially in the primary stage of socialism where the supply of material goods is not plentiful enough to allow distribution according to need and to put 'communal sharing' into practice, efforts must be made to guarantee equal sharing of the 'opportunities'.

(3) Common destiny and big power responsibility

For the time being, world polarisation, economic globalisation and society informatisation are gaining momentum and driving the world from isolation to overall development. When countries around the world with different systems, cultures and development stages display unprecedented interdependence and interwoven interests, disharmonious factors such as terrorism, natural disasters, financial risks and energy safety influence the world more profoundly. In the face of such universal problems, countries around the world comprise 'a community of common destiny' that will collaborate to address these universal problems.

The report of the 18th National Congress of the CPC initiated the human awareness of 'a community with a common future'. It pointed out that efforts should be made to 'consider the reasonable concerns of others when pursuing the interests of China, to foster the joint development of all countries when seeking to develop China, to establish a more equal and balanced new type of partnership for global development, to help others in the same situation as us, to share rights and liabilities and to enhance mankind's common interests'. Generally speaking, it is a viewpoint of interests and development aimed at addressing the challenges to mankind and a new viewpoint of co-existence encompassing the interdependent conception of international rights, a viewpoint of common interests, a viewpoint of sustainable development, a viewpoint of global governance and a new security outlook focused on how to realise cooperation and win-win. Since the 18th National Congress of the CPC, Xi Jinping has successively advocated building the 'Sino-Africa Community of Common Destiny' and the 'China-ASEAN Community of Common Destiny'.

The communities of common destiny are a vision and expectation, with the connotation of constantly enriching peaceful co-existence, the concept of improving co-existence and the development towards a higher stage of harmonious co-existence. It is the responsibility taken proactively by China during its step from a large country to a world power. The Chinese nation, in realising its great rejuvenation, always bears the world in mind and cherishes the spirit that 'all nations live side by side in perfect harmony', which fully reflects the inner impetus of the traditional culture of concord. The communities of common destiny fully reflect China's best vision to take its place on the world stage and establish a world of great unity. It also reflects China's strategic conception to integrate the interests of the

Chinese people with the common interests of people of other countries to expand the confluence of interests of all parties. From this perspective, the community of common destiny is the moral outlook on value brought forth by China to human civilisation and the ultimate care coordinated with harmonious co-existence. Xi Jinping pointed out at a workshop for foreign expert representatives working in China in December 2012 that our undertaking was win-win with the cooperation of all countries. The international community has increasingly become a community of common destiny. In the face of the complicated world economic situation and worldwide problems, no country will grow alone and outshine others. That requires that all countries help others in the same situation and make concerted efforts and mutual cooperation, consider the reasonable concerns of other countries in pursuing our own interests, stimulate joint development of other countries in seeking our own development, establish a more equal and balanced new type of global partnership, increase the joint interests of mankind and jointly build a more beautiful homeland on earth. The Fifth Plenary Session of the 18th Central Committee of the CPC deliberated on and approved the proposed plan for the '13th five-year plan' period and stressed that 'the opening and development had to comply with the trend that China's economy will become deeply integrated into the world economy, adhere to the mutually beneficial and win-win opening strategy, develop the open economy to a higher level, positively participate in global economic governance and public product supply, augment China's institutional right of speech in global economic governance and build a community of common destiny of wider interests.'

Countries in communities of common destiny all face shared crises and opportunities. Just as Xi Jinping said, whether China's peaceful development is successful largely depends on whether we can change the opportunities for the world into those for China and vice-versa, and move ahead amid benign interaction, mutual benefit and win-win results between China and other countries worldwide. To realise the Chinese Dream for the great rejuvenation of the Chinese nation, the Chinese people seeking rapid growth and their own interests should consider the appeals of other countries for their reasonable interests, constantly deepen mutual trust and benefits with other countries, seek win-win cooperation and demonstrate the responsibility of China as a great modern power.

Conclusion

Good Management of the World and Flourishing Culture

British historian Arnold Joseph Toynbee once said: "To prevent mankind from committing suicide, the Chinese nation developed its unique way of thinking for more than 2,000 years to make the fullest preparations." This 'unique way of thinking' originated from the fine cultural traditions created and inherited by the Chinese nation for thousands of years. In this long process, the Chinese culture has gone through numerous ordeals but has been able to be revived like a phoenix rising from the ashes, bloom gloriously and lead generations of Chinese people to move ahead toward self-improvement. The ups and downs of traditional Chinese culture over thousands of years tell us: Traditional culture constitutes the roots and soul of the nation, which should not be discarded but passed on steadfastly.

1. Three waves of craze for traditional Chinese culture

Traditional Chinese culture was subjected to criticism and negation for more than half of the 20th century. With the cultural revival spurred on by the reform and opening up, the mid-1990s witnessed the first wave of 'traditional Chinese culture craze' of the new China. In that period, the overall national strength of China was remarkably improved, people's living standard was fundamentally changed and the great cause of the reunification of China yielded substantial achievements: Hong Kong and Macau smoothly returned to China. The same period also saw the Taiwan straits crisis and the Taiwan issue come into focus. Finding a concept of shared values topped the agenda of Taiwan and the mainland. Traditional Chinese culture was the best bond linking Hong Kong, Macau, Taiwan and the Chinese mainland. The studies of Chinese ancient civilisation were able to arouse a sense of belonging among the Chinese and overseas Chinese all over the world to their own nationality. Hence, with the promotion of overseas and domestic experts and scholars, the first wave of 'craze for traditional Chinese culture' was aroused after the founding of the PRC. Although it was just the initial revival of traditional Chinese culture in terms of scale and nature, it marked the new identification of the Chinese with traditional Chinese culture after criticism and the ice-breaking development of traditional Chinese culture in the new China. 'Neo-Confucianism' came into being in that wave.

In the new century, Chinese culture was greeted with another wave of 'craze for traditional Chinese culture'. Some scholars such as Yu Dan, Yi Zhongtian and Wang Liqun interpreted the classic Chinese studies in a popular manner from the perspective of motivation and brought the classic Chinese studies out of their ivory tower so as to arouse the whole society to re-recognise the traditional cultural classics. Reading and interpreting classic Chinese studies has even become an elegant hobby of the grassroots people - a security guard once delivered a speech on what he had learned from *The Analects of Confucius*. Although comments were made that the wave of 'craze for traditional Chinese culture' was filled with uproar and media and market hype, it was undeniable that the 'craze for traditional Chinese culture' popularising the traditional classic studies further enhanced the sense of identity of Chinese nationals with traditional Chinese culture, boosted their intimacy with traditional Chinese culture, unavoidably exercised influence on their morality and implanted the concepts of 'self-improvement' and 'good management of family affairs' more deeply in the minds of modern people. According to expert analysis, the rise and continuation of the craze for traditional Chinese culture in the new century was fundamentally because of the accelerated modernisation and successful development of China and the change of the cultural psychology of Chinese nationals. After modernisation entered the fast lane of development and economic development succeeded, the cultural confidence of Chinese nationals gradually recovered and their cultural identity was enhanced accordingly. This wave of 'craze for traditional Chinese culture' stimulated the confidence of Chinese nationals in traditional Chinese culture and played a new role in strengthening the national cohesion and national soft power. In this wave, Chinese culture went global and showcased its glamour to the world. From 2004 when the first worldwide Confucius Institute was officially established in Seoul, Korea until the end of 2015, China established 500 Confucius Institutes and 1,000 Confucius Classrooms in 134 countries and territories with students totaling 1.9 million.

Conclusion

On the occasion of the countdown of China's construction to becoming an affluent country, the Chinese Dream for national revival has progressively been brought into reality. The third wave of 'craze for traditional Chinese culture' came in response to the needs of the times. Compared with the previous two, this wave seemed to be more vigorous, more comprehensive, deeper and longer lasting. That is because it was the top authorities that stimulated this wave. After the 18th CPC National Congress, Xi Jinping advocated promoting fine traditional Chinese culture on many important occasions. Especially, after socialist core values were proposed, he called on the whole society to explore the roots and soul of the modern core values from the traditional core values. Besides, he put forward strengthening the soft power of Chinese culture at a collective study meeting of the central committee political bureau. He held that the core values are the soul of cultural soft power and the emphasis of the construction of cultural soft power. That is the most important underlying element determining the nature and direction of culture. The cultural soft power of a country is fundamentally dependent on the vitality, cohesion and emotional appeal of its core values. Therefore, he proposed that: "Socialist core values should be practically applied in every aspect of social life. Through such measures as education, guidance, consensus propaganda, cultural edification, practice, cultivation and institutional guarantee, socialist core values should be internalised to be people's spiritual pursuit and externalised to be people's conscious action. All sorts of opportunities and occasions should be utilised to develop the living conditions and social atmosphere favourable for cultivating and carrying forward socialist core values so as to exert the ubiquitous influence of the core values anytime." To that end, the whole society must be clear about the connotation of socialist core values and about the fact that socialist core values are the products of the organic integration of fine traditional Chinese culture with the spirit of the times so as to generate cultural identification with and confidence in socialist core values, creatively translate them into the soft power of modern culture and materialise cultural self-improvement during the practice of socialist core values. In other words, the reform and opening up is driving China toward great order. The cultural mark of development towards great order is the evolution from the identification of the whole society with traditional culture towards self-confidence and cultural self-improvement.

2. Inspired by the 'craze for traditional Chinese culture'

From the trajectory of the three waves of 'craze for traditional Chinese culture' featuring 'cultural identity, cultural self-confidence and cultural self-improvement', we can notice the omen of the cultural revival of the Chinese nation. Cultural revival indicates national rejuvenation. By means of analysing the three waves of 'craze for traditional Chinese culture' after the reform and opening up and retrospectively with regard to some scenes of cultural prosperity in Chinese history, we may find that the fate of the Chinese culture is closely connected with the fate of the state. Great order throughout the land and national stability are both the good fortune of the state and its people, and opportunities for the development of national culture. Great disorder under heaven and national turmoil are the tragedy of not merely the state and its people but also the national culture. Especially, the studies of Chinese ancient civilisation taking Confucianism, Buddhism and Taoism as the principal are the indicators of historical changes. Great order under heaven promises prosperity for the study of Chinese ancient civilisation, if chaos prevails, then the opposite is true.

We can find here that it was the people that created fine traditional culture and the inheritance of fine traditional culture is tightly connected with the attitude of the ruling class. For instance, when Confucianism came into being, it was not accepted by the rulers in those years and even suffered the tragedy of being subjected to the 'burning of books and burying of scholars' when the Qin dynasty unified the country. However, in the Han dynasty, because of the identification with the political ruler at that time, Confucianism attained the status of exclusive dedication to Confucianism. In all the other dynasties, almost all the founding monarchs or those maintaining the achievements personally advocated and practiced Confucianism. When study of Chinese ancient civilisation thrived, the state necessarily flourished – study of Chinese ancient civilisation and the national fate were bound up with each other and interacted as both cause and effect. Otherwise, how could Zhao Pu say proudly that 'the world can be well governed with the top half of *The Analects of Confucius*'? Just as Xi Jinping said, fine traditional Chinese culture is our deepest cultural soft power. Now that the world is a vast orderly and flourishing community, modern CPC members must protect their inheritance gained through innumerable trials and hardships, take fine traditional Chinese culture as the roots and soul, and realise the Chinese Dream for cultural revival with the strength of the whole nation.

The modern 'craze for traditional Chinese culture' declares the awakening of the self-consciousness of the Chinese nation, reflects the rising self-esteem and self-confidence of the Chinese nation, and arouses the self-awareness of traditional Chinese culture. It boasts great significance for the revival and self-improvement of traditional Chinese culture. With the further growth of China and the further enhancement of cultural self-confidence, we anticipate that the present craze for traditional Chinese culture will embrace another wave. We should, like 'current leaders', bravely stand erect in front of the billows and 'keep the red flag in hand from getting wet'.

3. Seek the outstanding 'cultural yeast'

Excellent cultural tradition is a sort of cultural gene. It is a viewpoint repeatedly expounded in this book. We think that as long as a nation does not perish, its cultural gene will latently or evidently be shown in the future generations of this nation and cannot be expunged even should future generations want to do so. It has even been found to appear and influence people's words and deeds anytime and anywhere. This book discusses how the cultural gene of the Chinese nation exists in the core values of modern Chinese people and influences their words and deeds. However, when this book, a sister book of *The Vitality of the Chinese People – a Citizen's Textbook on Socialist Core Values* was completed, we didn't feel we had accomplished this mission. Considered carefully, it seems many fine cultural traditions of the Chinese nation have not been included. Even if sister books evolve to be a trilogy or more, it will be impossible to finish this task.

After completing this book and leafing through the piles of data on the desk, it suddenly occurred to me that so many classic Chinese studies and relevant interpretations in history and relevant works successively published now seem to expound more new views and values. They have inspired a new concept – that cultural tradition is not merely a cultural gene but the yeast indispensable for brewing – 'cultural yeast'. The genes are the DNA segments of hereditary effects supporting the basic structure and performance of living entities. Nevertheless, when a living species of the same genes perishes, the genes die out with it. But yeast does not. As long as yeast exists, even though the object perishes, the yeast will generate a new reaction and breed new species anywhere under appropriate environmental conditions. Cultural tradition is just like yeast. No matter whether the creators of the cultural traditions die out or not, it will come alive under suitable environmental conditions. The ancient Greek civilisation has long since died out, but their national culture still influences modern people. Confucius left us more than 2,000 years ago. But in China, his ideology, like genes, has been passed on by the Chinese nation for thousands of years. Moreover, it exerts wide influence on other nations in the world like yeast. Today, the establishment of Confucius Institutes worldwide is the result of the fermentation of the cultural yeast of the Chinese nation in the world.

We think that cultural tradition is not merely included in the nation like a cultural gene but also in all the cultural legacies like 'cultural yeast'. It will not vanish with the extinction of ethnic groups and individuals but will ferment in any nation. Definitely, 'yeast' can be distinguished into that of high quality and poor quality. High-quality yeast can be brewed with savoury, mellow wine while poor-quality yeast can only be used to brew sour, bitter wine. Cultural tradition is likewise. The introduction and creation of fine traditions brings about advanced culture imbued with the spirit of the times. Overlooking the inundation of decayed cultural traditions will generate flowers of evil. For this reason, when we inherit traditional culture, we should 'skim the cream and discard the dregs', find the high-quality cultural yeast and foster fine new national cultural traditions with the impetus of the spirit of the times.

The ideas of benevolence, 'people-oriented', honesty, righteousness, harmony and great unity are the fine yeasts of traditional Chinese culture and the yeast fostering modern core values. The accomplishments of our research group, namely, *The Vitality of the Chinese People – a Citizen's Textbook on Socialist Core Values* and *The Roots and Soul of the Chinese People – The Common Sense of Fine Traditional Chinese Culture*, were written just to stimulate these cultural yeasts to brew more mellow, good wine of culture favoured by the times.

Postscript

The Communist Party of China (CPC) has always placed top priority on carrying forward fine traditional Chinese culture. Since the 18th CPC National Congress, General Secretary Xi Jinping gave a series of important instructions on passing on fine traditional Chinese culture and cultivating socialist core values. He pointed out: Traditional Chinese culture is profound, and learning and mastering its ideological essence is good for establishing the correct world outlook, view of life and values. To help readers learn about and understand fine traditional Chinese culture and to further enhance their cultural self-confidence and self-confidence in their values, we made an in-depth study and compiled *The Roots and Soul of the Chinese People – The Common Sense of Fine Traditional Chinese Culture* based on *The Vitality of the Chinese People – a Citizen's Textbook on Socialist Core Values*.

This book is based on General Secretary Xi Jinping's requirements to 'clarify the history, the development thread and the basic orientation of fine traditional Chinese culture and to clarify the unique creativity, value, ideas and distinctive features of fine traditional Chinese culture' and to strive to 'deeply excavate and expound the value of the times of fine traditional Chinese culture stressing benevolence, 'people-oriented' thought, honesty, righteousness, harmony, concord and great unity' so as to introduce fine traditional culture into modern life and make it an important source of socialist core values and a strong impetus for economic and social development. The book adheres throughout to a style featuring universal readability, intellectual-cultural orientation and a high ideological level, and profoundly expounds the rich connotations of fine traditional Chinese culture through classic theories, historical records, verses and stories. Meanwhile, it recounts and argues through the realities of life, elucidates meticulously, enumerates appropriately and narrates in straightforward language, fully highlighting the characteristics of the times and the practical demands. The book is not merely reading material offering information on fine traditional Chinese culture but can also serve as an important extracurricular textbook of choice for primary and secondary school students.

Compilers of the Chinese edition of the book (listed alphabetically) are: Cheng Qiuying, Fan Xiaoming, Fu Zhiping, Jiang Caiyun, Li Yiming, Liu Hinghong, Liu Huanming, Liu Wangdao, Liu Wei, Liu Xinglin, Liu Zhenrong, Lou Ruixue, Lu Ming, Ren Junhua, Song Keyu, She Hongyun, Wang Hengyang, Wang Jinrui, Wang Yanhui, Xiao Jun, Xu Lixin, Yang Xian and Zheng Liqiao. The whole book in Chinese was finally compiled and edited by Fu Zhiping and Lu Ming. Here, special thanks should go to the leaders of the People's Publishing House and the editors of Section 1 of the Political Department of the People's Publishing House for their diligence in the rapid publication of the book.

Limited by the level and data of the author, any further corrections by readers and experts will be appreciated.

The Chinese editor
20 June 2016

Lightning Source UK Ltd.
Milton Keynes UK
UKOW06f0017020817
306504UK00001B/92/P